THE COMPLETE CRITICAL GUIDE TO
ROBERT BROWNING

Is Browning the most significant poet after the Romantics?

What does the study of Browning mean in the context of postmodern scepticism?

So many questions surround the key figures in the English literary canon, but most books focus on one aspect of an author's life or work, or limit themselves to a single critical approach. *The Complete Critical Guide to Robert Browning* is part of a unique series of comprehensive, user-friendly introductions which:

- offer basic information on an author's life, contexts and works
- outline the major critical issues surrounding the author's works, from the time they were written to the present
- leave judgements up to you, by explaining the full range of often different critical views and interpretations
- offer guides to further reading in each area discussed.

'This series has a broad focus but one very clear aim: to equip you with the knowledge you need to make your own new readings of crucial texts.

It is certainly the best introduction to the poetry of Robert Browning available today.'

Adam Roberts, *Royal Holloway,*
University of London

'The major strengths of *The Complete Critical Guide to Robert Browning* are its clarity, its comprehensiveness, and the judiciousness of critical and theoretical discourse. Because of these qualities it is useful to students and scholars alike.'

Thomas J. Collins,
University of Western Ontario

Th. dat. is Lecturer in English at the University of Buckingham. He is one of the editors of the Oxford *Poetical Works of Robert Browning* and the new editor of *Browning Society Notes.*

THE COMPLETE CRITICAL GUIDE TO
ENGLISH LITERATURE
Series Editors
RICHARD BRADFORD AND JAN JEDRZEJEWSKI

Also available in this series:

The Complete Critical Guide to Samuel Beckett
David Pattie
The Complete Critical Guide to Geoffrey Chaucer
Gillian Rudd
The Complete Critical Guide to Ben Jonson
James Loxley
The Complete Critical Guide to John Milton
Richard Bradford
The Complete Critical Guide to Alexander Pope
Paul Baines

Forthcoming:

The Complete Critical Guide to Charles Dickens
The Complete Critical Guide to D. H. Lawrence
The Complete Critical Guide to William Wordsworth

Visit the website of *The Complete Critical Guide to English Literature*
for further information and an updated list of titles
www.literature.routledge.com/criticalguides

THE COMPLETE CRITICAL GUIDE TO
ROBERT BROWNING

Stefan Hawlin

London and New York

First published 2002
by Routledge
2 Park Square, Milton Park, Abingdon, Oxon, OX14 4RN

Simultaneously published in the USA and Canada
by Routledge
270 Madison Ave, New York NY 10016

Routledge is an imprint of the Taylor & Francis Group

Transferred to Digital Printing 2006

Typeset in Schneidler by
HWA Text and Data Management, Tunbridge Wells

British Library Cataloguing in Publication Data
A catalogue record for this book is available from the British Library

Library of Congress Cataloging in Publication Data
Hawlin, Stefan
The complete critical guide to Robert Browning / Stefan Hawlin.
p. cm – (The complete critical guide to English literature)
Includes bibliographical references (p.) and index.
1. Browning, Robert, 1812–1889—Handbooks, manuals, etc.
2. Poets, English—19th century—Biography—Handbooks, manuals, etc.
I. Title. II. Series.
PR4231 .H39 2001
821′.8—dc21   2001032287

ISBN 0–415–22231–1 (hbk)
ISBN 0–415–22232–X (pbk)

CONTENTS

CONTENTS

SERIES EDITORS' PREFACE

The Complete Critical Guide to English Literature is a ground-breaking collection of one-volume introductions to the work of the major writers in the English literary canon. Each volume in the series offers the reader a comprehensive account of the featured author's life, of his or her writing and of the ways in which his or her works have been interpreted by literary critics. The series is both explanatory and stimulating; it reflects the achievements of state-of-the-art literary-historical research and yet manages to be intellectually accessible for the reader who may be encountering a canonical author's work for the first time. It will be useful for students and teachers of literature at all levels, as well as for the general reader; each book can be read through, or consulted in a companion-style fashion.

The aim of *The Complete Critical Guide to English Literature* is to adopt an approach that is as factual, objective and non-partisan as possible, in order to provide the 'full picture' for readers and allow them to form their own judgements. At the same time, however, the books engage the reader in a discussion of the most demanding questions involved in each author's life and work. Did Pope's physical condition affect his treatment of matters of gender and sexuality? Does a feminist reading of *Middlemarch* enlighten us regarding the book's presentation of nineteenth-century British society? Do we deconstruct Beckett's work, or does he do so himself? Contributors to this series address such crucial questions, offer potential solutions and recommend further reading for independent study. In doing so, they equip the reader for an informed and confident examination of the life and work of key canonical figures and of the critical controversies surrounding them.

The aims of the series are reflected in the structure of the books. Part I, 'Life and Contexts', offers a compact biography of the featured author against the background of his or her epoch. In Part II, 'Work', the focus is on the author's most important works, discussed from a non-partisan, literary-historical perspective; the section provides an account of the works, reflecting a consensus of critical opinion on them, and indicating, where appropriate, areas of controversy. These and other issues are taken up again in Part III, 'Criticism', which offers an account of the critical responses generated by the author's work. Contemporaneous reviews and debates are considered, along with opinions inspired by more recent theoretical approaches, such as New Criticism, feminism, Marxism, psychoanalytic criticism, deconstruction and New Historicism.

The volumes in this series will together constitute a comprehensive reference work offering an up-to-date, user-friendly and reliable account of the heritage of English literature from the Middle Ages to the twentieth century. We hope that *The Complete Critical Guide to English Literature* will become for its readers, academic and non-academic alike, an indispensable source of information and inspiration.

RICHARD BRADFORD
JAN JEDRZEJEWSKI

ACKNOWLEDGEMENTS

It is a pleasure to record my obligations and thanks: to the series editors Richard Bradford and Jan Jedrzejewski for their criticisms; to Michael Meredith and Adam Roberts for suggestions and corrections; to Liz Thompson at Routledge for her skilful comments on the first draft; to Philip Kelley for all he has taught me about Browning; and to John Drew, in the Department of English at Buckingham, for his advice and encouragement. I would also like to thank the staff of the Bodleian Library, and Joan Holah, Barry Clifton, and the staff of the University of Buckingham Library, for their efficiency in all matters. My greatest debt is to Marcella McCarthy for help and advice throughout the writing.

ABBREVIATIONS AND REFERENCING

Throughout the text, references to the poetry are from *Robert Browning: The Poems*, ed. John Pettigrew and Thomas J. Collins, 2 volumes (Harmondsworth, Middlesex: Penguin Books, 1981), abbreviated as *Penguin*. References to *The Ring and the Book* are to the accompanying Penguin volume, *Robert Browning: The Ring and the Book*, ed. Richard D. Altick (Harmondsworth, Middlesex: 1971).

Other abbreviations are:

Corr.	*The Brownings' Correspondence*, ed. Philip Kelley and Ronald Hudson to vol. viii, ed. Philip Kelley and Scott Lewis to vol. xiv (Wedgestone Press, Winfield, Kan., 1984–). This definitive edition so far reaches to 1847.
Longman	*The Poems of Browning*, ed. John Woolford and Daniel Karlin, 2 vols (London and New York: Longman, 1991). These volumes cover up to 1846. More volumes are to follow.
Ohio	*The Complete Works of Robert Browning*, ed. Roma A. King, jun., *et al.* (Ohio University Press, Athens, Ohio, 1969–).
Orr	Mrs [Alexandra] Sutherland Orr, *Life and Letters of Robert Browning* (London: Smith, Elder, 1891).
Oxford	*The Poetical Works of Robert Browning*, general editor Ian Jack and then Michael Meredith (Oxford, Clarendon Press: 1983–). This projected 15 vol. edition has so far completed vols i–v (the poetry and plays to 1855), and vols vii and viii (*The Ring and the Book*, Books I–VIII).

All references are to volume and page number.

For all other references the Harvard system is used; full details of items cited can be found in the Bibliography.

Cross-referencing between sections is one of the features of the series. Cross-references to relevant page numbers appear in bold type and square brackets, e.g. **[28]**.

INTRODUCTION

This is a study of Robert Browning (1812–1889), a poet who has been described as 'the most considerable poet in English since the major Romantics' (Bloom and Trilling 1973: 493). Growing up in the aftermath of Romanticism, he developed a poetry innovative in form and style, covering subjects ranging from murder, hatred, and decadence, to heroism and romance. Contemporary readers initially failed to appreciate his work, and only in the 1860s, when he was in his fifties, did it come to enjoy wide recognition. In the twentieth century, the reaction against things Victorian and the aesthetics of Modernism both lowered his reputation, but in the second half of the century he emerged once more as a major poet, particularly in relation to the confusions and scepticisms of postmodern thought.

Part I presents the main events of Browning's life and career: his conventional, if learned, middle-class upbringing; his adolescent rebellion in favour of Shelley's radicalism; his frustrated search for early literary success; his marriage to the most prominent woman poet of the day, Elizabeth Barrett Barrett; their life together in Italy, her death, and his final critical success. It also discusses the major contexts of his work: his fascination with acting and the theatre; his liberal politics; the profundity of his relationship with Barrett; and his deep engagement with the life and landscape of Italy.

Part II gives clear introductions to the early long poems. It then explains the nature of the dramatic monologue, the genre that Browning made his own. There follow introductions to the collections that lie at the heart of his achievement, *Dramatic Lyrics* (1842), *Dramatic Romances and Lyrics* (1845), *Men and Women* (1855), and *Dramatis Personae* (1864), in which he exploited the resources of the dramatic monologue to the full. There are further sections on *The Ring and the Book*, his 21,000 line epic, and on the late poetry, from 1870 onwards. This final phase is seen by some critics as a period of continued, sprightly inventiveness, and by others as a period of decline.

Part III reviews Browning's reputation in the century after his death, and then gives more detailed attention to studies on Browning from 1980 to 2000. Discussions of critical ideas are focused on particular poems, so that this section also serves to deepen an appreciation of key texts.

The Complete Critical Guide to Robert Browning takes a fresh look at Browning, while providing an up-to-date compendium on the state of knowledge about his life, his work, and responses to his work. More than most figures in the canon of English literature, Browning's reputation has fluctuated widely. Here readers have the means to make their own evaluations.

PART I

LIFE AND CONTEXTS

(a) THE EARLY YEARS: 1812–1832

(i) Childhood

Robert Browning was born into a modest, middle-class family on 7 May 1812. His father, also Robert Browning (1782–1866), was a clerk at the Bank of England, earning about £200 to £300 a year. His mother, Sarah Anna Wiedemann (1772–1849), was a devout Nonconformist Christian, of mixed German and Scottish descent, ten years older than her husband, 40 at the time of the poet's birth. He was baptized at a nearby Nonconformist (Congregational) chapel – later known as the York Street Congregational Church – where his parents worshipped. His only sister, Sarianna, was born two years later, in 1814. The famous historian, Thomas Carlyle, who knew Browning and his family in the 1840s, described the poet's parents as 'people of respectable position among the dissenters, but not rich neither' (Griffin 1938: 47).

During Browning's childhood, England's war with France ended at the Battle of Waterloo in 1815, and following this came a decade or so of social unrest and political unease. But the village of Camberwell where the Brownings lived, three and a quarter miles south of central London, was in many ways a secure and quiet environment. In the eighteenth century, and still in the early years of the nineteenth century, there were few bridges across the Thames, and south London as it now is had hardly developed at all. Camberwell was one of several villages in an open expanse of countryside:

> The village [Camberwell] is pleasantly situated, and the beauty of its environs, which command extensive prospects, and abound with richly diversified scenery, has made it the residence of several of the more wealthy merchants in the metropolis: it is paved, lighted with gas, and watched, under an act of parliament obtained in 1814, and the inhabitants are amply supplied with water from springs, and from the works of the South London Company.
>
> (Lewis 1831: i. 336)

At seven or eight years old, Browning became a weekly boarder at a nearby school in Peckham. Here he was taught until about the age of ten by the Misses Ready, and then afterwards by their brother the Reverend Thomas Ready, who gave him a traditional education in the Latin and Greek classics. Peckham, near to Camberwell, was also an attractive village, 'containing many spacious and excellent houses, forming one principal street' (Lewis 1831: iii. 514). Concrete details about his boyhood are scarce, but his later comments all suggest a happy time. In maturity, when he came to know Elizabeth Barrett, this is one of the things that struck him, particularly the contrast between their fathers: Barrett's dominant and authoritarian, his own mild and sweet-tempered.

The poet's paternal grandfather, also Robert Browning (1749–1833), seems to have been an ambitious and sometimes irascible man. He rose from relatively humble but prosperous origins in Dorset to become Principal Clerk of the Bank-Stock division of the Bank of England, a gentlemanly position, marrying on the way into the well-off colonial family of Tittle. After the death of his first wife (the poet's grandmother) in 1789, he married again in 1794, having nine children by his second wife (half-uncles and aunts of the poet). He seems to have expected Browning's father, the son of his first marriage, to aim for worldly success. To this end he sent him off to the island of St Kitts in the Caribbean, where his first wife's family had plantation holdings. Browning's father probably had a claim to part of these holdings as a consequence of his mother's death. Here, at roughly the age of twenty, Browning's father was (according to one account) revulsed by the system of slavery or (according to another) simply found the island's life out of keeping with his literary and artistic tastes. He returned to England, perhaps with the hope of training as an artist or writing, but – without any parental support for this – instead entered into a career at the Bank of England in 1803 and married in 1811. His literary and artistic tastes were a mainstay of his life: he was an omnivorous book collector, and indulged a passion for drawing, particularly caricature. His love of history, literature, and art are important factors in the poet's formation.

Browning's father encouraged his son's early knowledge of Latin and Greek literature, and also generally encouraged the reading of English literature, other European literatures, and history: '[Browning's father's] knowledge of old French, Spanish, and Italian literature was wonderful' (*Orr* 16). All kinds of texts, well-known and obscure, passed from father to son from a library of about 6,000 volumes. At various times in his childhood and youth, Browning had home tuition in music (from John Relfe, the master of the Queen's music), in French (from a M. Auguste Loradoux), and in Italian (from Angelo Cerutti). He also went to the renowned Dulwich picture gallery, with and without his father:

[I] used to go there when a child, far under the age allowed by the regulations – those two Guidos, the wonderful Rembrandt of

Jacob's vision, such a Watteau, the triumphant three Murillo pictures, a Giorgione music-lesson group, all the Poussins with the 'Armida' and 'Jupiter's nursing' – and – no end to 'ands' – I have sate before one, some *one* of those pictures I had predetermined to see, – a good hour and then gone away ... it used to be a green half-hour's walk over the fields.

(Corr. xii. 124)

Browning's musical ability was first fostered in childhood. In later life it showed itself in the sophisticated nature of the allusions to music in his poetry, in poems that contain musical extracts ('Pietro of Abano', 'A Parleying with Charles Avison'), and in letters in which (from memory and casually) he transcribes a tune. Throughout his life friends recall him sitting down and playing from memory at the piano or spinet.

At the end of his formal schooling at the age of 14, his home training was 'made to include everything which in those days went to the production of an accomplished gentleman ... dancing, riding, boxing, and fencing' (*Orr* 43) – something that is well reflected in the later poem 'A Likeness'. Poetry was only part of a wide field of activity:

I cannot remember the time when I did not make verses and think verse-making the finest thing in the world ... This itch for rhyming had not the least connection with the development of a poetic nature, but was the mere result of the notion that 'a poet' was the grandest of God's creatures; and all poets rhymed. When subsequently real and strong feeling called for utterance, either Drawing or Music seemed a much fitter vehicle than 'verses:' and for a long time I resorted to them, chiefly to music.

(Corr. iii. 264)

Through his youth, Browning received a good grounding in the canons of Greek, Latin, and English literature, but given that his father was (as Browning described him) a *'helluo librorum* [devourer of books]' (McAleer 1966: 193) he also came to know many works and writers that we may now consider secondary or obscure. Some biographies exaggerate this trait, making his education sound eccentric, but without going this far, it is a tendency worth bearing in mind, for Browning's formal schooling ended at fourteen; thereafter he spent just eight months at the recently-founded London University (October 1828–May 1829). So there are books in his childhood, which can be traced into his adult work in different ways, that many readers today are unlikely to have read or heard of. *Het Groot Schilderbeck* ('The Art of

Painting') by the Dutch artist Gerard de Lairesse, in the 1778 translation by J. F. Fritsch, was read 'more often and with greater delight, when I was a child, than any other [book]' (Kelley and Coley 1984: 118). Nathaniel Wanley's *Wonders of the Little World* (1678), a compendium of historical fact and anecdote, was another such text. The poetry of Francis Quarles; the plays of Nathaniel Lee – the list could be extended. Not only did Browning read widely but he had a retentive memory. In his 1736 edition of Nathaniel Lee's tragedy *Caesar Borgia* (1688), for example, he wrote in later life 'This was the first play I ever read'. In his correspondence with Elizabeth Barrett, in his thirties, he still remembered lines from this blood-and-thunder Restoration tragedy. He even recalled it again in his fifties when he was writing *The Ring and the Book* (see *Oxford* vii. 117n) **[100–15, 191–200]**.

(ii) Adolescent rebellion

Browning's adolescence is much discussed but relatively obscure, and his early years remain generally the least clear part of his biography. *Browning's Youth* (1977), by John Maynard, investigates every shred of information and combines it with meticulous research to give the fullest picture, but nonetheless what we miss is the poet's own voice in letters or reported speech. A simple contrast will serve: Keats died when he was 25, and there are roughly 320 extant letters that have come to act as a commentary on every nuance of his life and art. Had Browning died at a similar age – also in his first poetic maturity – we would have less than 50 surviving letters, and most of them, far from being profound excursions into the heart, are simple notes of courtesy or business.

Roughly at the age of 15 Browning had a momentous encounter with the poetry of Percy Bysshe Shelley (1792–1822). Shelley had died only five years before, drowned off the north-west coast of Italy, and his work was little known and not significantly in print. In either 1826 or 1827 Browning's cousin, James Silverthorne, gave him a copy of *Miscellaneous Poems* (1826), an unauthorized Shelley collection published by William Benbow, and thereafter Browning came to own the whole of the then available work, mainly in first editions. Though he had enjoyed the poetry of Byron since he was a boy, the poetry of Shelley had a much profounder impact. This seems to have been a poetry that thrilled him:

> Commerce has set the mark of selfishness,
> The signet of its all-enslaving power
> Upon a shining ore, and called it gold:

Before whose image bow the vulgar great,
The vainly rich, the miserable proud,
The mob of peasants, nobles, priests, and kings,
And with blind feelings reverence the power
That grinds them to the dust of misery.
(Shelley, *Queen Mab*, V. 53–60)

Browning's encounter with Shelley's work was direct and absolute, unmediated by literary criticism. For a time he seems to have been overwhelmed with his enthusiasm, one which, though moderated in the next years, and then qualified in middle age (as he learnt more about Shelley's desertion of his first wife Harriet), stayed with him for the rest of his life. Now, in his teens, he adopted a Shelleyan pose – atheism, vegetarianism, political radicalism – and took delight in parading it in front of his elders.

Browning later recalled to Elizabeth Barrett how he lived 'a couple of years & more on bread and potatoes' in imitation of Shelley's vegetarianism (*Corr.* xi. 76). He was friends during this period with the Flower sisters, Eliza (1803–46) and Sarah (1805–48), who later lived with his future friend and mentor, the Reverend W. J. Fox. Sarah Flower was a poet and actress, and is now remembered for her authorship of the hymn 'Nearer, My God, to Thee'. In 1827 Browning, aged about 15, argued with her about religion, deploying his new-found scepticism. She plaintively told Fox that 'My mind has ... lost sight of ... a firm belief in the genuineness of the Scriptures ... It was in answering Robert Browning that my mind refused to bring forward argument, turned recreant, and sided with the enemy' (*Corr.* ii. 354). The poet's first authoritative biographer, Alexandra Orr (who relied on the memories of his sister Sarianna) noted how this period of Shelleyanism offended his mother. In 'after-life' Browning only spoke of this 'period of negation' as an 'access of boyish folly, with which his maturer self could have no concern' (*Orr* 42).

This rebellion can be both overstressed and underplayed. Browning's first published poem, *Pauline* (1833), written five years later, still has Shelley as a crucial presence. Throughout his life, we can trace his on-going involvement with Shelley. Often, in letters, he remembered Shelley's poetry easily. In 1839 he lent the publisher Moxon a Shelley volume, probably to help him with an edition of Shelley's poetry. During his courtship of Barrett in 1845–6, he lent her various of Shelley's works. And in October–December 1851 he wrote the so-called *Essay on Shelley* (1852). This list could be extended, even to the touching detail recalled by his valet in old age, William Grove, that late in life the two books he read most were Plato's *Republic* and Shelley's poetry: 'Undoubtedly Shelley was the English poet he loved best' (Grove 1927: 9).

The man who emerges from these years into his late teens and early twenties was serious, confident, urbane, with also, perhaps, a touch of the dandy, and certainly, in everything, a 'gentleman'. In general terms, his politics was liberal and progressive, though not seriously or radically left-wing. His early works centre 'almost invariably on the resistance to despotism, whether of the eighteenth-century *ancien régime* (*King Victor and King Charles*), or the feuding aristocratic dynasties of thirteenth-century Italy (*Sordello*)' (Woolford 1988: 1), but actually, as politics manifests itself here, anything as simple as political commitment is shrouded in ambiguity. Sometimes, in youth, he appears just sophisticated and detached. In a letter written when he was 22 to his friend the Bourbon-sympathiser André Victor Amédée de Ripert-Monclar, he analyses the implications of the fall of the Whig ministry in 1834, and seems unperturbed by one of the outcomes he predicts: a coalition between the arch Tory, the Duke of Wellington, and the radicals in parliament. He wants to stress the internal stability of English politics as against the volatility of France (*Corr.* iii. 108). One modern critic, acknowledging in his work the 'passing references to contemporary political struggles', nonetheless calls Browning a 'bourgeois poet' because of his lack of direct engagement with 'real conditions', 'unionisation; public demonstrations; and other direct challenges to capitalist authority' (Bristow 1991: 64–5).

In old age Browning spoke of 'the audacious obstinacy which had made him, when a youth, determine to be a poet and nothing but a poet' (Garrett 2000b: 144), but the decision may not have been so absolute. In 1829 he attended the medical lectures of the well-known Dr James Blundell at Guy's Hospital in London. Certainly in these years also, and indeed afterwards, a career in the law may have seemed a possible choice, given the friends he had who were young lawyers. Both his father and grandfather were in banking. Two of his half-uncles, William Shergold Browning (1797–1874) and Reuben Browning (1803–79) worked for Rothschild's bank in Paris and London, another obvious path to follow. It may be that he thought of some kind of work in diplomacy; in February 1834 he accompanied Chevalier George de Benkhausen, Russian consul-general in Britain, on an emergency embassy to St Petersburg. This trip does not feature largely in the biographies, mainly because little is known about it. But it is indicative of the kind of confident, outgoing person he had become that he could travel all the way across northern Europe by horse and carriage, see the forests of Russia, and the ice cracking on the Neva, and mingle for a short time in the St Petersburg society of the Tsar and Pushkin.

In these years the theatre and music were his abiding passions. In October 1830 he attended a performance of *Hamlet* at the Haymarket Theatre, with William Charles Macready (1793–1873), the great actor (and future actor-manager), in the title role; the performance so moved him that he kept it as one of his 'most vivid recollections' (*Corr.* iii: 251). In May or June 1832 he attended twice, with his cousin James Silverthorne, the first performances in England of Beethoven's opera *Fidelio* (*Corr.* xi. 29). On 22 October of the same year he saw the famous, if by then terminally-ill, actor Edmund Kean in his great role as Richard III at the King's Theatre, Richmond, a performance which he felt inspired him in the writing of *Pauline*. We know that he shook Kean's hand, and in May 1833 he attended the actor's funeral.

> He was a passionate admirer of good acting, and would walk from London to Richmond and back again to see Edmund Kean when he was performing there. We know how Macready impressed him, though the finer genius of Kean became very apparent to his retrospective judgment of the two; and it was impossible to see or hear him, as even an old man, in some momentary personation of one of Shakespeare's characters, above all of Richard III, and not feel that a great actor had been lost in him.
>
> (*Orr* 52)

(b) THE YOUNG WRITER: 1832–1846

(i) First works

Published anonymously in March 1833, *Pauline* marks the tentative start of Browning's official career [47–50, 137–40]. It had been begun in October 1832 (or perhaps a little earlier) and both its publication and advertising were paid for by his aunt, Christiana Silverthorne. It received very little notice. Probably in the summer of the next year, 1834, he conceived *Sordello*, though its ambition and scale, and his on-off work on it, meant that it took five years to bring to completion [53–8, 145–50]. In the meantime, probably starting in October 1834, he wrote *Paracelsus*, a verse drama about the great sixteenth-century mage and alchemist, a sustained work that, on publication in August 1835, earned him his first serious notice in the London literary world [50–3, 141–5]. In November 1835, at the home of the Rev. W. J. Fox,

11

he was first introduced to the actor Macready (whose *Hamlet* had so impressed him in 1830) and so commenced his engagement with the contemporary theatre.

In the ten years from 1836 to 1846, he wrote five plays for the theatre, three poetical dramas (for reading not the stage), the long narrative poem *Sordello*, and two volumes of short verse: eleven works in all. Though the exact chronology of writing is unclear, it seems likely that Browning frequently had more than one work on hand at the same time. This impetus, and the relatively few letters surviving from this early period, tell the story of a young, ambitious writer eager to create and sustain an audience. Quite simply, he worked hard, and towards the end of this time, with significant set-backs and popularity proving elusive, we hear often of headaches and weariness.

Throughout these years Browning moved easily within a small circle of young friends and their wives, literary friends and acquaintances, and in the circle around Macready at the theatre. One significant contact was with the Unitarian preacher and political activist Rev. W. J. Fox, who wrote the only serious review of *Pauline*, and through whom, as its editor, Browning placed five short poems in *The Monthly Repository*, a journal on the side of political and social reform. His closest male friends were Alfred Domett, Joseph Arnould, Christopher Dowson, and his cousin James Silverthorne. Among the literary figures of the age, he knew, in greater or lesser degrees, the historian Thomas Carlyle, the feminist Harriet Martineau, Charles Dickens and his future biographer John Forster, the minor poet Richard Hengist Horne, the lawyer and dramatist Thomas Noon Talfourd (whose play *Ion*, now obscure, was a success in 1836), and Bryan Waller Procter (alias 'Barry Cornwall') also now an obscure writer though his *Dramatic Scenes* inspired the great Russian writer Pushkin.

In public Browning seemed an enthusiastic figure, full of talk, easily able to charm, confident and outgoing. So, in 1835 or 1836, Eliza Bridell-Fox recalls a visit to the house of her father, W. J. Fox:

> I remember ... when Mr. Browning entered the drawing-room, with a quick light step; and on hearing from me that my father was out, and in fact that nobody was at home but myself, he said: 'It's my birthday to-day; I'll wait till they come in,' and sitting down to the piano, he added: 'If it won't disturb you, I'll play till they do.'... He was then slim and dark, and very handsome; and – may I hint it – just a trifle of a dandy, addicted to lemon-coloured kid-gloves and such things.
>
> (*Orr* 92–3)

So, also, at a New Year's Eve party of 1835/36, at Elstree, Macready recorded that

> Mr. Browning was very popular with the whole party; his simple and enthusiastic manner engaged attention and won opinions from all present; he looks and speaks more like a youthful poet than any man I ever saw.
>
> (Toynbee 1912: i. 267)

At Carlyle's home in July 1842 he met the American transcendentalist Bronson Alcott, with results the Scottish historian considered comic. As Carlyle wrote to John Sterling:

> Alcot came to see me again the other day; little Paracelsus Browning, a dainty Leigh-Huntish kind of fellow, with much ingenuity, vivacity and Cockney gracefulness, happened to be here; and answered his solemn drawling recommendations of vegetable diet with light Cockney banter and logic; whereupon Alcot, at parting, told me 'he would never come to me again!'
>
> (*Corr.* vi. 369)

There are hints, however, of another Browning, more volatile, less secure. Throughout these years his works were published at his father's expense, in cramped, ill-printed pamphlets (a cheap format), and we know from later evidence that his failure to create a wide readership was something that annoyed and even embittered him. In a letter to Barrett, referring to 1836, he recalls the contrasting receptions of his *Paracelsus* and Talfourd's *Ion*. Beneath the light-hearted manner, it is not hard to catch the frustration. To some extent, he exaggerates the negative reception of his own work, an indication of the extent of his hurt. He had clearly hoped for a burst of fame:

> 'Paracelsus,' printed a few months before, had been as dead a failure as 'Ion' a brilliant success ... I know that until Forster's notice in the 'Examiner' appeared, *every* journal that thought worth while to allude to the poem at all, treated it with entire contempt ... and that first taste was a most flattering sample of what the 'craft' [i.e. the Reviews] had in store for me – since my publisher and I had fairly to laugh at *his* 'Book'... in which he was used to paste extracts from newspapers & the like – seeing that, out of a long string of notices, one vied with its predecessor in disgust at my 'rubbish', as their word went.
>
> (*Corr.* xi. 232)

It is hard to tell exactly how wounded Browning was given the small number of extant letters from the 1830s. Sometimes he was buoyed up by positive comments in the Reviews. More often he was confused by the criticisms of his work, in particular the disastrous reception of *Sordello* (1840), the narrative poem on which he had laboured long and hard. The charge of unintelligibility that was levelled at *Sordello* was to become one of the ongoing criticisms, and at various times we can see him trying to throw off this image and write in a more accessible manner. In the year of his death, 1889, talking privately to the critic Edmund Gosse, he spoke of 'the desolateness of his early and middle life as a literary man' (Garrett 2000b: 144).

(ii) The theatre: a dead end?

A vital biographical source for these years is Macready's *Diaries* (Toynbee 1912). There was a mutual friendship between the young poet and the older actor. Browning knew Macready's stature, how he held the stage, and also how he was genuinely reviving the quality of Shakespearean production both in terms of his own acting and also in terms of his respect for Shakespeare's texts. As, from 1836 onwards, he came to know the actor better, we can clearly see his ambition to be a playwright, with the quality of Macready's acting as the vehicle for his success.

In May 1836 Browning intended to finish *Sordello* in a couple of months, and then settle to playwriting. He appealed to Macready:

> if, before then [July], any subject shall suggest itself to you – any character or event with which you are predisposed to sympathize – I will give my whole heart & soul to the writing a Tragedy on it … should I succeed, my way of life will be very certain, and my name pronounced along with yours.
>
> (*Corr.* iii. 173)

Browning wrote his historical drama *Strafford* quickly in the summer or early autumn. As Macready then took it up and moved towards its performance in May 1837, we see the 43-year-old actor subjecting the 25-year-old poet to a process of revision that caused him considerable stress:

> *March 21st.* [1837] – Browning came with me into the study, and with much interruption over the discussion of points and passages, we read through his tragedy of *Strafford* [one revision had already

taken place] ... *March 29th*. – Browning called and brought me the play of *Strafford*; he looked very unwell, jaded and thought-sick ... *April 7th*. Forster and Browning both came to my room – Browning with some of the passages to be supplied – very feebly written. Forster and he had rather a warm altercation ... *April 22nd*. – Browning ... apparently suffering from over-excitement.

(Toynbee 1912: i. 380–9)

With Macready in the lead role, the play received its first performance on 1 May 1837 at Covent Garden Theatre, and then just three more performances. Macready, who had been convinced it would fail completely, was relatively pleased at its reception, but, given the shortness of the run, it could not be regarded as a popular triumph. In the following years Browning was on the edge of Macready's 'court', seeing him perform and going back-stage to praise him, receiving complimentary passes to the theatre, and being available for informal play-readings when Macready wanted to test the quality of a new script. Browning, in turn, aimed one play after another at Macready, but with hardly any success.

In August 1839 he was at Macready's lodgings: 'His object, if he exactly knew it, was to learn from me whether, if he wrote a really good play, it would have a secure chance of acceptance' (Toynbee 1912: ii. 22). In September Macready turned down *King Victor and King Charles*. Less than a year later, Browning was beginning to broach the matter of another play, *The Return of the Druses*, in the wake of the failure of *Sordello* in the spring of 1840. In a letter probably of July, he assured Macready that his 'spick & span new Tragedy' has '*action* in it, drabbing, stabbing, et autres gentilesses [other pretty tricks]' (*Corr*. iv. 293). Then he went to see Macready:

August 27th. [1840] – Browning came before I had finished my bath, and really *wearied* me with his obstinate faith in his poem of *Sordello*, and of his eventual celebrity, and also with his self-opinionated persuasions upon his *Return of the Druses*. I fear he is for ever gone.

(Toynbee 1912: ii. 76)

Macready's rejection of the play did not deter Browning from trying again a year later. The result, *A Blot in the 'Scutcheon*, was his clearest attempt to write for popular taste, to work with some of the more obvious melodramatic conventions of the contemporary theatre. As Macready sat on the play through 1842, Browning continued to press him, while at the same time charming him with two poems for his

15

little son William, who was sick: 'The Cardinal and the Dog' and the (now famous) 'Pied Piper of Hamelin'. William Macready jun.'s pencil drawings for these poems, which he enclosed in thank you letters to Browning, are naive but delightful, and are beautifully reproduced by Kelley (*Corr.* v. 331, 350–1).

Browning's relationship with Macready finally broke down in February 1843 over tensions generated around *A Blot in the 'Scutcheon*, in particular because of the way in which – as Browning saw it – the play was unfairly treated in rehearsal. Forty years later, Browning wrote a supposedly objective account of what happened:

> When the Drury Lane season began, Macready informed me that he should act the play when he had brought out two others – 'The Patrician's Daughter,' and 'Plighted Troth;' having done so, he wrote to me that the former had been unsuccessful in money-drawing, and the latter had 'smashed his arrangements altogether:' but he would still produce my play ... I had no notion that it was a proper thing, in such a case, to 'release him from his promise;' on the contrary, I should have fancied that such a proposal was offensive. Soon after, Macready begged that I would call on him: he said the play had been read to the actors the day before, 'and laughed at from beginning to end:' on my speaking my mind about this, he explained that the reading had been done by the Prompter, a grotesque person with a red nose and wooden leg, ill at ease in the love scenes, and that he would himself make amends by reading the play next morning – which he did, and very adequately – but apprised me that, in consequence of the state of his mind, harassed by business and various trouble, the principal character must be taken by Mr. Phelps; and again I failed to understand, – what Forster subsequently assured me was plain as the sun at noonday, – that to allow at Macready's Theatre any other than Macready to play the principal part in a new piece was suicidal, – and really believed I was meeting his exigencies by accepting the substitution.... He wanted me to call it 'The Sister'! – and I have before me, while I write, the stage-acting copy, with two lines of his own insertion to avoid the tragical ending – Tresham [the main character] was to announce his intention of going into a monastery!
>
> (*Orr* 119–21)

And so the litany of complaint continues. Whether we see Browning as the nagging, touchy playwright, or Macready as the subtle, egotistical actor – he left Samuel Phelps in the principal role, so contributing to the play's failure – is less important than the larger issue that the letter reveals: the hurt of the 30-year-old Browning struggling to get his play produced. It is also more evidence, if it were needed, of his intimate knowledge of the theatre: the extent of his behind-the-scenes experience, his familiarity with actors and actresses, and with the processes of rehearsal. Even when his friendship with Macready was over, Browning did not give up. Shortly after this failure he started work on *Colombe's Birthday*, aiming directly at another prominent actor, Charles Kean (son of the great Edmund Kean). In March 1843 he read aloud his play to Kean and his wife, still pressing his ambitions.

What conclusions can we draw from this? It is important to emphasize that none of the plays written directly for the theatre have significant merit. *Strafford* (1837), *King Victor and King Charles* (1842), *The Return of the Druses* (1843), *A Blot in the 'Scutcheon* (1843), and *Colombe's Birthday* (1844) will be read and analysed by experts in nineteenth-century theatre, but they are unlikely to be at the centre of a living interest in Browning's work. The great early poems – those in *Dramatic Lyrics* (1842) and *Dramatic Romances and Lyrics* (1845) **[66–80, 150–68]** – at first seem to be produced almost incidentally or just tangentially to his project in the contemporary theatre, but really they grow out of the same passionate interests in acting and actors and live theatre. (In old age, when Browning saw the great Tommaso Salvini play *King Lear*, he is reported to have remarked: 'It makes one wonder which is the greater, the poet or the actor' (Garrett 2000b: 113).) In the 1830s, at the time when Browning was first developing the dramatic monologue, cross-overs and connections are not hard to see. When, for example, in June 1837, Browning said to Macready that his recent *Hamlet* had been 'a magnificent revelation' he was not just flattering (*Corr.* iii. 251). We know that he had watched carefully many of Macready's performances in different roles, and of course the acting skills of all the better actors around Macready. He was knowledgeable about the techniques of theatre, the timing of speeches, the nature of dramatic gesture and poise, the use of pause, the nature of theatrical climax and, crucially – in relation to *Othello* and other works – the workings of dramatic irony. All these things find their way into the early dramatic monologues.

The dramatic monologue **[60–6]**, or as Browning called it, 'dramatic lyric' – best exemplified here by his most famous work 'My Last Duchess' **[67–70]** – is a highly theatrical form occupying (paradoxically) a very untheatrical space. It is built upon the essential elements of live theatre: the pacings, turns, and rhythms of actor-spoken speech, yet it exists as a lyric, a private work in a volume of poems to be privately consumed. More than anything else, dramatic monologues (at least in Browning's early use of them) are fairly short. It is as though the largeness of theatrical time and space finds itself shrunk, made dense and elliptical, in the framework of a fifty- or hundred-line poem.

(iii) First journeys to Italy

Italy is uniquely important to Browning's life and works taken as a whole – he lived there for twelve years and wrote a great deal of poetry set there. Browning made two early trips to Italy. Partly, as well as other purposes, they served as holidays from the struggles described above. The first journey, in 1838, had as its main aim to complete *Sordello* 'among the scenes it describes' (*Corr.* iv. 24), though he is not actually known to have advanced the poem on this trip.

He sailed from London in early April 1838, on a merchant ship, and arrived in Venice on 1 June. He was hugely impressed by the city, particularly after the long sea trip, and on his return he gave 'glowing descriptions of its beauties, the palaces, the sunsets, the moon-rises' to Eliza Bridell-Fox (Garrett 2000b: 34). In Venice he stayed in lodgings for two weeks before making a tour around the Veneto. This took him from Venice to Mestre, Treviso, and Bassano, then to Asolo, San Zenone, and Possagno (up on the hills edging the plain), and then via Vicenza and Padua back to Venice. He had *Sordello* at the front of his mind, but this trip was at least partly a pilgrimage in the footsteps of Shelley and Byron. Shelley's 'Lines written among the Euganean Hills', from *Rosalind and Helen*, was one of his favourite poems, and in June 1838 he visited these beautiful rolling hills south-west of Padua.

Even this first trip, when he was in Italy for only a month, had an enormous impact. *Sordello* (1840) – as it struck one contemporary reader – 'is a perfect storehouse of Italian scenery and exotic fruits, plants, and flowers' (Horne 1844: ii. 185–6). *Pippa Passes* (1841) is set in the small hill-top village of Asolo, which so impressed him on this trip: he visited the Rocca, the 'turret' of Part III of *Pippa Passes*, on 20 June 1838. In *Dramatic Lyrics* (1842) both 'My Last Duchess' and 'In a Gondola' can be described as 'Italian' poems.

His second Italian journey was a source of inspiration for three of the important poems of the volume *Dramatic Romances and Lyrics* (1845): 'Pictor Ignotus' [70–2, 161–5], 'The Bishop Orders His Tomb' [75–6], and 'The Englishman in Italy'. This time he sailed in early August 1844, arriving in Naples in late September. He travelled in the beautiful Sorrento peninsula south of Naples, the countryside of which is so vividly brought to life in 'The Englishman in Italy'. He saw some of the standard sites for travellers, Vesuvius and Pompeii for example, before going north to Rome. Details of this trip are scarce, but we know that he made friends with an Italian couple, and also that he visited Shelley's grave in the Protestant Cemetery at Rome. Subsequently, he travelled north to Pisa, Livorno, and Florence, and then made his way home through Germany and the Low Countries. At Livorno he met Edward John Trelawny, the friend of Shelley and Byron, indeed the man who had supervised the cremation of Shelley's body on the beach near Viareggio in 1822. Again, he was seeing the art and architecture of Italy, but he was also (as on his first trip) on pilgrimage to his Romantic predecessors.

(iv) Courtship

In 1842, R. H. Horne decided to write an updated version of William Hazlitt's *The Spirit of the Age* (1825), and give a survey of the significant writers and intellectuals of his own time. In his *A New Spirit of the Age* (1844) he examined Dickens, Bulwer-Lytton, Macaulay, Carlyle, and Wordsworth, writers that informed opinion considered to be obviously major, but he also included lesser lights: William Harrison Ainsworth, John Banim, Anna Jameson, Harriet Martineau, and others. Browning is discussed in a joint chapter with J. W. Marston, though immediately Horne refers to 'the comparatively little known works of Mr. Browning' (Horne 1844: ii. 155).

In reviews of *A New Spirit of the Age* the lack of mention of Browning is striking. He was known to the cognoscenti, but, compared to Dickens or Macaulay, his reputation was tiny. *The Weekly Chronicle* admitted that 'a very limited number of readers' would be acquainted with his work, *The Church of England Quarterly Review* that 'we know nothing of Mr. Browning's poetry, except from the quotations in the volume before us' (*Corr.* viii. 375, 409). Nonetheless Browning's inclusion was its own limited kind of success. He knew Horne personally and had actually helped him with some of the epigraphs for the volume. Another poet whose aid Horne solicited was the invalid Elizabeth Barrett, who also appears in *A New Spirit*, paired in a chapter with Caroline Norton (then hailed as 'the Byron of poetesses').

Browning came to meet Elizabeth Barrett (1806–61) via the agency of John Kenyon, a wealthy man-about-town and dilettante of literature. Kenyon was Barrett's second cousin, and a regular visitor at her sick room. He was also a friend of Browning's, whom he considered 'strikingly upright & loyal in all his ways' and 'impeccable as a gentleman' (*Corr*. xii. 259). He had been to school with Browning's father and he knew Browning's family.

While Browning was away on his second Italian journey, Elizabeth Barrett had published her two-volume *Poems* (1844), a vivid collection that quickly extended her reputation. Kenyon gave a copy to Browning's sister, Sarianna, and Browning, on his return to England in about mid-December, read the poems and was deeply moved by 'the fresh strange music, the affluent language, the exquisite pathos and true new brave thought' (*Corr*. x. 17). The volumes would have struck him all the more because in one poem, 'Lady Geraldine's Courtship', there was a generous, complimentary allusion to his own work (ll. 165–6). Barrett was one of the cognoscenti who was able to see the worth of his writing, and on 10 January 1845, at Kenyon's urging, he wrote to her in the fullest and most direct terms. A correspondence resulted, leading to their first meeting on 20 May 1845. Just over a year and three months later, after a further 91 meetings, and a total correspondence of 572 letters, Robert Browning and Elizabeth Barrett married secretly at St Marylebone Church on 12 September 1846.

The Brownings' courtship and marriage has been popularized and mythologized in numerous romantic and fictionalized accounts, in, for example, Rudolf Besier's play *The Barretts of Wimpole Street* (1930), the later film of this, in Virginia Woolf's *Flush* (1933), and – nearer our own time – in Margaret Forster's *Lady's Maid* (1991), an imagined view of the marriage from the perspective of Barrett's maid. The love correspondence has become famous, and some critics see it as a work of literary merit in its own right. Romantically-inclined biography has thrived on it, but it has also provoked Daniel Karlin's *The Courtship of Robert Browning and Elizabeth Barrett* (1985), a serious psychological and literary treatment of the development of the relationship. What lies behind all this interest is the fact that two significant poets had fallen in love, and that in the years of their marriage – through to Barrett's death in 1861 – they both produced the majority of their best poetry. The emotional dynamic of their love contributed to the quality of the writing they both accomplished in the 1850s.

(v) Elizabeth Barrett

The woman who Browning met in May 1845 was 39 years old, had bad lungs and could hardly walk. As someone apparently significantly disabled, she spent the winters immured in her second-floor room at 50 Wimpole Street. Her 60-year-old widowed father prayed with her each night. She was supported by her father's stern and distant love, and by the love of her six brothers and two sisters living in the same house.

From a sheltered, privileged childhood, she had passed, through a period of relative normality, to this cloistered existence. When Browning first entered her room he was struck with pity at her pinched life, the dust and lack of fresh air. By contrast, Barrett was a witty, sophisticated, and deeply humane literary intellectual. She had written a significant body of poetry, culminating in *Poems* (1844). She was fluent in Greek, Latin, and French. Her erudition was apparent in her essays on the Greek Christian poets. She conversed with some of her correspondents – Mary Russell Mitford in particular – about the contemporary French novelists Honoré de Balzac, George Sand, Frédéric Soulié, Victor Hugo and many others, in wide-ranging terms. The realism of this French literature was in some ways an escape from certain kinds of English puritanism and restriction, a window on a larger world that her status as a gentlewoman denied. In 1844 Horne could rightly say of her that

> probably no living individual has a more extensive and diffuse acquaintance with literature ... there is probably not a single good romance of the most romantic kind in whose marvellous and impossible scenes she has not delighted, over the fortunes of whose immaculate or incredible heroes and heroines she has not wept; nor a clever novel or fanciful sketch of our own day, over the brightest pages of which she has not smiled inwardly, or laughed outright, just as their authors themselves would have desired.
>
> (Horne 1844: ii. 135)

Barrett had suffered significant bereavements: the early loss of her mother in 1828, and the early deaths of her two eldest brothers, Edward and Samuel, in 1840. For Flush, her spaniel, she had a deep, humorous, and sentimental affection.

The Barrett family was of a much higher social status than Browning's, and certainly saw itself as a grand clan. Though she published as Elizabeth Barrett Barrett, her brothers urged her to use the correct form Elizabeth Barrett Moulton-Barrett. The Barretts' wealth had been created in Jamaica, where a Barrett had been one of the seventeenth-century colonists. Through the eighteenth century, led by powerful, strong men, the family had built up extensive sugar plantations in the north of the island – in the region of 30,000 to 40,000 acres – run, of course, with the usual slave labour. The sons of the family sometimes had black mistresses with whom they had children, and the major historical treatment of this – written in the 1930s, by the American academic Jeannette Marks, at a time of course when America itself was beginning to reassess issues of 'race relations' – reads like a strange factual version of Faulkner's novel *Go Down, Moses*. It is uneasy about the extent of the cross-racial sexual relations it reveals, and evasive about the cruel consequences that resulted for mixed-race children. A more recent account of this can be found in Barrett (2000).

At the end of the eighteenth century the family's fortunes declined when three of Barrett's great-uncles died in succession, leaving a problem over inheritance and the continuance of the line. At that point, the poet's great-grandfather, Edward Barrett (1734–98), had succeeded in passing the bulk of the family wealth through to his daughter's children. Those children, Barrett's father, Edward Moulton-Barrett, and his brother Sam, had come to England in 1792 to be brought up as gentlemen, and also to avoid the high mortality rate suffered by whites in the Caribbean climate. Legal disputes over inheritance, the use of attorney managers to control the estates in the absence of the heirs, and the abolition of slavery (enacted in Jamaica in the 1830s, but in prospect long before), all lessened the family wealth, and the consequence was one of the great traumas of Barrett's youth. In 1832 her father had had to sell the flamboyant house and large estate, Hope End Mansion near the Malvern hills, where she had been brought up, and settle – after various residences – in a relatively modest house at 50 Wimpole Street, London. The Barretts were still a high-status family, even if Edward Moulton-Barrett had had to compound with his creditors 'at great cost to his income for the rest of his life' (Marks 1938: 368).

The famous love letters of the two poets do not make light or sentimental reading. This is a sophisticated, thoughtful, and profoundly emotional correspondence in which Browning and Barrett gradually dismantle the doubts and inhibitions that block their intimacy. The syntax of both poets – though particularly Browning's – is frequently opaque to a first reading, but on both sides what could be called the emotional syntax, the involved process by which doubts and fears are expressed and soothed, is sometimes even harder to untangle.

Simple insecurities were easy to solve: they both discovered they were Nonconformist in religious affiliation. As the possibility of marriage clearly arose, Browning – who had no income – offered to take up a profession in order to maintain them; Barrett refused this, insisting that he keep wholly to his vocation as poet. It is as this discussion came to a head that she revealed her personal income, £300 to £400 a year, from investment of a legacy from her grandmother and from the annual return from shares in a merchant vessel inherited from her uncle, Samuel Moulton-Barrett. (It was, in fact, on this money that Browning and Barrett lived their comfortable, middle-class life abroad in the coming years.)

The biggest single fear to be exorcised was Barrett's. Her sense that Browning might be deceiving himself, that he might have fallen in love with a fantasy, that he might not be looking hard enough at the disabled, older, and none too beautiful woman before him. Browning's persistence and warmth gradually overcomes this, and at such moments, on either side, their letters break into passion. Browning's heightened writing here has precisely the contorted lyricism that can be so eloquent in his poetry:

> for the one thing you must believe, must resolve to believe in its length and breadth, is that I do love you and live only in the love of you.
>
> I will rest on the confidence that you do so believe! You *know* by this that it is no shadowy image of you and *not* you, which having attached myself to in the first instance, I afterward compelled my fancy to see reproduced, so to speak, with tolerable exactness to the original idea, in you, the dearest real *you* I am blessed with – You *know* what the eyes are to me, and the lips and the hair – and I, for my part, know *now*, while fresh from seeing you, certainly *know*, whatever I may have said a short time since, that *you* will go on to the end, that that arm round me will not let me go, – over such a blind abyss – I refuse to think, to fancy, *towards* what it would be to lose you now! So I give my life, my soul into your hand – the giving is a mere form too, it is yours, ever yours from the first – but ever as I see you, sit with you, and come away to think over it all, I find more that seems mine to give, – you give me more life and it goes back to you.
>
> (*Corr.* xii. 153)

The final obstacle remained the attitude of Barrett's father. Much has been hypothesized about why Edward Moulton-Barrett did not want his children to marry. As the question of marriage arose in the correspondence, Barrett was well aware of her father's little-stated but adamant prohibition: she called it an 'obliquity of the will' or 'eccentricity'. John Kenyon called it a 'monomania'. Some have suggested that, in the wake of his wife's death in 1828, Edward Moulton-Barrett had developed a quasi-incestuous bond with his daughters. A more probable explanation is that he was a relatively lonely man who had suffered a series of disasters: the early deaths of his wife and his only brother, his financial difficulties, and, in one terrible year, 1840, the deaths of his two eldest sons. A sense of things falling apart, and his idea of father-as-leader – backed up by a Biblical literalism that saw fathers as patriarchs to be unquestioningly obeyed – is perhaps enough to explain his attitude. Barrett only confided some aspects of her developing relationship to her sisters, Henrietta and Arabella, not to her brothers, in case they should reveal it by accident, and her father knew nothing of it at all, only that (as he thought) Browning was an occasional (rather than regular) visitor to his house.

Amid the many emphases that could occur at this point, perhaps a literary one is the most important. This was to be a marriage of two poets, both differently but seriously committed to their art. Even during the courtship one subject of their letters was the poems that Browning was preparing for publication as *Dramatic Romances and Lyrics* (1845). ('Pictor Ignotus' **[70–2]**, 'The Bishop Orders His Tomb' **[75–6]**, 'The Laboratory' **[78]** and 'The Lost Leader' **[78–80]** are all originally from this volume.) Barrett saw the poems of this volume in manuscript, and – while continually asserting their quality and her faith in his genius – offered criticisms, queries, and suggestions about their wording. Most of these were adopted into the final versions. (The text of her comments is reproduced in full in *Corr.* xi. 375–92.) After this, she also commented on the plays *Luria* and *A Soul's Tragedy* (1846).

(c) THE ITALIAN YEARS: 1846–1861

(i) 'Italy ... *my* university'

Robert Browning and Elizabeth Barrett married secretly at 11.00 a.m. on Saturday 12 September 1846 at St Marylebone Church, with Barrett's maid, Elizabeth Wilson, and Browning's cousin, James Silverthorne, as the witnesses. On the marriage certificate they are described as 'Bachelor, Gentleman' and 'Spinster' 'of Full age'. They both returned to their ordinary lives for a week, and then, on the following Saturday afternoon, rendezvoused at Hodgson's bookshop in Great Marylebone Street before catching the 5.00 p.m. train from Vauxhall to Southampton. Barrett would insist, rightly, that there was nothing improper in this – 'There was no elopement in the case, but simply a private marriage' (*Corr.* xiv. 14) – nonetheless, if not technically an elopement, its social impact was pretty much as shocking. Browning's family knew about the wedding and the circumstances that made secrecy necessary. But the Barretts had no idea: Barrett's sisters may have guessed in the intervening week, but they told no one. On the Saturday the couple left for Italy, Barrett posted a letter to her eldest brother George, explaining and justifying her actions, and enclosing a further letter for her father. The circle of their friends and acquaintances only learnt of the wedding by the simply phrased adverts that appeared in the newspapers on the following Monday (21 September), by which time the newly-weds were already in Paris.

The Brownings stayed a week in Paris while Barrett recovered some of her strength, and then headed down through Lyons to Marseilles, and then by steamer to Livorno. For their first Italian winter they settled at Pisa, in an apartment near the Duomo and the Leaning Tower, enjoying in solitude their first months together, though also having to weather the emotional storm of Edward Moulton-Barrett's complete rejection of his daughter. In April 1847 they moved to Florence, and – after various toings and froings between apartments, including the one they eventually ended up in – in May 1848 they settled in a spacious, seven-room apartment on the first floor of the Palazzo Guidi (which they called Casa Guidi) in the south of the city, near to the Palazzo Pitti and the Boboli gardens. Though they were sometimes away from it for extended periods – at Paris, at Bagni di Lucca, and at Rome for example – this was their main home until Barrett's death thirteen years later.

In old age, noting that he had not been to a major public school, or to Oxford or Cambridge, Browning said 'Italy was *my* university' (Garrett 2000b: 137). Its impact on him was broadly threefold. First, it was a country where – even though he had relatively few Italian friends or acquaintances – he was exposed to a different cultural, social, and religious milieu. The living, breathing Italy of the 1840s and 50s filtered its way into his imagination. The broad-brimmed straw-hats worn by Tuscan women, the Roman custom of offering iron implements for sale spread out on the pavements, the 'figpeckers' pecking the first crop, the Romans' love of roast chestnuts and roast porcupines: this rich, Balzac-like vein of perception and description accumulated during his years of residence. The physical impact is obvious in 'Up at a Villa – Down in the City', 'Old Pictures in Florence', and 'De Gustibus –', written while in Italy, but *The Ring and the Book* (published in 1868–9) is still saturated with such memories even though it was written after his permanent return to England. Henry James could say that its 'quantity' of Italian atmosphere 'is like nothing else in English poetry … a perfect cloud of gold-dust' (James 1914: 318).

The Brownings, though Protestant and Nonconformist in affiliation and sensibility, did not shut themselves off from the environment of

Italian Catholicism. They heard Catholic preaching: on one occasion, for example, the preaching of an impassioned Dominican monk in Pisa, on another that of the English convert Henry Manning (the future Cardinal) in Rome. They saw the processions and celebrations of the Catholic feastdays (memorably evoked in 'Up at a Villa'), and once attended Christmas Mass at St Peter's, Rome. They saw the great fireworks to celebrate the feast of St John the Baptist, and they saw, and sometimes attended, parts of the Carnival festivities that preceded the quiet of Lent. Barrett noticed how in Florence the different classes mixed unselfconsciously at celebrations, in a way different from in England. Compared to England, this was a world of different colour and light, of different social texture and reality, to Barrett (initially) almost a fairytale world, to which she opened up rather like Lucy Honeychurch in E. M. Forster's novel *A Room with a View* (1908).

Then there was the Italy of history. This certainly comprised the classical past, but most importantly the Renaissance, to a lesser extent the Baroque. For Browning, the galleries and churches of Florence became a textbook in which he learnt, really and in detail, the art of the Renaissance. He read extensively in Giorgio Vasari's *Le Vite de' più eccellenti pittori, scultori, et architettori* (*The Lives of the Painters*), the sixteenth-century work that first summarized the achievements of Italian art from Giotto to Michelangelo. He also read in a similar work of the seventeenth century, Filippo Baldinucci's *Notizie de' professori del disegno* (*Accounts of the Experts in Design*), in effect a massive encyclopaedia of artists' biographies.

Readers who know only the giants of the Renassiance, like Michelangelo and Raphael, may be surprised that Browning chose lesser figures like Fra Filippo Lippi and Andrea del Sarto to write about, but these painters are prominently represented in the galleries and churches where he often walked, in the Uffizi, for example, and the Pitti Palace. He knew their art intimately long before he thought to dramatize their lives. Moreover, he had developed his own interpretations of Renaissance art, and his own complex sense of how art and religion interact [175–81].

The third aspect of Italy that affected Browning was the political. The Brownings were not socialist or radical in their political thinking; they were opposed, for example, to the French socialist thought of Charles Fourier, Louis Blanc, and Pierre-Joseph Proudhon – thinkers who had some impact on Marx – but they were politically liberal in broad terms. The Italy of 1846 was in many ways little different from the Italy of Shelley and Byron: the political landscape was still determined by the settlement of the Congress of Vienna (1815) from the end of the Napoleonic wars. There was no such thing as 'Italy' as a nation state. The peninsula was divided into kingdoms and dukedoms, most autocratic, and most directly or indirectly under the influence of the Austrian Empire (what Shelley so vividly called 'the Celtic Anarch').

To put it simply, England in the first half of the nineteenth century had a constitution but only a small measure of democracy. Across the Italian peninsula there was even less true constitutionalism and even less democracy, and to liberals like the Brownings, it presented a dismal political picture. Tuscany, where the Brownings lived, was ruled by the Austrian Grand Duke Leopold II of Habsburg-Lorraine. In 1847 he took some measures to liberalize restrictions on the press, but he was still basically an autocrat.

Across this Italy, in 1848, while the Brownings were resident in Florence, swept the year of revolutions. The monarchs and the Pope were forced to grant new or more liberal constitutions. There were insurrections in Venice and Milan, throwing off the Austrian yoke. The king of Piedmont risked a nationalist war against Austria, and Grand Duke Leopold II eventually fled Florence, just as the Pope had fled Rome. In 1849, between February and July, there was a Republic in Rome. These hopes for a more liberal politics were bound up with the cause of Italian nationhood, the Risorgimento.

Gradually, however, the liberal dawning was crushed and the conservative regimes reasserted themselves. The Brownings experienced these turmoils vividly, but it is Barrett, and not Browning, who brings it directly into her poetry. It is she, in other words, who continues directly a Shelleyan mode of political poetry, the hopes for *'bella libertà'* (blessed liberty) and the shocks and disappointments to this cause. In May 1849, she, with Browning, saw the Austrian army marching into Florence to re-establish the conservative regime of Leopold II. Her description of this in *Casa Guidi Windows* (1851) conveys brilliantly what we might now think of as the fascistic impact of this event:

> Then, gazing, I beheld the long-drawn street
>   Live out, from end to end, full in the sun,
> With Austria's thousands. Sword and bayonet,
>   Horse, foot, artillery, – cannons rolling on,
> Like blind slow storm-clouds gestant with the heat
>   Of undeveloped lightnings, each bestrode
> By a single man, dust-white from head to heel,
>   Indifferent as the dreadful thing he rode,
> Like a sculptured Fate serene and terrible.
>   As some smooth river which has overflowed,

Will slow and silent down its current wheel
  A loosened forest, all the pines erect, –
So, swept, in mute significance of storm,
The marshalled thousands, – not an eye deflect
To left or right, to catch a novel form
  Of Florence city adorned by architect
And carver ...
(Part ii. 299–315)

In his poetry, at least, Browning is rarely interested in politics in this way, and there is no comparable passage of political verse by him from this period that is as open, Shelleyan, and living as this. (Compare, for example, the different nature of political allusion in 'Old Pictures in Florence'). This contrast can help us to understand his very different development in these years.

(ii) Italy, creativity, and love

As Browning entered on his married life in Italy there is a fallow period in his writing. If we telescope and simplify somewhat, we could say that between 1846 and 1852 he wrote relatively little new poetry, and what he did write is relatively unimportant to his future reputation. Initially, at least, he was absorbed in his new marriage and the intimacy and love it brought him.

Between 1846 and November 1849 the only new poem he is known to have written is 'The Guardian Angel'. On 9 March 1849 his only son, Pen, was born. At the end of the same month he heard the news of his mother's death from England. This tragic coincidence and his profound grief seem to have led – at the end of 1849 – to the writing of *Christmas-Eve and Easter-Day* (1850), a meditation on the different denominations of Christianity, agnosticism, and the arguments for faith, a meditation that is only thinly couched in dramatic terms. It is his least characteristic work, and most critics have considered it a failure. From then till 1853 he is only known to have written the now-titled *Essay on Shelley* (1852), a short prose work, originally an introduction to a small batch of 'Shelley letters' most of which were quickly shown to be forgeries.

Then, suddenly, creativity blazed. In Florence in 1853, and again in 1854, he wrote the bulk of the poems of the two-volume *Men and Women* (1855) **[80–100]**, his central work, in periods of composition that seem at various times to have been highly intense and productive. Between June 1851 and October 1852 the Brownings had been staying in Paris, with two trips over to England. Now, back in the quiet of Florence, with socially (as Browning said) 'no life, no variety', he made a conscious artistic effort. His comments in letters noted the lyrical nature of these poems, their sheer variety and (in many cases) brevity, and again addressed the issue of his recalcitrant audience:

> I have not left the house one evening since our return. I am writing, a sort of first step toward popularity (for me!), 'Lyrics' with more music and painting than before, so as to get people to hear and see ... something to follow, if I can compass it! (24 February 1853).
> I am trying if I can't take people's ears at last, by the lyrical tip; if they have one (17 March 1853).
>
> (Oxford v. xiv, xv)

In the next year, when writing was more advanced, he noted that the new poems were 'of all sorts and sizes and styles and subjects' (5 June 1854) (*Oxford* v. xviii). The emphasis on lyric is interesting: he was conscious that he was *not* writing a long poem, or – as more usual for him – a play. He was developing the aspect of his work demonstrated in *Dramatic Lyrics* (1842) and *Dramatic Romances and Lyrics* (1845).

Men and Women (1855) is most famous for its blank verse dramatic monologues about painting, 'Fra Lippo Lippi' and 'Andrea del Sarto' [84–8], but, as Browning's comments perhaps make clear, the majority of poems are stanzaic dramatic monologues, many focused on love and relationships [96–100]. Their male and female speakers – Browning is, as usual, writing dramatically – are in very different kinds of relationship. As well as being about the intensity of young passionate love ('Love Among the Ruins'), and the stability of established married love ('By the Fire-Side'), these poems are also about disappointments, misunderstandings, jealousies, and desertions: examples would be 'A Lovers' Quarrel', 'A Woman's Last Word', 'Any Wife to Any Husband', and 'In a Year'. No simplistic conclusion can be drawn from this, that, for example, there were covert disappointments in Browning's own marriage. Rather we should conclude that the process of being opened out by love, of being made vulnerable and alive in this particular way, extended his emotional range and allowed him to think (in dramatic terms) about different kinds of situation and relationship.

Sometimes it is clear that the relationship between biography and art, between the root in biography and the flower of the poem, is inter-involved, almost deliberately inverted or deceptive. So, for example, 'Any Wife to Any Husband' has as its speaker a woman who is dying, hoping that her husband will stay loyal to her memory and not remarry.

She is jealous, prospectively, of an imagined future wife, but also disturbed by what her knowledge of her husband's character tells her about him now: the present quality of his love. Since Barrett was seriously ill at various times during the marriage, the poem might seem to have an obvious biographical resonance: Browning imagining what she might fear about him. Yet this is not a new theme, it was precisely these kinds of emotional insecurities that Browning and Barrett spent a long time exorcising from each other, both during their courtship and afterwards, building a deeper trust.

At one point in the courtship letters, for example, Barrett expressed the fear that, in effect, she has been warming up Browning for another, more suitable wife. She is an invalid, she is not good enough for him: but he has learnt something through his relationship with her, and can now go on to a fuller, more natural marriage to another woman. She raises the spectre of this insecurity (in an atmosphere of growing trust) in order to have it banished:

> Dearest beloved, when I used to tell you to give me up, & imagined to myself how I should feel if you did it, ... & thought it would not be much worse than it was before I knew you ... (a little better indeed, inasmuch as I had the memory for ever) ... the chief *pang* was the idea of another woman ... ! From *that*, I have turned back again & again, recoiling like a horse set against too high a wall.
>
> (*Corr.* xii. 274)

Here, as elsewhere, the love correspondence is remarkably honest in its emotional analysis, and a good guide to the quality of the relationship that resulted. The nature of such prospective jealousy, and the sexual feeling it implies, can be acknowledged, and so (in some sense) tamed. It is this kind of emotional material, reconsidered and reworked, that feeds into Browning's dramatic poems about love and relationships.

In these years the Brownings shared deeply the experience of being poets together. Both of them were working at full tilt through parts of 1854, Browning on the poems of *Men and Women*, and Barrett on what she called her 'novel-poem' *Aurora Leigh*. In April 1855 she commented on the manuscripts of his *Men and Women* (Huxley 1929: 216). Likewise, early in 1856, Browning saw the working manuscript of *Aurora Leigh* and praised it, even breaking down in tears when he was moved by the story. Again, however, their writing seems to be taking them in different imaginative directions. Barrett was writing an epic of contemporary life, about a woman writer's friendship with a working-class girl who is raped, a work – as she described it – 'taken from the times, "hot and hot"' (March 1855) (Reynolds 1996: 331). In *Aurora Leigh* issues of class division, poverty and deprivation, women's social position, and the role of the woman writer all loom large. By contrast, much of Browning's work has a lyrical focus, or enters into past historical eras, or, in the case of 'Childe Roland', into a mainly imaginary world. Compared to hers, his work is more aesthetic and introspective, almost guarded against easy assimilation to the contemporary world by historical reference, the lyric impulse, and internal dramatic complexity. Even when poems do have contemporary settings (as in the case of 'A Toccata of Galuppi's' or 'Bishop Blougram's Apology') they nonetheless seem to turn in upon themselves. Perhaps this is one factor that explains the different critical receptions of these works. The reception of *Men and Women* in 1855 was disastrous, with the majority of reviewers demonstrating little significant understanding of what Browning had achieved, whereas *Aurora Leigh* in 1856 was both critically and popularly acclaimed. It went through five editions in the next four years.

In December 1856, not long after the publication of *Aurora Leigh*, John Kenyon died and left the poets a significant legacy in his will: £4500 to Barrett and £6500 to Browning, hence ensuring financial security. This, and the poor critical reception of *Men and Women*, may be factors explaining Browning's relative reluctance to write during the rest of the 1850s.

At Florence, and at Rome in the winters, he settled to the life of a gentleman abroad, bringing up his small son with Barrett, and enjoying evenings out in those parts of the expatriate communities he found congenial. As Barrett's *Aurora Leigh* became more and more popular, he must have been struck by the different reception of his own more stylistically and dramatically intricate art. In her letters to others Barrett expressed a sense of injustice on his behalf. In these years, in Rome, he took up clay modelling in the studio of the American sculptor William Wetmore Story (1819–95), who became one of his closest friends. He also practised drawing twice a week under the supervision of Emma Landseer Mackenzie. Sometimes he socialized heavily. In January 1859, for example, Barrett reports that he 'has gone out every night for a fortnight together, and sometimes two or three times deep in a one night's engagements. So plenty of distraction, and no Men and Women' (Kenyon 1897: ii. 303).

In the late 1850s Barrett's health declined. The death of her father in April 1857 affected her deeply, partly because of the way in which he had never endorsed her marriage or acknowledged his grandson.

The death of her sister, Henrietta, in December 1860, was another crisis that undermined her health and strength.

In June 1859 the peninsula of Italy entered into a period of war that ended a year and nine months later in the official inauguration of the Kingdom of Italy. Retrospectively, the achievement of the political unification of Italy (the Risorgimento), the establishment of Italy as a nation state, can look inevitable, but it did not appear so at the time, particularly as initially some of the main players did not want it. In June 1859 Napoleon III of France came in on the side of the Piedmontese against the Austrians, so commencing the period of change. The Brownings lived through the excitements and disappointments of the ensuing months: through the Peace of Villafranca in July 1859 (which halted the Franco-Piedmontese war against the Austrians and initially appeared to halt the cause of unification), through the plebiscites of early 1860, Garibaldi's military campaign in the south (May–October 1860), and the Piedmontese occupation of Umbria and the Marches. By late in 1860 only Rome and its surrounding region were left outside the new constitutional Kingdom of Italy, a kingdom which was officially proclaimed in March 1861.

Barrett was a passionate supporter of the Risorgimento, and, despite her weakening health, she turned these events directly and quickly into poetry, writing out her admiration for Napoleon III (who set events in motion) and celebrating various aspects of the heroism of the political struggle. Browning, who shared her enthusiasm for unification, was none the less not an admirer of Napoleon III. Prior to the Peace of Villafranca he worked on a poem on 'the Italian question' which he then abandoned as it 'no longer suited the moment' (Kenyon 1897: ii. 368–9). In the spring of 1860 he worked on some 'lyrics', presumably poems that were eventually published in *Dramatis Personae* (1864). It is probably now also that he made a prose-sketch for the poem that eventually became *Prince Hohenstiel-Schwangau* (1871), his attack on Napoleon III.

These two hints of his attempting to write on 'the Italian question' and on Napoleon III suggest he may have been trying to match the excitement of Barrett's politically-committed poetry, and that something blocked or would not allow fruition. Barrett could write openly the cause of *bella libertà* and her passion for Italy, he could not. Besides this, at this time, he was anxious about her health. This was particularly weak during the winter at Rome from late November 1860 to May 1861, but, given her general record of illness, not predictably fatal. Her photograph, in May 1861, shows her standing, gaunt but composed. After their return to Florence in early June, she died after a short illness on the 29th. The evidence suggests that Browning was profoundly traumatized, experiencing a heart-broken grief so intense as to be near to a breakdown.

(d) WIDOWERHOOD AND OLD AGE: 1861–1889

(i) Recognition at last

At 49 years old, Browning was a young widower, and he now returned to England to rebuild his life, to continue his career as a poet, and to bring up and educate his 12-year-old son.

There is a sense at this point that the intensity of his writing life was one way of living through the early years of grief. In early 1862 he prepared for publication the *Last Poems of Elizabeth Barrett Browning* (March 1862). In May he and Pen settled at 19 Warwick Crescent, (near Paddington), London. In August, a little over a year after Barrett's death, he began writing again, '... & mean to keep writing, whether I like it or no' (18 August 1862) (McAleer 1951: 119).

It is difficult to reconstruct the chronology of the poems that were published as the volume *Dramatis Personae* (1864) **[80–100]**. Some were written before Barrett's death, mainly in 1860 and 1861, others were written after it, but the datings of some poems (notably 'Caliban upon Setebos' and 'A Death in the Desert') are suppositious. This volume is poised across the central crisis of his life. Some of the light verse in the volume has been much praised by Christopher Ricks. About 'Youth and Art', for example, he speaks of how Victorian light verse 'offers unique combinations of acumen and pathos' (Ricks 1987: xxix). Such poems sit oddly with the dark irony active in other poems, and the lack of open, fulfilled poems about love. The uneasy feel of the volume as a whole reflects to some extent Browning's emotional circumstances at this time: as he had written painfully to Isa Blagden, 'And now the past & present & future, pleasure & pain & pleasure, for the last taste of all, are mixed up like ingredients of a drink' (9 September 1861) (McAleer 1951: 87).

After the publication of *Dramatis Personae* in May 1864, and after an August–September holiday with his father, his sister, and Pen in the south-west of France, Browning plunged into the writing of his 21,000-line masterpiece, the work he would eventually call *The Ring and the Book* **[100–15]**. From the start he clearly intended something special, but he had no idea how long it would preoccupy him or the dimensions it would reach. In October 1864 he wrote with characteristic optimism to Julia Wedgwood: 'I have got the whole of that poem, you enquire about, well in my head, shall write the Twelve books of it in six months, and then take breath again' (Curle 1937:95). Five years would be the actual time it would take him to complete the work.

If, as the evidence suggests, he was setting out on a conscious *tour de force*, it is interesting how much he deviates from Barrett's example. In *Aurora Leigh*, her equivalent long work, she not only wrote an epic of contemporary life, she also theorized that kind of epic. She argued that it was the poet's duty to deal in contemporary subject-matter, 'to represent ... this live, throbbing age', not delve back into history, resuscitate old times (see *Aurora Leigh*, v. 154–221). Resuscitating old times, however, is exactly what Browning did.

He had become fascinated by a collection of Latin legal documents of 1698, bound in one volume, which he bought at a flea market in Florence in 1860 (or possibly 1859). They told the story of the vicious murder, by a middle-aged aristocrat, Count Franceschini, of his teenage wife Pompilia Comparini, whom he accused of adultery and elopement with a priest. In 1863, through friends in Florence, he acquired another account of the murder with the thrilling title 'Morte dell'Uxoricida Guido Franceschini Decapitato' ('The Beheading of the Wife-Slayer Guido Franceschini') which seems to have clinched his resolve to work on this material.

While English politics of the 1860s ran its course, culminating in the second Reform Act of 1867, Browning led himself to 'a novel country', an imagined world of Rome in the late-seventeenth century, 'from the level of to-day | Up to the summit of so long ago' (i. 1331–2). As the work grew by thousands of lines, it is difficult to overestimate the hard work involved. He was writing on his own, without Barrett's emotional support, without her critical eye. He did not use, or feel able to use, an amanuensis, as for *Men and Women*, and the whole of the poem was written out and redrafted in his own writing, even though he admitted to having difficulties in 'seeing' his verse in this form. Moreover, he still felt partly that he was working in isolation, that he was 'unpopular', that there was no obvious or eager audience waiting his efforts. Actually, from about the *Selections* (1863) and the 3-volume *Poetical Works* (1863), the critical tide had begun to turn in his favour, but he seems to have felt this little. In January 1867, for example, he wryly described himself to Euphemia Millais as 'the most unpopular poet that ever was' (Millais 1899: i. 440), and he made a joke of his unpopularity in *The Ring and the Book* itself, in the direct address to the 'British Public, ye who like me not' (i. 410).

Browning's sense of his unpopularity reached back a long way, to the receptions of *Paracelsus* and *Sordello*, through to the poor reception of *Men and Women*. This makes his imaginative choices in *The Ring and the Book* all the more striking. Rather than make an obvious accommodation with his audience, he launched into difficult territory, not only in terms of subject-matter – an obscure seventeenth-century murder-case – but also in its treatment. *The Ring and the Book* is organized into ten independent but interacting monologues, spoken by nine characters, all giving different views of the same events. In other words, it is a complex work of ironic construction. It is not as obviously experimental as some of the masterpieces of Modernism, but, like those works, it makes significant demands on the reader.

In 1866 Browning's father died, and in 1868 he lost his beloved sister-in-law Arabella Barrett. In these years, he was struggling, with the aid of tutors, to bring Pen up to the standards in Greek and Latin required for university entrance. He had become friends with Benjamin Jowett (1817–93), the famous Greek scholar and the future master of Balliol College, Oxford – in academic terms the best college of the university – and he hoped that Pen would be able to go there. In fact, in the 1860s and 70s, Pen was often a worry to his father. He failed the entrance exam to Balliol College, and eventually entered Christ Church, which had less exacting standards. Here, in 1870, he twice failed the examinations and had to withdraw from the university. From his father's point of view he was a dilatory adolescent; only some time later did he eventually settle to becoming a painter and sculptor.

The Ring and the Book was published in four volumes from November 1868 through to February 1869, and this is usually seen as the defining moment of the change in Browning's critical reception. The volumes were widely reviewed, and though there was still some carping about style and subject-matter, there was also a sense that Browning had arrived as a poet, that he was one of the major writers of the age, and that he should be listened to. So, Robert Buchanan, in *The Athenaeum*, described the poem as 'the supremest poetical achievement of our time', one containing 'a wealth of nature and a perfection of spiritual insight which we have been accustomed to find in the pages of Shakespeare, and in those pages only' (Buchanan 1869: 399–400), and this hyperbole reflects a general mood of praise.

The reasons for this sense of re-evaluation are complex. G.R. Hudson, who has examined carefully contemporaries' views of Browning's work, sees this triumph as something that had emerged gradually. She argues that even in the negative receptions of *Christmas-Eve and Easter-Day* and *Men and Women* 'there was also a receptivity that foreshadowed future approval':

> *The Ring and the Book* would not have had the recognition it deserved without the preceding slow and steady acclimatization to the original qualities of Browning's poetry ... There had been no sharp turning point in the growing acceptance and appreciation of the intellectual, spiritual, and dramatic in Browning's character portrayal.
>
> (Hudson 1992: xiv)

There were other, clearer reasons for the changed situation. Browning was no longer a poet resident abroad, he had been in London and in London society since 1861. He was the widower of Barrett, a much-admired poet. In 1867 he had been elected an Honorary Fellow of Balliol College, Oxford, a fact that was proudly displayed on the title page of the six-volume *Poetical Works* of 1868, an edition which itself helped to consolidate his reputation. Fresh judgements seemed required in the face of the obvious *tour de force* of his new 21,000-line poem.

(ii) The 'Saturated, Sane' public man

Through the last nineteen years of his life, through his sixties and seventies, Browning practised his art assiduously, publishing fifteen new volumes, most of considerable length. There are undoubtedly wonderful things within this vast body of late poetry **[115–24]** – particularly *Red Cotton Night-Cap Country* (1873) and some of the poems in *Asolando* (1889) – but the majority of critics have sensed a loosening of imaginative grasp, a failure of inspiriting vision. T. S. Eliot, for example, caustically remarked: 'One can get on very well in life without having read all the later poetry of Browning or Swinburne' (Eliot 1957: 48). A minority of significant critics, however, champion the later work as showing continued imaginative richness and interesting experimentation with genre and style. (Notable among these are Clyde de L. Ryals, Michael Meredith, and Adam Roberts.) This debate over the quality of the late work has no easy resolution.

Now, more than in the 1860s, Browning became a figure in society, a more public figure. He dined out a great deal, attended concerts and social functions, and was invited to the country houses of friends and acquaintances in the upper class and aristocracy: to Naworth Castle by George Howard (future Earl of Carlisle), to Highclere Castle by the Earl of Carnarvon, to Belton House by Lord Brownlow, to Alton Towers by the Earl of Shrewsbury, to Hatfield House by Lady Salisbury. Disraeli thought him 'a noisy conceited poet': 'all the talk [was] about pictures and art, and Raffaelle, and what Sterne calls "the Correggiosity of Correggio"' (Garrett 2000a: 169). The novelist Henry James, setting out in London society, was disappointed by one of his literary heroes: 'Browning is a great chatterer but no Sordello at all' (30 March 1877):

> [Browning's] talk doesn't strike me as very good. It is altogether gossip and personality and is not very beautifully worded. But evidently there are two Brownings – an esoteric and an exoteric. The former never peeps out in society, and the latter has not a ray of suggestion of *Men and Women*.
>
> (8 April 1877) (Edel 1962: 330)

This idea, that there were two Brownings, the public persona, the 'saturated, sane, sound man of the London world', and behind this the 'inscrutable personage' who wrote the great poetry, came to haunt James and led eventually to the writing of his 'The Private Life' (1892), a short story in which the character Clare Vawdrey seems quite literally split in two (James 1903: ii.88–9). Some critics are annoyed that James's view is so often repeated, but it is both an indication of how Browning struck his contemporaries in later life, and an interesting reading of his character.

Browning was nonetheless much liked, and we can see him at various dinners with the figures of the age, with William Ewart Gladstone (the Liberal prime minister), with Benjamin Jowett, and with Arthur Stanley (the admired Dean of Westminster Abbey). We also see him at a range of public and private events: the celebratory dinner for the opening of a new building at Balliol College, Oxford, in 1877; as sponsor at the baptism of Tennyson's grandson (christened Alfred Browning Stanley Tennyson in recognition of the poets' friendship) in 1879; and at the funeral of George Eliot in 1880. In these years he was awarded various kinds of recognition and honour. In 1879 he received the honorary degree of LLD from the University of Cambridge. In October 1881 F. J. Furnivall founded the Browning Society to forward the appreciation of his work, at that time a unique honour for a living poet. In 1882 he was awarded an honorary DCL at the University of Oxford. The list could be extended. Through these years he kept up regular writing habits: as his valet touchingly reports, 'regardless of the time he had come in the night before – it was seldom later than half-past twelve or one – my orders were to call him every morning at seven o'clock' (Grove 1927: 9).

One feature of Browning's last years was the long holidays he took at the end of each season. These usually comprised the whole of August and September, and sometimes part of October, occasionally they went on into December. The habit began in the 1860s, after the death of Barrett, and initially involved his father, his sister, and Pen. After his father's death in 1866, and Pen's coming of age, it was usually just him and his sister, sometimes in the company of friends.

These holidays were both sources of rejuvenation and also sometimes inspirations to his work. In the 1860s his preferred destinations were seaside villages in Brittany or on the Loire coast: Sainte-Marie du Pornic, Le Croisic, and Audierne (this last, on the tip of Brittany). The first two of these provided him with stories and backgrounds for his work. From 1870 he switched to the Normandy coast: in 1870, 1872, and 1873 he stayed at St Aubin-sur-Mer (above Caen) near the home of this close friend, the French critic Joseph Milsand (1817–86). Here he learnt the story of Antoine Mellerio (who had lived nearby) which he reworked, in fictional form, for *Red Cotton Night-Cap Country* [116–18]. From 1878 onwards, mountainous regions in south-east France, Switzerland, or Italy, became his favourites, and often thoroughly remote villages and locations. In 1881 and 1882, for example, he and his sister stayed at St-Pierre-de-Chartreuse, a tiny hamlet on the Chartreuse Massif (not far from the Grande Chartreuse monastery). In 1883 and 1885, they stayed at Gressoney-Sainte-Jean, just under the massive Alpine peak Monte Rosa. These holidays were now usually two-part affairs: a month or so in the mountains, followed by time in Venice as the final destination.

A deeper look at these last years would involve some consideration of Browning's wider thought, particularly his politics. Browning described himself as a liberal, and we know that he disliked Disraeli and his administration of 1874 to 1880. His own sonnet 'Why I am a Liberal' was first published in a collection of statements entitled *Why I Am a Liberal, Being Definitions by the Best Minds of the Liberal Party* (1885); it preceded a statement in prose by Gladstone. It is, however, not a profound affair – one critic describes it as 'curiously inchoate' – and when we can locate his political views exactly they are an uneasy mixture of conservative and progressive, a misreading of some significant issues. Ireland and the position of women are two cases in point, and they can be used as indications of this final phase.

Browning was against the cause of Irish home rule and any self-determination for Ireland. The whole of the island of Ireland was at this time linked constitutionally with England and Scotland as the United Kingdom of Great Britain and Ireland. Structural social injustice there, particularly relating to land tenure, rents, and property, economic unfairness and educational inequality, meant that the cause of Irish home rule had become a potent force by the 1880s, and Gladstone (whom Browning profoundly admired) responded to this with a Government of Ireland Bill to give a measure of internal autonomy to Ireland within the British Empire. The Bill was rejected by the Commons in 1886 and subsequently the issue split the Liberal party. Browning was against Gladstone on this matter:

> He was ... a passionate Unionist ... It grieved and surprised him to find himself on this subject at issue with so many valued friends; and no pain of Lost Leadership was ever more angry or more intense, than that which came to him through the defection of a great statesman [Gladstone] whom he had honoured and loved, from what he believed to be the right cause.
>
> (Orr 374–5)

On the political position of women his stance was also unprogressive. In these years there was the beginning of serious pressure to improve the legal status and dignity of women within society. In 1886, for example, a bill giving women the vote passed its second reading in the House of Commons (though it got no further at this stage). In 1889, the last year of his life, Browning was contemplating a play about 'Women's Emancipation', apparently one that would show why women should *not* get the vote. In describing this, Alexandra Orr, his close friend, stresses what we would now call the absence of sexism in his dealings with women, his unconventionality, and physical warmth. She goes on, however:

> This virtual admission of the equality between the sexes, combined with his Liberal principles to dispose him favourably towards the movement for Female Emancipation. He approved of everything that had been done for the higher instruction of women, and would, not very long ago, have supported their admission to the Franchise. But he was so much displeased by the more recent action of some of the lady advocates of Women's Rights, that, during the last year of his life, after various modifications of opinion, he frankly pledged himself to the opposite view. He had even visions of writing a tragedy or drama in support of it. The plot was roughly sketched, and some dialogue composed, though I believe no trace of this remains.
>
> (Orr 396)

Venice, as we have seen, was the final destination of most of Browning's holidays in the last years of his life. In 1885 he negotiated to buy the Palazzo Manzoni on the Grand Canal, a deal which only fell through when structural faults were discovered. Subsequently, in 1888, Pen Browning purchased the huge Palazzo Rezzonico on the Grand Canal and began to renovate it. In these rather splendid surroundings, after a short final illness, Browning died on 12 December 1889. His body was brought back to England, and his funeral was in Westminster Abbey on 31 December, a well-attended public event, fully reported in *The Times*. He was buried within the Abbey, in Poets' Corner.

(iii) Interpretations

So far Browning has not provoked a high-profile or 'star' biography on a par with Peter Ackroyd's *Dickens* (1990) or Hermione Lee's *Virginia Woolf* (1996). Perhaps he seems a tamer commodity. For most of his life he was – with occasional periods of inactivity – a dedicated, practising poet, focused upon his art and its problems.

His biography has not produced, either, any radical disputes: differences of interpretation have tended to be minor. Some critics have questioned the idealized 'legend' of his marriage. They point out, for example, that he and Barrett had significant disagreements about Napoleon III and also about the value of spiritualism, and that – as Barrett's health declined – they were forced to live at different paces. Though these critics do not usually want to read either Barrett's or Browning's poems about unhappy relationships as overtly autobiographical, they do move partially in this direction. So, for example, Majorie Stone:

> For all the wedded happiness they undoubtedly did experience, the Brownings themselves in their poetry represent love and marriage as being much more complex and conflicted than their hagiographers assume both states to be.... Would not the painful feelings of neglect expressed in [Barrett's] 'My Heart and I' be likely to occur in an ageing and physically declining woman, several years older than her healthy husband, as he necessarily, and at her own urging, went out into the society he craved and needed to feed his creativity?
>
> (Stone 1998: 227, 216).

This position is a corrective to simplified romantic views, but does not overturn the general happiness of the marriage. The series of letters that Browning wrote to relatives and friends reporting the exact circumstances of Barrett's death are intensely poignant, and reflect the quality of their intimacy.

The other significant issue in the biography is the interpretation of Browning's character. Many people who met him seem to have been struck by his hale manner, his talkativeness and ebullience, his general air of *not* being temperamental, introverted, or wayward in any way, not being like *their* idea of a poet. The comments of Henry James and Benjamin Disraeli (quoted previously) are typical, and could be paralleled by others. This, in turn, has provoked two kinds of response. First, the instinct either to exaggerate or celebrate this fulsomeness – which is rather the tendency in Chesterton (1903) – or alternatively to read Browning's character as essentially naive in some respect – the implication of Santayana's famous essay 'The Poetry of Barbarism' (1900). Another response, only occasionally applied, has been to try to crack the carapace of heartiness, to see weaker, darker, or more disturbed aspects beneath it.

Betty Miller's psycho-biography *Robert Browning: A Portrait* (1952) is the main work in this direction. Miller sees a fundamental split between the poet's 'intellectual' and 'moral' nature, hinging on his 'secession' from Shelley. She attaches great importance, in other words, to Browning's adolescence, when he gave up Shelley's atheism and political radicalism in response (as she sees it) to his deep love for his mother and respect for her religion. Browning, in other words, tamed himself back into a more conventionally Christian awareness, though, as Miller argues, at a considerable psychological cost: the secession from Shelley 'was the primary inspiration of the poet's life-long obsession with the psychology of the charlatan, the quack, the second-rater and the "apparent failure"' (Miller 1952: 12). Miller's Browning is a weak, vulnerable person, overly dependent on his mother, then transferring this emotional dependency to Barrett.

Suggestive as this argument is, it now seems too drastic in the lines it draws through the life. Again, it is useful as a corrective. Browning's life looks like a highly normative, middle-class progression towards a certain kind of success, achieving just the kind of 'respectability' that – in the poem of that name – he derides. There are many hints, though, of the deeper (if of necessity) hidden patterns of his inner life. One of the most poignant is his late conversation with Edmund Gosse (quoted in section b.i) where he spoke of the long-drawn 'desolateness of his early and middle life as a literary man': he was in his fifties before he received really significant recognition. There was also a vein of vehemence and passion in his character that was capable of flashing out into

41

anger; there are many significant instances. The most obvious are his arguments with Forster and Macready over his plays (see section b.ii), his denunciations of the spiritualist Daniel Dunglas Home as a trickster, his anger towards his critic Alfred Austin in *Pacchiarotto* (1876), and his fury concerning a slighting remark made about Barrett (see 'To Edward FitzGerald', *Penguin* ii. 972, 1155–6). Many of his late poems are built on strong oppositions between purity and lust, tragedy and comedy, soul and body, which again suggest a passionate, driven nature. The title of Daniel Karlin's study *Browning's Hatreds* (1993) draws attention to the intensity that is one of the roots of his power as a writer.

Further reading

The standard scholarly biography is William Irvine and Park Honan's *The Book, the Ring, and the Poet* (1974). Less comprehensive, but nonetheless adequate to most needs is Clyde de L. Ryals's *The Life of Robert Browning* (1993). Hudson (1992) is a good account of how critics reviewed Browning's work in his own lifetime. There are specialized studies of Browning's youth by Maynard (1977), of his intellectual environment by Armstrong (1993), of the influence of Italy by Korg (1983), and the influence of France by Gridley (1982). Karlin (1985) is the most detailed reading of the courtship letters of 1845–46.

Of the older biographies, Orr's (1891; revised edition by Frederic G. Kenyon, 1908) has value as being written by someone who knew Browning well in the last part of his life and who spoke directly with Browning's sister Sarianna. Griffin (1910; 3rd edition 1938), Miller (1952), Ward (1968, 1969), and Donald Thomas (1983) are all still helpful. Two recent works are useful. Martin Garrett's *A Browning Chronology* (2000a) is more than its title suggests, and reads like the notes towards some future and excellent biography; it does, however, contain some inaccuracies. The same author's *Elizabeth Barrett Browning and Robert Browning: Interviews and Recollections* (2000b) makes available the most vivid descriptions and memories of the poet by his contemporaries, from otherwise hard-to-obtain sources.

Browning's own letters and the extensive correspondences of Barrett are the most important sources for his life. These letters appeared piecemeal through the twentieth century, usually in good editions. The most important collections are those edited by Hood (1933), Curle (1937), DeVane and Knickerbocker (1951), McAleer (1951), Kintner (1969), Peterson (1979), and Meredith (1985). These are gradually being superseded by the true giant of Browning scholarship, the (to date) fourteen volumes of *The Brownings' Correspondence* (1984–), edited first by Philip Kelley and Ronald Hudson (to vol. 8), and then by Philip Kelley and Scott Lewis (to vol. 14). This definitive project aims to publish all the known letters of both Browning and Barrett, and also all known letters to them from other people. The end-sections of each volume give biographies of the main correspondents and also lists of 'supporting documents' that help to elucidate the background. In addition these sections contain reprints of all known contemporary reviews of the two poets' work. For the period it covers – at this time up to 1847 – *The Brownings' Correspondence* presents a wealth of information within a context that allows readers to interpret the life for themselves.

PART II

WORK

(a) EARLY LONG POEMS

The first important movement in Browning's poetry is represented by the three long works written between 1832 and 1840, *Pauline* (1833), *Paracelsus* (1835), and *Sordello* (1840). During these same years Browning was experimenting in other directions. His first dramatic monologue was probably 'Porphyria's Lover', which may have been written as early as 1834 (it was published anonymously in *The Monthly Repository*, a liberal-radical journal in 1836), and with his play *Strafford* (1836) Browning began his intense but unsuccessful involvement with the theatre **[14–18]**. However, *Pauline*, *Paracelsus*, and *Sordello* remain a powerful testament to Browning's preoccupations as a developing writer, and are interesting for readers whose concerns lie in this area. The reputed difficulty of these works, particularly *Sordello*, has led to the witty description of them as 'three great dragons guarding a hoard of gold', the gold being 'the more accessible middle period work' (Roberts 1996: 16). Some readers may want to pass straight on to the 'middle period' work **[60–100]** but there are of necessity losses in doing so. What follows is an attempt to show, in a brief space, what these might be.

(i) *Pauline*

Pauline **[137–40]**, a quasi-dramatic confessional poem of just over a thousand lines, imagines a poet-speaker outlining the course of his life to Pauline, a beautiful woman whose love has helped him recover from depression. Browning published this poem anonymously in March 1833, and at the time of its appearance and for many years afterwards almost no one knew who wrote it; it passed into obscurity after only a few reviews. Browning chose not to reprint it for over thirty years. When he finally did so, in the 1868 *Poetical Works* – under pressure from the likelihood of unofficial editions – he wrote in a preface that he only acknowledged it 'with extreme repugnance' since it was 'a boyish work', lacking 'good draughtsmanship' and 'right handling' (*Penguin* i. 3). These comments, in their full context, are a small instance of the passion we identified in Part I, d. iii. '*Extreme* repugnance' is an unusually strong expression in this context, as though he were intent on warning the reader off, a kind of 'Do not enter' sign. He was aware, perhaps, at some level, that *Pauline* was genuinely revealing about his initial entry into literature.

The full title of *Pauline* is *Pauline: A Fragment of a Confession*, a 'confession' in this sense being originally a religious genre in which the autobiographer explained how he found his way back to God. A 'confession' may describe the passage of a life from sin through to some better, fuller understanding: St Augustine's *Confessions* (400) is the most famous instance. Gradually the genre came to be less overtly religious, describing the development of the autobiographer's whole being. Rousseau's *Confessions* (1782) and De Quincey's *Confessions of an English Opium Eater* (1822) are examples of this.

The subtitle *'Fragment of a Confession'* seems immediately to pose the question as to exactly how autobiographical *Pauline* is. Some critics have tended to see it as unmediated autobiography, Browning scrutinizing his own adolescence, and his development from childhood to early adulthood; there are certainly vivid, quasi-autobiographical passages (see for example ll. 313–35). In later life Browning himself wanted to insist that it was not in the least autobiographical, but purely dramatic, that the poem's speaker was fictional, as separate from the real Robert Browning as any of his other imaginary speakers. As many critics believe, these options are extremes. The poem is a blending of autobiography and fiction, or – more properly – an autobiography shaped and stylized into fictional form.

Browning is exploring the nature of his early encounter with Shelley's poetry **[8–9]**, and, in relation to this, his powerful sense of an imaginative and spiritual defeat. In bald terms, this sense of defeat relates to the way in which young Robert Browning cannot be young Percy Bysshe Shelley. The poet-speaker strives to take over Shelley's mantle. He aspires to be a poet in Shelley's vein, with the accompanying radical politics, utopian vision, and high lyricism. However, he finds this task impossible, and, after a period of cynicism and despair, he comes to a different understanding of life, a Christianized Romanticism: an aspiration towards transcendence that is now couched in terms of a yearning towards God.

The poem shows the transition from the radicalism of Shelley to the liberalism of Browning. Browning is not simply dismissing or debunking Shelley. He is converting his example to his own needs, or assimilating Shelley within a different, apparently more Christianized world-view. *Pauline*'s emotional intensity hinges on the ambivalence he feels about doing this. Shelley is celebrated as a utopian poet of high emotion and spiritual vision, so that when the poet-speaker feels he cannot directly take on the same role, there is a sense of collapse, of living in an aftermath, of struggling, in a confused way, to find a replacement for a lost ideal.

Here is the beginning of the passage in which the poet-speaker celebrates Shelley as the 'Sun-treader':

> Sun-treader, life and light be thine for ever!
> Thou art gone from us; years go by and spring
> Gladdens and the young earth is beautiful,
> Yet thy songs come not, other bards arise,
> But none like thee: they stand, thy majesties,
> Like mighty works which tell some spirit there
> Hath sat regardless of neglect and scorn,
> Till, its long task completed, it hath risen
> And left us, never to return, and all
> Rush in to peer and praise when all in vain.
> The air seems bright with thy past presence yet,
> But thou art still for me as thou hast been
> When I have stood with thee as on a throne
> With all thy dim creations gathered round
> Like mountains, and I felt of mould like them,
> And with them creatures of my own were mixed,
> Like things half-lived, catching and giving life.
>
> (151–67)

The other central passage concerning Shelley celebrates the inter-relation between Shelley's poetry and his utopian politics (404–29). Following Shelley's example, the poet-speaker tells how 'I was vowed to liberty, | Men were to be as gods and earth as heaven, | And I – ah, what a life was mine to prove!' (425–7). When this direct imitation of Shelley's example proves impossible, the poet-speaker discovers a different kind of idealized vision, a faith in God:

> But I have always had one lode-star; now,
> As I look back, I see that I have halted
> Or hastened as I looked towards that star –
> A need, a trust, a yearning after God:
> A feeling I have analysed but late,
> But it existed, and was reconciled
> With a neglect of all I deemed his laws,
> Which yet, when seen in others, I abhorred.
> I felt as one beloved, and so shut in
> From fear: and thence I date my trust in signs
> And omens, for I saw God everywhere; ...
>
> (292–302)

It would be easy to see the movement from idolizing Shelley to Christian faith as one from a 'Romantic' to a 'Victorian' sensibility, but actually all of these early long works – *Pauline*, *Paracelsus*, and *Sordello* – negotiate so strongly with Shelley and Romanticism, that they should actually point us in a direction that breaks down simple ideas of periodization. Browning is sometimes called a 'post-Romantic' as opposed to a 'Victorian' poet, but on the evidence of *Pauline* we could just as easily call him a 'late Romantic', or perhaps 'a third-generation Romantic'. Shelley's poetry was centrally concerned with the struggle towards a kingdom of justice, a utopia where corrupt political structures, and resulting inequalities and suffering, would be abolished. Browning surrendered the political overtness of this, and moderated Shelleyan radicalism to liberalism, but the emphasis on struggle and aspiration are still there, only now with the goal being either the Good or God.

(ii) *Paracelsus*

Paracelsus **[141–5]** was the first publication to bear Browning's name, and it appears to be a more carefully worked composition. It is a five-act dramatic poem about the alchemist and occult-philosopher Paracelsus (1493–1541), a figure who – in Browning's interpretation – straddles the transition from medieval to modern. The poem could be compared, in some respects, with Byron's *Manfred* (1817) or with Mary Shelley's *Frankenstein* (1818). Paracelsus sets off on a quest for total knowledge, a superhuman understanding of the world. Initially he is moderately successful, but not successful enough to satisfy his own overwhelming ambition, and his driven single-mindedness ages him prematurely. Taken as a whole, the work has the self-conscious air of a first determined attempt to break into the literary world. In this respect it was partially successful. In May 1836 Browning attended the celebratory dinner for Talfourd's *Ion* – with among others William Wordsworth, the older writer Walter Savage Landor, and the dramatist Mary Russell Mitford. Here, among the other toasts, he was himself toasted as 'the youngest poet of England' (*Orr* 82).

In different terms, and by different means, *Paracelsus* reprises the pattern of aspiration and defeat that is central to *Pauline*. The young Paracelsus sets off with the Promethean ambition of achieving total scientific and religious knowledge, some undefined sense of supreme knowledge, and – though this seems a secondary aim – of giving this knowledge to humankind to improve its lot. This is his absorbing quest, for which he is willing to appear eccentric and to sacrifice the common joys of life. He aims 'To grasp all, and retain all' (i. 245), to find 'the

secret of the world, | Of man, and man's true purpose, path and fate'
(i. 276–7). He wants 'to KNOW' (i. 733), 'to comprehend the works of
God, | And God himself, and all God's intercourse | With the human
mind' (i. 533–5). In Part I, he burns with idealism as he explains these
aspirations to the happily-married and conventionally-religious Festus
and Michal. Festus, in particular, queries the nature of his ambition.

The demur proves well founded. In each of the succeeding scenes
we see Paracelsus in states of disillusionment and confusion. He achieves
more and more knowledge and greater European celebrity, but all the
time he is having to adjust his understanding of the quest, to re-
understand what it is to be a human being. His aims prove to have
been conceived in too simplistic terms: he has excluded love, joy, and
beauty. With this realization, he has to adapt his quest, but habit makes
it almost impossible for him to do so.

Essentially Browning is concerned with analysing what he sees as a
wrong kind of single-mindedness. In this context, the character of
Paracelsus can be considered side by side with the poet-speaker of *Pauline*
and with Sordello. All three protagonists set off on quests which have
at their root a simplified understanding of the world and of themselves.
Inevitably they are forced to develop their views, to accommodate more
of the complex nature of reality. They have to modify the absolute
nature of their quests.

Paracelsus is, as it were, a would-be angel setting off into the
stratosphere – or, to put it politically, a rebel against the status quo –
who is gradually dragged back to earth by a developing sense of the
complexity of life, its limitations, and the needs of love. His premature
physical ageing and decay – on which emphasis is laid – is a symbolic
revenge on his hubris, an expression of his failure. Browning wrote
Paracelsus as a poetic drama (to be read and not performed), but he
seems to have held in his mind a vivid theatrical image of his protagonist
as a wild-eyed, emaciated, rambling scientist-mage.

Part II is set in 1521 in the house of 'a Greek Conjurer' in Constan-
tinople, where Paracelsus, now cynical and confused, meets the poet
Aprile. Aprile has set out on a quest 'to LOVE', which in its monomania
and imbalance is the parallel of Paracelsus's quest 'to KNOW'. Browning
explained this in one of the fullest critical comments on any of his
works, which he wrote as an explanatory note for his French friend
Ripert-Monclar. The note is valuable not only for the light it throws
on *Paracelsus* but also for its wider implications in reading the early
works. In the following extract, Browning does not define what he
means by 'love', but, taking the passage in conjunction with *Paracelsus*
itself, 'love' seems to be a compound of aspects of romantic love,

Christian love, emotional joy, and aesthetic pleasure – a range of ways in which individuals can be drawn out of themselves.

> [concerning *Paracelsus*, Part II] Paracelsus has long since abjured Love: his acquisitions in Knowledge are therefore never a *success*, – never complete in themselves – never in any degree final or satisfactory. He does not see this so long as his youthful energy holds on untired – but 14 years have elapsed since the night of his leaving Würzburg, his health is gone, his youth fleeting, and he is no nearer the end he has proposed to himself than at first: this end being *such an amount of Knowledge as will effect the perfect happiness of mankind*, WITHOUT LOVE. He has ventured, or been compelled, to confront this sad truth for the first time on the Evening he is introduced in this Second Part … *What has been wrong in his system?*
>
> This is answered by the sudden appearance of Aprile, *the nature that only Loves*: Aprile has at last discovered the insufficiency of *mere love* … and, taking in his heated fancy, Paracelsus for one of the *perfect natures* he has been contemplating and for whom he feels the achievement of his own designs is destined, he unveils to him his own nature – his effort to Love infinitely, dispensing with Knowledge, and the cause of his failure. Then the truth flashes on Paracelsus, and he *attains* a Knowledge of his own error, – the reverse of Aprile's.
>
> And then Paracelsus determines to *accept Love* – to offer the Knowledge he possesses already to the world and to receive the world's Love in return … not understanding that *to Love* is as much a science as *to Know* – that he has neither learnt *how to love Men* – nor how to discover the *elements of love* in the hatred, envy and uncharitableness he is about to provoke, though he dreams not of them.
>
> (1835) (*Corr.* iii. 420)

This passage could be read as a reworking of Shelley's preface to *Alastor* (1816), including its ringing final sentence: 'Those who love not their fellowbeings live unfruitful lives, and prepare for their old age a miserable grave' (Hutchinson and Matthews 1970: 15). It is always clear that Browning considers Paracelsus's quest heroic, almost necessary, yet at the same time it leads the scientist-mage into a progressively enveloping spiritual wasteland, through which he battles on till death.

Echoes of this theme can be heard much later in Browning's career in better-known poems like 'A Toccata of Galuppi's' **[94, 170–5]**,

'Childe Roland' **[94–6, 181–7]**, and 'A Grammarian's Funeral'. In *Paracelsus* itself there are lines that seem like fragments or notes anticipating these later poems. Paracelsus has 'subdued' his life to 'one tyrant all- | Absorbing aim', giving up all other joys and 'lusts', 'but foreseeing not | The tract, doomed to perpetual barrenness' that will be his resulting emotional landscape (ii. 109, 152–3, 115–6). In saying this, he sounds like the knight in 'Childe Roland to the Dark Tower Came', struggling through his actual physical wilderness. When Paracelsus speaks of 'this wolfish hunger after knowledge' that has resulted in a 'harassed o'ertasked frame' and 'grey hair, faded hands, | And furrowed brow' (ii. 124, 72, 220–1) he reminds us of the grammarian in 'A Grammarian's Funeral'. Later, when he tells us how he has excluded joy, aesthetic pleasure, and love from his quest for knowledge, so that 'life, death, light and shadow, ... were bare receptacles | Or indices of truth to be wrung thence, | Not ministers of sorrow or delight' (ii.156–9), he reminds us of another questing scientist, the speaker of 'A Toccata of Galuppi's', who seeks to 'triumph o'er a secret wrung from nature's close reserve' (32) . There are other potential echoes, all pointing to how deeply this theme was rooted in Browning's imagination. It represents a more difficult and harder version of the Shelleyan quest for transcendence.

(iii) *Sordello*

Sordello **[145–50]** remains the enigma in Browning's oeuvre, more famous for its supposed unintelligibility than for anything else. This is a densely-written narrative poem which, in six books, tells the life of the troubadour poet Sordello (*c.* 1200–*c.* 1250), a figure Browning probably first encountered through his brief appearance in Dante's *Divine Comedy* (*Purgatorio*, vi–ix). If we take Paracelsus, then Sordello, and then several of the other historical figures treated in the early work, it might initially appear that Browning was fascinated only by the obscure. To someone of his wide learning, however, these were not obviously minor figures. (In 1837 he contemplated a tragedy on the death of Marlowe, until he felt he was pre-empted by a one-act play on the same subject by R. H. Horne. His early work might appear different at first view if *The Death of Marlowe* had come to fruition.) However, the relative obscurity of Paracelsus and Sordello does serve one important purpose. Their biographies are distant enough to be shrouded in conjecture and myth. As Browning goes back and researches the past and then – using his findings – brings these figures to life, he is able to use them as vehicles to discuss some of his own deepest preoccupations. In *Sordello*, as in *Pauline* and *Paracelsus*, the issues he airs are the nature of poetry, the role of the poet, and his own situation as a writer coming to maturity in the aftermath of the great Romantics.

These works, in other words, are self-reflexive, attempts at self-understanding. This is hardest to see in the case of *Sordello* because of its complexity. *Sordello* brings to life the north-east of Italy in the early thirteenth century, focusing on the political struggle between the factions of the Guelfs and Ghibellins, (that is to say) between those on the side of the Pope and those on the side of the Emperor. Individual incidents in the political struggle – as for example, the siege of Ferrara in 1222–4 – are brilliantly evoked. Sordello's life is marked by the political violence and confusion of his times, and, amidst these, he has to evaluate which side in the conflict is politically progressive.

There is evidence that Browning undertook a great deal of historical research to recreate Sordello's life and times, and this is filtered into the narrative in ways that are often vivid and exciting. But he did not feel constrained to treat the historical facts in a scholarly or objective way. As Ian Jack remarks, despite Browning's extensive research, 'the poem is profoundly unhistorical, and while Browning uses the names of actual personages his principal characters have little or nothing in common with their originals' (*Oxford* ii. 175). Facts are adjusted or transposed to suit his purposes, and the central premise of the plot, that Sordello was the son of the great Ghibellin chieftain Taurello Salinguerra, is an invention. In this vivid historical romance, a partly gothic story about how Sordello finds out the identity of his true father, the past is a screen onto which Browning projects his own most urgent concerns.

Paracelsus is a significant step up in terms of literary sophistication from *Pauline*, and *Sordello* represents a further advance. Composed off and on over a period of six years, it is the young Browning's consciously most ambitious work, one he hoped would make his name. In writing it, however, he so profoundly worked his way into his own inner emotional and spiritual spaces, that inadvertently he left a possible audience behind. Browning did not intend the poem to be obscure, and was profoundly stung by the implication, in some of the reviews, that he had been difficult by design. Even an experienced reader, however, can find *Sordello* challenging simply at the level of basic meaning, and in both the *Longman* and *Oxford* texts – the two best annotated texts for reading the poem – the editors sometimes indicate lines they still find puzzling or susceptible to two or more interpretations, even after the most careful scrutiny.

This being said, the level of difficulty can be exaggerated. Those who persist may come to feel that it is very nearly a masterpiece, albeit flawed and not fully achieved. It presents a great historical panorama, the struggles of Guelf and Ghibellin in the thirteenth century vividly brought to life, and there is a great deal of picture-painting of medieval scenes that – drawing on earlier medievalism – clearly anticipates Pre-Raphaelitism. This is a world of aristocratic ladies, castles and fierce sieges, of minstrels and troubadours, warriors and monks. Beginners require an outline of the story, though even this presents problems. As the Longman editors remark, 'Browning employs suppression, ellipsis, flashback and digression with a freedom that comes close to that of the novel' (*Longman* i. 360). What follows is an economic simplification, a bare outline of the plot.

An outline of *Sordello*

Book I: The opening throws us back into the world of thirteenth-century Lombardy, gives us glimpses of later parts of the story, and then introduces us to the central conflict between Guelfs and Ghibellins. The story proper, beginning at line 374, takes us to the lonely castle of Goito, somewhere near Mantua, the childhood home of the poet Sordello. The rest of the Book is concerned with Sordello's early life, how he grows in poetic sensibility amidst the beautiful surroundings of Goito, and how he is gradually filled with poetic ambition. Sordello aspires to the highest ideal, to be nothing less than an Apollo (the god of poetry). As Orr paraphrases it, he craves for 'that magnitude of poetic existence, which means all love and all knowledge, as all beauty and all power in itself' (Orr 1896: 33). Browning's gloss is even more emphatic: 'He [Sordello] means to be perfect'. Sordello is essentially another quester in the mould of Paracelsus.

Book II: Sordello travels to Mantua, where a 'Court of Love' (a kind of medieval poetry contest) is taking place. Here, emphatically, a picture of the gracious Pre-Raphaelite Middle Ages comes to the fore. Sordello is able to stand up and, impromptu, beat one of the best poets of the day, Eglamour, thrusting himself into the limelight and becoming the official minstrel of the lady Palma. But subsequently this Book explores his confusions of aim, his egotism, and his self-doubt, all of which gradually undermine his suddenly achieved success. Sordello wants to strive towards a better kind of poetry, but poetic experiment fails and he writes a populist poem about Simon de Montfort. Now there is collapse and confusion: 'internal struggles to be one, | ... frittered him incessantly piecemeal' (ii. 694–5).

Political changes take place in the wider world. Ecelin II, head of the Romano family, retreats to a monastery and signals the end, within the family, of his aggressive Ghibellin (i.e. anti-Papal) policy. The great warrior-chieftain Taurello Salinguerra, an ally of Romano, tries to persuade Ecelin to change his mind, but is dismissed. He proceeds to Mantua, where Sordello (as official poet) should be ready 'to sound the great man's welcome' (ii. 928). Sordello, however, has retreated in disillusionment to Goito, his childhood home.

Book III: At Goito, Sordello enjoys a 'sweet and solitary year' away from the pressures of his public role, but, in meditation on his life, he realizes what has gone wrong with his quest: 'he should have embraced ordinary human experience ... instead of rejecting it, and he regrets that he left Mantua' (*Oxford* ii. 518). At just this point he is summoned to Verona, as he thinks to compose a marriage-song for one of the Guelf–Ghibellin alliances, the marriage of the lady Palma (Ghibellin) to Count Richard (Guelf). In fact that alliance has been abandoned. Taurello Salinguerra (ultra-Ghibellin in policy) has dissuaded Palma from this marriage, and when Sordello arrives in Verona, Palma declares her love for him.

Palma knows the truth of Sordello's birth. He is not the son of a humble archer who died bravely in one of the Guelf–Ghibellin skirmishes. Unknown to everyone, he is actually the son of Taurello Salinguerra, the greatest warrior of Italy. She does not tell this to Sordello at this time. Instead, she and Sordello, disguised as minstrels, escape from Verona and head for Ferrara. Palma is taking Sordello to see Taurello Salinguerra, who will speak to him of the importance of the Ghibellin cause. Sordello is now persuaded that he might join with Palma in the leadership of the Ghibellin party in Lombardy, become 'Gate-vein of this heart's blood of Lombardy, | Soul of this body' (iii. 556–7). He has come out into the world, no longer standing aside from life and politics, but becoming involved in it. Book III ends with a long authorial aside relating to Browning's time in Venice in 1838.

Book IV: Ferrara, the 'lady-city', is in 'rueful case' (1–2), fought over by Guelfs and Ghibellins. Alone in Taurello's palace garden, Sordello rethinks his life, becoming concerned for the overall welfare of humankind, the necessity for a 'mighty equilibrium' of happiness (261). Filled with this ideal, he goes to see Taurello, but after a short interview with the great warrior, he comes out shocked and disconcerted, 'older by years' (332).

We now go back to see Taurello Salinguerra in his 'presence chamber', the state apartment where he has just received Sordello, and where he has now finished receiving various ambassadors. One ambassador, from the Emperor, has brought him the 'badge' of the Imperial Prefecture (the symbol of authority over the Ghibellin party in Lombardy) either directly for himself or for his nominee. This is a turning-point in Taurello Salinguerra's life. There is a vivid physical description of him (417–68), and then he himself, in a long soliloquy, reviews his character and career. We learn again of the tragic death of his wife and son in a Ghibellin–Guelf skirmish in Vicenza, and of how, subsequently, he poured his energies into the Ghibellin–Romano cause, but always as follower not leader. He is a grand, canny warrior, knowledgeable about the world, analysing his own political reticence.

As night falls, Sordello asks Palma to explain the Ghibellin cause to him. He is trying to understand Taurello Salinguerra, who he had assumed was on the people's side, but whose conversation suggests otherwise. As he talks to Palma he becomes convinced that neither the Guelf nor the Ghibellin faction is truly progressive. He dreams of building up a new Roman republic, a kingdom of justice: in this way he would set himself above the contemporary political struggle, safe in an unfulfillable idealism.

Book V: Sordello's musings continue with his dawning realization that idealism can be false, that humankind's social and political progress is necessarily slow and incremental, that his duty is to enter his historical moment, to do the small thing that can make a difference. He decides, on balance, that the Guelfs (the Papal faction) are more on the side of the people, more progressive, and so (in Browning's gloss) he 'takes his first step as a Guelf' to persuade Taurello of the truth of his opponents' cause.

At this point Sordello has given up a certain amount of egotism, committed himself to the Guelf cause, entered into history. He makes a great 'outpouring' speech before Taurello and Palma, proclaiming that the poet is 'earth's essential king' and on the side of 'the multitude' (v. 506, 534), and develops complex ideas about the role of the poet and the future of poetry: 'from his own desire to dedicate poetry completely to the service of mankind, Sordello projects a further progression beyond his own lifetime in the reciprocal development of poetic form and audience contribution' (*Longman* i. 690–1 n).

Sordello's speech before Taurello Salinguerra and Palma has a wholly unexpected effect. Taurello senses the love of Palma for Sordello, and foresees their marriage. Suddenly, and on instinct, he gives Sordello the Emperor's badge and proclaims him leader of the Ghibellin-Romano cause in Lombardy, a mighty political position.

And then, miraculously (and with gothic aplomb) Taurello and Sordello instinctively recognize each other as father and son. Palma reveals how Adelaide (the step-mother figure of the poem) concealed the survival of Sordello as a baby for her own wicked ends, and brought him up without a knowledge of his true identity. All this now overwhelms Sordello. He has been offered the leadership of the faction he regards as politically unprogressive, and he finds himself having to reassess his whole identity in the light of the knowledge that Taurello is his father. Taurello and Palma withdraw to give him time to think.

Book VI. And so, finally, a battle begins within Sordello's soul. His nature has been wounded, lacking some great love or clear ideal by which to guide it, and now he has to decide between (on the one hand) the attractions of political power and the ties of love and blood and (on the other hand) the cause he considers right, the side of the people and their suffering. He is torn, weighed down by the thought of how little he can bring to the people's cause, and the complexities of his 'novel duty' to serve them. Yet he craves some earthly happiness for himself, the possibility of enjoying the life of power and pride that Taurello has held out to him: 'how | This badge would suffer you improve your Now!' (319–20). His mind is overwhelmed by conflicting arguments, and (seemingly) in this condition he dies. When Palma and Taurello find his corpse, the imperial 'badge' is beneath his foot, suggesting that he may finally have spurned the temptations of power. As Browning makes clear, in dying of extreme stress and tension at this point – in failing to act positively within his historical moment – Sordello has cost humanity dearly in terms of its overall political progress (828–51).

(iv) Conclusions

In struggling with the inherent difficulties of *Sordello*, it is easy to lose sight of how it fits within the larger pattern of Browning's early work. It is worth stressing what these three early works have in common: a pattern of aspiration and defeat. Each of the protagonists sets off on an idealistic quest, which then runs into difficulties, has to be reassessed or transformed, and ends in a complex mixture of triumph and defeat. Many commentators have felt that at some level this pattern involves a reappraisal or readjustment of Browning's inheritance from Romanticism, particularly his engagement with Shelley.

Together these works enact both an emotional and a political thwarting. The poet-speaker of *Pauline* sets off to follow in Shelley's poetic and political footsteps, and finds that this leads to emotional disaster: he has to find a different way in which to be a poet. Paracelsus, with his distinctly Shelleyan ideal of finding *'such an amount of knowledge as will effect the perfect happiness of mankind'*, is forced to accommodate an awareness of limitation, both political and emotional. Finally Sordello, the protagonist of the most explicitly political of these works, moves from a relatively solipsistic idea of poetry to an engagement with politics and history. But just at the point where he has taken up a progressive political stance, he finds himself blocked – overwhelmingly it would seem – by the father-figure of Taurello, and by the complex web of loyalties and counter-loyalties which this encounter with Taurello provokes.

In this recurring pattern it is hard not to see a deep-seated response to Shelley. It is as though Browning felt an inclination towards a Shelley-like role as a poet, but could not fully take it up; or, as if he felt that – in his own personal circumstances and in the wider history of the 1830s – a Shelley-like role was somehow an impossibility. In *Pauline*, the poet-speaker (to some extent an embodiment of Browning himself) yearns directly towards Shelley as a kind of god-like figure, an immortal 'Sun-treader' (151). In *Paracelsus* the protagonist yearns towards a trans-cendent knowledge that will improve humankind's lot – a directly Shelleyan role. In *Sordello* the troubadour protagonist comes near to understanding the nature of a clearly defined and committed political idealism, and then simply dies. Shelley's left-wing idealism went hand in hand with a poetry of great lyric intensity and beauty, an extra-ordinary emotional and spiritual aspiration. Browning seems to find this kind of idealism impossible, and in the process has to forge a different aesthetic.

At the same time as he was working on *Paracelsus* and *Sordello*, Browning was starting to develop his use of the dramatic monologue and beginning to explore the nature of the irony that went with it. (These things are analysed in the next two sections **[60–6]** and **[66–80]**.) In the short dramatic monologues of the 1830s and 1840s he explores a world of moral ambivalence and perversity. At first sight, these ironic monologues would appear to be the inverse of the quest for idealistic vision. However, the monologues and the quest poems have a complex relation to each other, and it would be clearer to see them as two aspects of the same creative impulse: the searching scrutiny of moral perversity is the inverse image of the quest for transcendence and truth.

The quest for transcendence represented in *Pauline, Paracelsus*, and *Sordello* never left his work, but rather was changed into other forms, into the themes that are central to his major poetry: the struggle for individual virtue, for religious faith, and for love. The quest for transcendence, thwarted in these early long works, would eventually break surface again in overt terms in the theological preoccupations of *The Ring and the Book*. In the meantime, his explorations of criminality and madness and moral perversity, and his insistent use of irony, constitute an examination – among other things – of the world's resistance to ideals, all the blocks to the illuminated vision of the 'Sun-treader'.

Further reading

The best introductions to these poems are the prefaces to them in the *Oxford* edition (vols i and ii) and in the *Longman* edition (vol. i). Readers need all the help they can get with *Sordello*, and the extensive annotation in the *Longman* edition in particular provides the best possible entrance into the poem's complexities. The critical treatments in Tucker (1980) and Ryals (1983) are excellent. Ryals sharpened and improved his readings in *The Life of Robert Browning* (1993): for *Pauline* see pp. 11–20, for *Paracelsus* pp. 24–32, and for *Sordello* pp. 41–55. These accounts are also good places to start reading.

Tucker's 'Browning as Escape Artist: Avoidance and Intimacy' in Woolford (1998) is a particularly fine reading of *Pauline* in the deconstructive mode. Drawing on the work of Jacques Derrida, Froula (1985) has seen *Sordello* as more connected with modernist poetics than with romantic: her essay 'Browning's *Sordello* and the Parables of Modernist Poetics' is conveniently reprinted in Gibson (1992) and is often referred to by later critics. Two good recent discussions are in Sarah Wood's *Robert Browning: A Literary Life* (2001): chapter 1 '*Pauline* and Mill' and chapter 2 '*Sordello* and the Reviewers'. John Stuart Mill (1806–73), the philosopher, was given *Pauline* to review, and wrote extensive and negative comments on his review copy. Shortly afterwards this copy came back to Browning, who then further annotated it with his replies to Mill. (Mill's actual journal article was never written.) (See *Penguin* i. 1022.) By setting Mill's response in context, Wood is able to show how his 'outraged and judgmental' reading of *Pauline* fails to come to terms with the poem's strangeness, and so to suggest her own approach.

(b) THE DRAMATIC MONOLOGUE

Dramatic Lyrics (1842) and *Dramatic Romances and Lyrics* (1845) contain nine or ten poems central to an understanding of Browning's work.

Before coming to them directly, we need to think about their genre: the dramatic monologue. Abrams defines it like this:

> A **dramatic monologue** is ... a type of lyric poem that was perfected by Robert Browning. In its fullest form, as represented in Browning's 'My Last Duchess,' 'The Bishop Orders His Tomb,' 'Andrea del Sarto,' and many other poems, the dramatic monologue has the following features: (1) A single person, who is patently *not* the poet, utters the entire poem in a specific situation at a critical moment: the Duke is negotiating with an emissary for a second wife; the Bishop lies dying; Andrea once more attempts wistfully to believe his wife's lies. (2) This person addresses and interacts with one or more other people; but we know of the auditors' presence and what they say and do only from clues in the discourse of the single speaker. (3) The main principle controlling the poet's choice and organization of what the lyric speaker says is to reveal to the reader, in a way that enhances its interest, the speaker's temperament and character.
>
> (Abrams 1993: 48)

One way of thinking of the dramatic monologue would be as a play that had shrunk to one speech by one character. From that one speech we can infer a wider dramatic situation, but the speech is all we have of the larger reality. Intrinsically, this is a concentrated genre, lending itself to certain kinds of intensity.

Both Browning and Tennyson came upon the genre in the 1830s. You could say – though it would be slightly misleading to do so – that it is invented in this decade. Some critics have been concerned to see the dramatic monologue in relation to forms which anticipated it, and *not* to see it as totally or radically new. Alan Sinfield (1977), for example, sees it as evolving out of 'the complaint', the dramatic epistle, and the humorous colloquial monologue – in other words, out of poems like Thomas Gray's 'The Bard', Alexander Pope's 'Eloisa to Abelard', and Robert Burns's 'Holy Willie's Prayer'. Of Pope's 'Eloisa to Abelard', he says: 'I believe it satisfies the most demanding criteria [to qualify as a dramatic monologue] with the exception of the actual presence of an auditor'. For Sinfield, Tennyson and Browning 'are the heirs and in major ways the beneficiaries of these three traditions' (Sinfield 1977: 51). Examples of the dramatic monologue by Tennyson are 'Ulysses', 'Tithonus', and 'St Simeon Stylites' (all of 1833). These, however, are not as fully or vividly dramatic as Browning's monologues, nor does the form dominate Tennyson's work as it does Browning's.

There are many other potential backgrounds to the development of the dramatic monologue. The movement of aesthetic trends, practices, and ideas creating the conditions in which a genre can emerge and be explored are impossible to trace in full, but the following are some hints. Another background is the Romantics' passion for drama. With the exception of Blake, all the six major Romantic poets wrote plays or fragments of plays. An integral part of Romanticism was a deep critical interest in Shakespeare, and this led on to the great Shakespearean acting of Edmund Kean and William Macready, acting which fascinated Browning **[11]**. The best plays by the Romantic poets are Shelley's *Cenci* (1819) – a work that Browning greatly admired – and the plays of Byron, but even these are not fully successful as plays for the stage. Putting the matter baldly, it is fair to say that the Romantic poets were fascinated by the drama, but unable to write plays that were successful in explicitly dramatic terms. It is as though other aspects of their preoccupation – their politics, for example, or their concentration on lyric subjectivity – were a bar to a fully successful drama.

One way of keeping a certain lyric intensity without having to develop a large dramatic structure was the playlet or one-scene play. Bryan Procter (1787–1874), alias Barry Cornwall – a friend of Browning's – produced his *Dramatic Scenes* in 1820, a work which had a significant impact on Pushkin in Russia. These were short pieces that presented the climaxes of drama without any earlier exposition. Browning himself wrote a few such works – 'In a Balcony' in *Men and Women*, for example – and would perhaps have written more. We know, for example, that R. H. Horne anticipated him in a short play he intended to write on the death of Marlowe (Garrett 2000a: 28).

Browning also particularly admired the prose genre of the 'imaginary conversation', which had been developed by the older poet Walter Savage Landor (1775–1864). Landor had explored the possibilities of this genre at length in a series of works well known to Browning. As used by Landor an imaginary conversation usually comprised two people from history – Diogenes and Plato, Vittoria Colonna and Michelangelo, Milton and Marvell – talking to each other. The conversation would be grounded in a sense of historical reality, but could develop beyond it just as Landor chose, with, crucially, the conversation itself having an overall dramatic shape and rationale. Browning does something similar in the dramatic monologue. Some of his characters, though located in history, are still essentially imaginary; they are supposed to be typical in some way. ('Pictor Ignotus' and 'The Bishop Orders His Tomb' are examples of this.) But others – as with Landor – are real people from history brought to life in a way that, usually obliquely, reflects some of Browning's own preoccupations: 'Johannes Agricola in Meditation', 'Fra Lippo Lippi', and 'Andrea del Sarto' are good examples of characters based on real historical figures. In Landor the imaginary conversation is just that, a two-way exchange, though sometimes one speaker dominates while the other acts as a sounding-board or provoker of argument. In Browning's monologues the second speaker disappears altogether, but acts as a silent presence, shaping the dramatic situation as a whole, or implicitly affecting the contents and manner of the monologist's speech.

The dramatic monologue, then, is a crystallisation of some of these trends. It is a cross or hybrid of the genres of drama and lyric. A lyric poem is 'any fairly short poem, consisting of the utterance by a single speaker, who expresses a state of mind or a process of perception, thought, and feeling' (Abrams 1993: 108). Usually, of course, this is in some sense the poet himself. But in the dramatic monologue the process of perception, thought, and feeling are not (directly) the poet's own, but that of an imagined character, and they come into being in a particular setting at a given moment in time: a dramatic context.

Irony is another crucial ingredient in the dramatic monologue as Browning practises it. In fact one of the most important things that can be said about Browning is that he is a profound ironist, and that irony is an important part of the post-Romantic moment that he occupies. Browning's characters are often projecting one image of themselves, yet, through the ironic structure of the poem and the distance it imposes, they are revealed to readers in a way that con-tradicts their self-image. 'My Last Duchess' is the most famous case. The Duke projects an image of himself as grand, sophisticated, flexible of attitude and manner, a connoisseur, a complete man. As readers, we deduce a jealous or deranged psychopath, eaten out with insecurity, showing that 'savage indifference that cohabits with an occasional magnanimity' (Hill 1991: 57).

The best known theorizing of Browning's irony is Robert Langbaum's *The Poetry of Experience* (1957), which, though critical trends have superseded it, states its central idea so well that it remains a point of reference. Langbaum argues that Browning's use of irony generates a tension between sympathy and judgment in our responses to his monologists. The fact that a Browning character speaks for him- or herself *apparently* unmediated by the poet, allows us to be drawn into their world, their mindset, their view of things. From one point of view, we empathize with the speaker because of how we are fully exposed to his or her total personality, the persuasions of voice and manner of speaking. We see only with his or her eyes. From another viewpoint, irony acts to distance us from the speaker, reintroduces our moral awareness, and makes us judge the speaker for who he or she really is. These two processes take place simultaneously. In 'My Last Duchess' the apparent flexibility, warmth, and sophistication of the Duke's voice draw us empathetically into his world. We participate imaginatively in the egotism, hauteur, and largesse of a proud Renaissance Duke. However, the irony of the monologue continually undermines this perspective, and awakens our critical faculties. While the Duke tells us of his reasonableness, we see his irrationality; while he implies his generosity to his first wife, we see his blind desire to control another human being within the confines of his own will.

A later theorizing of irony, still of value, is Wayne Booth's *A Rhetoric of Irony* (1974). Booth defines what he calls 'stable irony'. It must be (1) intended, (2) covert, 'intended to be reconstructed with meanings different from those on the surface', (3) it must be fixed 'in the sense that once a reconstruction of meaning has been made, the reader is not then invited to undermine it with further demolitions and reconstructions', (4) it must be finite, (5) it expects or invites us to share the poet's wider beliefs, views, or assumptions; (6) it invites us to make 'a leap or climb to a higher level ... The movement is always toward an obscured point that is intended as wiser, wittier, more compassionate, subtler, truer, more moral, or at least less vulnerable to further irony' (Booth 1974: 5–6, 33–6). Again, this definition works well for 'My Last Duchess'. We are clearly invited to share some of Browning's ideas about the princely courts of the Renaissance, that they combined high culture with political and emotional ruthlessness. The 'leap or climb to a higher level' is also apparent. The Duke sees himself as a magnanimous connoisseur of art. As we decode the irony, we see him as a sadist who reduces people to objects.

Booth has a lot of interesting things to say about the nature of irony. He points out, for example, that all authors – even the least didactic – ask us to join them in whatever opinions, views, attitudes, or emotions they present or imply: 'the reader will find himself choosing, perhaps unconsciously, to accept or reject the pose, or stand, or tone, or claim to poetic craft':

> But irony dramatizes this choice, forces us into hierarchical participation, and hence makes the results more actively our own ... Irony obtrudes itself and thus obtrudes its author's claim to skill. It risks disaster more aggressively than any other device.
>
> (Booth 1974: 41)

This 'aggressive' aspect of irony is obviously applicable to Browning's work, but, as we shall see, it is complicated by other factors. Booth defines Browning's irony as 'stable irony' because he feels that as readers we are always able to decode it easily. We can be sure that we know exactly what the poet intends us to think of a particular character, because – like all stable ironists – Browning expects us to decode what his characters say in the context of moral norms that we can be certain we share with him. By and large, this is true, but in fact some of Browning's poems have provoked debates of interpretation hinging on exactly the extent of the irony deployed. ('Count Gismond' is a case in point [76–8, 165–8].) These debates point to the intrinsically slippery or elusive nature of irony: when one thing is said, but another thing is to be inferred (but not stated), a necessarily complex space is opened up. This aspect of Browning's work has come to fascinate post-structuralist critics battling with their own kind of larger philosophical scepticism.

Further reading

The dramatic monologue has provoked a vast literature since it is in many respects a curious, innovative genre. It seems best to select from this literature ruthlessly. Two excellent earlier accounts are by Mason (1974) and Sinfield (1977); these are the best places to start wider reading. Mason investigates the ways in which early-nineteenth-century drama tended to put 'poeticity before action' and sees this as one of the important backgrounds to the form. Sinfield, referred to above, is particularly concerned to see the genre as connected with earlier genres.

Two important articles by Rader (1976) (1984), the second reprinted in Gibson (1992), carefully define what exactly a dramatic monologue is and make distinctions between variations in the form. In the 1980s discussions became more overtly theoretical, considering 'the nature of consciousness, the extent to which language is constitutive of reality, and the status of first-person utterances' (Drew 1990: 35). One important work here is Slinn (1982). Tucker's 'Dramatic Monologue and the Overhearing of Lyric' (1985), reprinted in Gibson (1992), is one of the subtlest accounts of the dramatic monologue in relation to ideas of lyric form. The most ambitious attempt to explain exactly the origins of the dramatic monologue is Martin (1985), who takes a Marxist approach, seeing the form evolving out of some aspects of Romantic literary strategies. Bristow (1991), chapter 2, aptly called 'Dramatising Lyric', is probably the best account of the 1990s. An interesting, mischievous essay is Maynard's 'Browning's Duds of Consciousness (or) No Gigadibs, No Bishop' (1998a), which turns much discussion on its head by looking at the listeners within the monologues, the people who have to endure the great tirades that come at them, 'these poor creatures of shade, these backstagers upstaged by the great ones of the monologues' (p. 62).

(c) *DRAMATIC LYRICS* AND *DRAMATIC ROMANCES AND LYRICS*

The poems in these volumes of 1842 and 1845 can usefully be considered together, since little separates them chronologically or stylistically, and they are essentially part of the same poetic moment. They show the first flowering of Browning's use of the dramatic monologue **[60–6]**. These poems are dramatic in form, highly-coloured, and often (though not always) ironic. There is a group of poems here that are celebratory, passionate, positive, and heroic: as for instance 'Cavalier Tunes' (a group of boisterous drinking-songs), 'The Englishman in Italy' (which gives a beautiful evocation of an Italian landscape), and 'How They Brought the Good News from Ghent to Aix' (a highly rhythmical poem describing messengers galloping to bring the good news of victory to the town of Aix). However, the great poems of these volumes explore a darker world, focused on a subject-matter concerned with what is aberrant and socially marginal: poisoning, murder, heresy, hatred, failure, and madness.

The most famous poem, 'My Last Duchess', explores the psychology or psychopathology of an Italian Renaissance duke, who has had his first wife murdered. This duke is matched by other disturbing characters: the aristocratic lady in 'The Laboratory', giving a fortune to a chemist for a phial of poison with which to murder her husband's mistress; the religious maniac in 'Johannes Agricola in Meditation' who believes God has destined him to heaven whatever sins he may commit, and who gloats over the millions that he imagines to be burning in Hell; 'Porphyria's Lover', a working-class man who strangles his mistress in order to keep her true and faithful. Browning – a middle-class poet – none the less explores a subject-matter full of transgression, deceit, and marginality, consciously or unconsciously affronting bourgeois values.

(i) 'My Last Duchess'

'My Last Duchess' **[155–61]**, probably written in 1842, is the most highly-achieved of this group of poems. Generations of critics have marvelled at how, in a bare fifty-six lines, a character so rich and vital steps before us. Browning is thought to have based the poem's speaker on Alfonso II (1533–97), fifth Duke of Ferrara and last of the Este line, an aristocrat infamous for his imprisonment of the Renaissance poet, Torquato Tasso (see Friedland 1936). Browning's Duke, however, though inspired by history, transcends any specific identification.

As we attend closely to this monologue, we come to understand the full dramatic situation in which it takes place. The Duke, egocentric, vengeful, and possessive, has had his first duchess quietly murdered because she failed to focus her whole existence on him. Now he is negotiating for a second marriage with a Count's daughter. At the exact point at which we hear him speak, he has taken the Count's envoy or messenger up to the first-floor of his palace in order to look at some of his art treasures. Ostensibly this is a moment of relaxation, a break from the negotiations concerning the dowry that must accompany his next wife. Actually it is an opportunity for the Duke – suave and urbane as he appears – to vent a powerful set of obsessions on his unsuspecting hearer: the circumstances of his *first* marriage, and what he thinks went wrong with it.

At the start of the monologue the Duke draws back the curtains on a private, especially-prized portrait of his first wife, 'my last Duchess' (1), and invites the envoy to sit down to look at it (5). In the manner of a connoisseur, he invites the envoy to contemplate the beauty of the painting: Frà Pandolf, the artist, seems to have captured an intense likeness, a particular expression: a passionate 'earnest glance', a 'spot of joy' (8, 14–15). At first the Duke only appears concerned with the aesthetic realm, rather in the manner of later veneration of Leonardo da Vinci's *Mona Lisa*, so here – for a time – the main emphasis appears to be on the painter's skill in capturing an exquisite facial expression. Then, disturbing undercurrents emerge. The Duke maintains his smooth tone, but gradually we sense his underlying, deadly annoyance. Discussing the lovely portrait of his first wife is leading him into an account of his marriage to her, and the words he uses to describe her create a very different image of the lady.

As far as he is concerned, his first wife was too easily made happy, too spontaneous, lacking in aristocratic hauteur or sang-froid. She took pleasure in many aspects of her life at court, and (as the Duke insists) failed completely to focus on him sufficiently. She *should* have been focused on him, and on the importance of his aristocratic lineage – his 'nine-hundred-years-old name' (33). When she failed in this, he did not condescend to reason with her, or explain how her behaviour annoyed him. He simply had her quietly executed, and so moved on to the possibility of a second marriage. After he has euphemistically told the envoy how he 'gave commands' (45), i.e. gave orders for her murder, he gestures at the portrait in order to remark that 'There she stands | As if alive' (46–7). The irony is abrupt and chilling.

A first reading disconcerts. It is clearly a macabre gothic study. But what has it got to do with us or with a world of more ordinary emotion? We are presented with a highly-coloured investigation into the psychology of a murderer. The poem also evokes a particular historical epoch, the splendour of the Renaissance enlightenment in a sixteenth-century ducal court. But how can we get nearer to it? Is it forever to be shut off in its own world of inter-involved irony?

Criticism has explored various themes or angles, the most important being the issue of control. The Duke would have us believe that his first wife was overly spontaneous or flirtatious in the way she responded to court life. Her face would light up with happiness at so many things: 'my favour', i.e. a token he had given her (25), a sunset (26), some cherries presented to her by one of the courtiers (27–8), Frà Pandolf's stylized compliments while he was painting her (16–19) – all these things gave her joy. The Duke clearly implies that *only he*, or perhaps his gifts, should make his wife happy, and he sees her behaviour as undiscriminating, almost – in her lack of focus on himself – teetering on the brink of sexual infidelity. As readers we decode the irony. Far from seeing the duchess as a naïf or a wanton with a suffering husband, we actually see a vital, spirited, innocent-hearted woman married to a monster of egotism and jealousy.

The ironic structure gives us various insights into the Duke's real character. It is only he, for example, who is allowed to draw back the curtains over the duchess's portrait, an almost sexual gesture of revelation. Now, as it were, he has her in his power. He controls access to her and she is only seen when he wants it. The last three lines (54–56) represent an aggressive ironic thrust, all the more so for the way they are disguised as an apparently throw-away remark. In non-ironic terms, the Duke simply indicates to the envoy another of the masterpieces of his art collection: Claus of Innsbruck's bronze figurine of the sea god Neptune taming a sea-horse. In fact, we cannot but read this gesture in the terms set up by the poem. The sea-horse is a delicate, fantastic, and feminine creature; Neptune is – in traditional depictions – vast, muscular, and bearded. Neptune's 'taming' of the sea-horse suggests a display of power and sadism that corresponds to what the Duke believes he has achieved with regard to his last Duchess. He has conquered her wayward nature and reduced her to a work of art. The feminine and the erotic have been reined in, ruthlessly brought under control. The Duke has tamed his wife from an uncontrollable three dimensions to a very controllable two.

In this context, the word 'object' (53) has always seemed important:

> I repeat,
> The Count your master's known munificence
> Is ample warrant that no just pretence
> Of mine for dowry will be disallowed;
> Though his fair daughter's self, as I avowed
> At starting, is my object.
>
> (48–53)

The twisted syntax can give the first-time reader problems. What the Duke is saying to the envoy is: 'I know your master the Count is generous with his money, and therefore that when I make a claim for a large dowry, he will meet it'. And then, as if he finds all this discussion of money distasteful, he assures the envoy that really, of course, his only aim or object is the daughter herself, her qualities of character and appearance. But 'object' is a double-edged word. The Duke has reduced his first wife to an object, from a live woman, to a painting in his art collection. Whatever he professes, we feel sure that his new wife will have a good chance of suffering the same fate.

Yet – a question several critics have asked – how successful is the Duke in this act of control, this sadistic reduction of a live human being? In telling the envoy about his last duchess, he repeats once more the story of how his temperament and character could not deal with a real woman. In the course of his account the duchess again escapes him, so that – at the centre of the monologue, particularly lines 25–31 – we see her as she was in life, riding her white mule round the terrace, enjoying the sunset or the cherries. The Duke may have reduced her to a portrait, a death-in-life, but even in the portrait – in its intense verisimilitude – she comes back to life and annoys him all over again. The Duke seems to some critics a little like Coleridge's ancient mariner. Does he endlessly repeat his story to whoever will hear? Is he never fully able to reduce his wife to the dead object he seems to desire?

From this point, some critics go further and read the monologue in terms of reading itself, the act of interpretation, or the act of seeing. The Duke has sought to impose (ruthlessly) one reading, one interpretation, on his last duchess and on his relations with her, but that interpretation does not satisfy him, and seems undermined by her continuing presence and vitality. So also, in pornography – the ultimate reduction of woman-to-object – the flattened image can only ever irritate the restless spirit, which secretly desires the real life (intimacy, warmth, relationship) that it has sought to exclude. In these, and other ways, this great poem itself has proved patient to criticism, but never been fully pegged down or controlled by it.

By now it should also be clear that the ideas of Langbaum and Booth about the functioning of irony, outlined in II (b), useful as they are in first approaching these poems, have limitations in our actual experience of reading them. This is something that can be proved again in relation to the other major poems. These monologues move us away from an obvious public realm into the inner worlds of their own peculiar dramas. As we will see, Wordsworth's late poetry offers a useful point of contrast. Rather than existing in the public realm of social evaluation and exchange, of morality and didacticism, Browning's poems invite us into profound and strange emotional empathies. They are intense, coloured, and ironic. In one sense they anticipate aspects of aestheticism later in the century, the involutions of Walter Pater's essays or the paradoxes of Oscar Wilde.

(ii) 'Pictor Ignotus'

'Pictor Ignotus' **[161–5]** well demonstrates this complexity. The title is Latin for 'Painter unknown', a phrase commonly used in museums to designate an unascribed painting. The phrase can stand for any artist who does not become famous in his or her lifetime, whose style is not so distinctive or celebrated as to be always identifiable. It has been suggested that, when Browning wrote this monologue, he was thinking of the painter Fra Bartolommeo (c. 1475–1517). Some aspects of the poem seem to fit perfectly. Fra Bartolommeo's surname was unknown, and he was commonly called just 'il Frate' (the Friar). If we accept this identification, then the painter who is becoming famous in line 1 – the 'youth' – would be Raphael, and the 'voice' of line 41 would be that of the great Dominican religious reformer Girolamo Savonarola (1452–98), who attacked the worldliness of Florentine art. Other critics have pointed out the limitations of these identifications, which – though suggestive – are not absolute or exact.

The monologue's speaker is a shy painter who has deliberately avoided artistic originality, and so deliberately avoided fame. He has chosen to continue with an idealized style of painting when about him bolder painters are exploring the possibilities of a greater realism, making their pictures really life-like, and winning celebrity as a result. (The opposition here between a purist or conventional style of religious art, and a style that lets in more that is life-like, strongly anticipates the central dichotomy of 'Fra Lippo Lippi'.) The painter in the poem contrasts himself with 'that youth ye praise so' (13), an artist of celebrity status like Raphael. He asserts that he himself could paint in the youth's more achieved, more life-like manner:

And, like that youth ye praise so, all I saw,
  Over the canvas could my hand have flung,
Each face obedient to its passion's law,
  Each passion clear proclaimed without a tongue
                                                    (13–16)

Had he painted on canvas (and not frescoes on walls), his work could have been carried to great states or little towns, 'to Pope or Kaiser, East, West, South, or North' (28), so spreading his name throughout Europe. Even when he died, he would 'linger' on earth through his much-loved pictures and his on-going fame (37–9). During his life the painter has come near to this kind of celebrity, but then – on the brink – has been affected by a spiritual crisis. The 'cold faces' of people thronging round his paintings made him feel as vulnerable as a nun shrinking from soldiers (47–8). The noisy mechanisms of celebrity were unreal, and so he retreated to executing 'cold calm' frescoes in churches and monasteries (57–62) with conventional subject-matter treated in an unoriginal way. These frescoes will 'moulder on the damp wall's travertine [limestone]' (67), and will be seen only by a few.

From this we might conclude that Browning is simply showing us an imaginative and spiritual coward, a painter refusing to fulfil his talents. He is analysing the psychology of failure, the psychology of someone who declines to access the new technical and stylistic innovations stirring around him, sticking to accepted ways. The poem is about an artist in sixteenth-century Italy, but its subtext could be said to be about the situation of a Romantic or post-Romantic poet in the nineteenth century. Is Browning implicitly celebrating his own sense of originality through this negative portrait? Just as the Romantic poets tried new forms and styles of writing – breaking away from the conventions of the eighteenth century – so we can read this monologue as Browning's implicit self-celebration as a post-Romantic innovator. He is examining the psychology of an unoriginal artist who refuses to be stirred by the times, to ride the zeitgeist.

As we enter more closely into sympathy with the speaker, the monologue's ironic structure seems more ambivalent. We can feel (as post-Romantics ourselves) that there must be something wrong about an artist who refuses to fulfil himself, to innovate and explore new styles. The monologue's ironic structure seems to judge the limitations of the speaker from the outside. However, we are lead into the details of the speaker's mindset so intensely that we come to see real reasons, real integrity, in his *chosen* failure. An art aspiring to be truly religious which (stylistically) becomes an unquestioning celebration of the world and which generates the brash realities of celebrity-status may really be losing touch with itself. (One thinks of the emptiness that surrounds the modern cult of celebrity, and the extent to which art implicated in this cult can simply become a commodity, a facet of the marketplace, compromised in its own standards and ideals – perhaps an awareness that Browning anticipates.)

> These [people] buy and sell our pictures, take and give,
> Count them for garniture and household-stuff,
> And where they live needs must our pictures live
> And see their faces, listen to their prate,
> Partakers of their daily pettiness
>
> (50–4)

'Prate', with the rhyme-word 'hate' (55), is a strong word. The speaker rejects the world of the rich patron, the picture dealers, the connoisseurs, the loud critics. Is this nervous inhibition, or rather integrity? We could certainly see his refusal to enter his historical moment as a combination of egotism and cowardice. But perhaps – just as easily – we could see it as what Pound called 'the intelligence at bay', a worthy suspicion of 'fame', a sense that there are values even more important than 'great art'. The speaker's final question to the famous contemporary with whom he contrasts himself is vivid: 'Tastes sweet the water with such specks of earth?' (72)

This two-way focus, the poem's involved and ambivalent ironic structure, is worth detailed analysis because it gives us a paradigm for the other crucial poems in these volumes. In 'Johannes Agricola in Meditation', 'Porphyria's Lover', 'Soliloquy of the Spanish Cloister', 'The Bishop Orders His Tomb', and 'The Laboratory' we are drawn into states of mind that initially seem only morally faulty, but which gradually seem to embody within them things beautiful or genuine or admirable. Our second awareness does not completely overthrow our first – they exist in creative tension – but the second awareness may come to seem the more important, even if it seems to be making us empathize with what is villainous or hateful.

Again, there are anticipations here of Wilde and others later in the century. An apparently moral position is undermined by irony in order to reach out towards a truer and more nuanced morality. In one of his later dramatic monologues, 'Bishop Blougram's Apology', Browning theorized this apparent combination of morality and perversity in a revealing way:

> Our interest's on the dangerous edge of things.
> The honest thief, the tender murderer,
> The superstitious atheist, demirep [loose woman or prostitute]
> That loves and saves her soul in new French books –
> We watch while these in equilibrium keep
> The giddy line midway: one step aside,
> They're classed and done with.
>
> (395–401)

(iii) 'Porphyria's Lover'

Taking up one phrase from the quotation above, we could well say that 'Porphyria's Lover' **[155–6]** presents a speaker who could aptly be described as a 'tender murderer'. The monologue's story is violent and abrupt: a working-man, or at least someone of modest circumstances, the lover of a middle-class girl, murders her when she comes to his cottage, strangling her with her own hair. At the end of the poem he sits, apparently calmly, with her corpse leaning against him in a sort of pseudo embrace (49–60).

'Porphyria's Lover' was originally published in the journal the *Monthly Repository* in 1836, where it was paired with 'Johannes Agricola in Meditation'. When Browning reprinted these poems, slightly revised, in *Dramatic Lyrics* (1842) he gave them the joint general title '*Madhouse Cells*', as though he felt the need to give a signal to otherwise confused readers. '*Madhouse Cells*' (which Browning later dropped) seems part warning, part interpretation, but taken too literally it can lead to a reductive reading: 'The speaker is mad. This poem is a disturbing but vivid examination of his psychopathology'. Again, though, our actual experience of reading the monologue is different. We are drawn into the speaker's mindset, and curiously partake of his erotic, sadistic fantasy. At some level we realize that he is not simply 'mad' in the sense of 'other', 'unknowable', 'satanic', totally different from ourselves.

His mindset is an exaggeration of feelings or tendencies that we may all have experienced.

What makes this come alive, of course, is that he is a *tender* murderer, his whole perspective is (in some sense) gentle or feminized. His language is delicate, sometimes almost prettified:

> No pain felt she;
> I am quite sure she felt no pain.
> As a shut bud that holds a bee,
> I warily oped her lids: again
> Laughed the blue eyes without a stain.
>   (41–5)

The first half of the monologue centres on the speaker's description of how Porphyria, his middle-class lover, comes into his cottage and sets about making it comfortable. The reader can sense his unbearable tension – enacted by the storm rocking the elms in the grounds of the big house (3) – because he has no control over when Porphyria will come to him. The wonderful vignette of lines 6–21 shows through *his* eyes her loveliness, her tenderness, her sexual warmth. His desire to freeze this exquisite moment, to bind Porphyria irrevocably to him, to capture the erotic frisson, is one we can all understand. It is a perverse marriage, not a mutual alliance entered into with freewill, but the total control of one partner by the other. It is an artist-like instinct to seize, frame, or find the form in, one particular arrangement of things. The diseased mind works with good images and ideas (physical warmth, eroticism, domesticity, loyalty, tenderness) even if it terribly distorts them.

What makes the monologue chilling is the relationship between its achieved, verbal perfection and its disturbing subject-matter. The poem has a beautiful verbal surface – witness, for example, the lovely change of rhythm (to a trochee) at the beginning of line 21: 'Murmuring how she loved me'. This seems to enact the soft voice with which Porphyria whispers to her lover. The combination of aesthetic perfection and sadistic subject-matter might even suggest a comparison with a picture like Aubrey Beardsley's 'Salome with the Head of John the Baptist' (1894), whose loveliness of design seems eerie or free-floating in relation to the decapitated, bloody head. A twentieth-century work that comes near to its emotional effect is Thom Gunn's 'Troubadour' sequence in the volume *Boss Cupid* (2000), in which the poems are imagined as spoken in the person of the mass-murderer Jeffrey Dahmer.

(iv) 'Soliloquy of the Spanish Cloister', 'The Bishop Orders His Tomb'

The other poems in the group we are considering all press the reader into the inner worlds of their speakers in similar ways. 'Soliloquy of the Spanish Cloister' **[151–5]** is spoken by a twisted monk who hates one of his fellow monks, the saintly Friar Lawrence. In one sense the ironic structure works against the speaker: he appears as essentially an embittered man perversely attacking a loving, spontaneous, and warm-hearted monk. The speaker destroys flowers (24), reads a pornographic novel (57), and sings black-magic chants to raise the devil ('*Hy, Zy, Hine*', 76). But then again, his energy and worldliness come to seem attractive, and Friar Lawrence's character limited: a rather tedious version of supposed virtue.

The paradox of 'The Bishop Orders His Tomb' is even more striking. This is the death-bed speech of a Renaissance bishop, not concerned with the salvation of his soul, but with orders for his own costly, sumptuous tomb. Although he is a supposedly celibate bishop, it quickly becomes clear that he is addressing his sons, the product of a long-term relationship with an illicit mistress. It might appear at first that the monologue's intention is primarily satirical. From Browning's firmly Protestant viewpoint (we suppose) it is an examination of the decadence and worldly excess of the Roman Catholic Church in the Renaissance, the world of Julius II's Rome (the world the Reformation opposed).

The kind of Protestantism in which Browning had been brought up was wary of the physical embodiment of religious mystery: it did not believe in great ritual and ceremony in relation to religious observance, and it was cautious about the sensuousness of religious art and sculpture as a means of coming near to God. It prided itself on a certain kind of simplicity and directness. In the 1830s and 1840s the Oxford Movement within the Anglican Church was perceived by the majority of Protestants to be moving the Anglican Church towards the Roman Catholic Church, leading (as Protestants saw it) to more ritualized, sensuous, and elaborate forms of worship, a tendency they deprecated. When Browning sent this monologue to *Hood's Magazine* in 1845 (where it was first published) his accompanying letter seems to evoke this context: 'I pick it out as being a pet of mine, and just the thing for the time – what with the Oxford business [i.e. the Oxford Movement]' (18 February 1845) (*Corr.* x. 83). This would seem to countenance a satirical, anti-Catholic reading of 'The Bishop Orders His Tomb'. Yet, as the reader enters into the poem's imaginative world, the bishop too provokes sympathy. The poem can come to seem anti-Protestant in its reverberations, or – to be more accurate – an attack on a limited kind of pietism. The bishop's speech seems a wonderful baroque celebration of sex, language, colour, ritual, and the sensuous beauty of marble and precious stones:

> Peach-blossom marble all, the rare, the ripe
> As fresh-poured red wine of a mightly pulse ...
> And have I not Saint Praxed's ear to pray
> Horses for ye, and brown Greek manuscripts,
> And mistresses with great smooth marbly limbs?
> (29–30, 73–5)

So far in this section we have concentrated on the poems concerned with perversity and criminality, because they are in many respects the strongest. There is, however, a countervailing tendency. It is not as striking as the interest in moral perversity and decadence – with some exceptions it results in less memorable poetry – but it is none the less an important part of these volumes' total dynamic. This contrary tendency is an interest in extreme virtue, aggressive heroism and chivalry: 'Incident of the French Camp', 'Through the Metidja to Abd-el-Kadr' and 'How They Brought the Good News' would all be examples. However, the most interesting poems in this group are 'Count Gismond' and 'The Lost Leader'.

At first this contrary tendency may seem simply to move in an opposite direction from the moods and concerns outlined above, as though Browning, having given some time to the study of crime and decadence, was determined to balance it with an interest in virtue. In fact, however, though these poems do not have ironic frameworks, they are still focused on a certain kind of intensity. Their coloured, highly-charged dramas are still part of the same exploration of an inner, aesthetic world.

(v) 'Count Gismond'

In the original volume of *Dramatic Lyrics* 'Count Gismond' **[165–8]** was paired with 'My Last Duchess' under the joint title *'Italy and France'* (see *Penguin* i. 1077). It would be possible to conclude from this that 'Count Gismond' is simply intended as a study of virtue and true marriage in contrast to the evil of the Duke. We need, however, to think of the kind of virtue we are dealing with. This is a poem of 'love at first sight' and the very bloody defence of good against evil. It is so heroic and chivalrous that – back in the days of New Criticism – one critic, John Hagopian (1961), suggested that it should be read ironically and that the speaker of the poem was guilty of hypocrisy and fornication. Implicitly, to Hagopian, a non-ironic reading was too fulsome to countenance since it would indicate an almost embarrassing celebration of the good, the wise, the religiously true, with trial-by-combat magically ringing out a just verdict.

The story of 'Count Gismond' is told by the Countess Gismond, happily married with a loving husband and two sons. From this domestic bliss, she looks back to the traumatic events on the day her marriage started. She was a young lady at the French court, single and with no thought of marriage. It was a festival day, a day for tournaments, and she was due to be crowned as the May queen (40), a pretty, courtesy title. Unknown to her, her two jealous cousins have conspired to have a certain Count Gauthier denounce her before the whole court for fornication with himself. This duly happens. She is defenceless, an orphan in fact, with no one to believe or stand up for her, when – suddenly – Count Gismond steps forward to defend her honour. He challenges Gauthier to a combat, spears him through, and then drags him in front of the lady and the crowd to recant his lie. After a few deep words of love, Gismond carries the lady away to the 'South' (114) – the country of the troubadours – to marriage and happiness with himself.

If this summary makes the poem appear sentimental, a fragment of medieval romance, the shock comes in its highly-charged eroticism. Gismond recognizes the speaker's true virtue instantaneously. He accuses Gauthier of lying, 'then struck his mouth | With one back-handed blow that wrote | In blood men's verdict there' (74–6). Gismond's squire puts on his armour while he stamps his foot in an almost sexual gesture of impatience: the speaker notes 'my memory leaves | No least stamp out' (88–9). Gismond 'flew' at Gauthier, killing him with one blow through the chest (94–6). Afterwards, as he carries away the lady-speaker to marriage, she remembers how 'His sword (that dripped by me and swung) | A little shifted in its belt' (111–12), a phallic image, mixing and accepting connections between virility and controlled violence. At the end of the monologue, where we learn that the speaker is telling her story to her confidante Adela, she has to coyly change the subject as her adored husband approaches. She begins to talk about her tercel (a male hawk), symbolic of her husband's physicality and virility, now trained into marriage.

Browning, as we saw in I. a. ii., was not a political radical in the mould of Shelley, or at least he seems not to have been politically committed in Shelley's way. Given his Nonconformist, middle-class background, he was also at a distance from the other pole of contemporary debate: the conservative religious humanism represented by Wordsworth, Coleridge, and John Henry Newman. In these circumstances, one way of seeing him is as a restless liberal poet, seeking out deeper perspectives through a complex ironic engagement with aspects of contemporary discourse.

The intense eroticism so evident in 'Count Gismond' is a feature across the poems we have been examining, and can be seen as a masking of political unease: compare, for example, 'Soliloquy of the Spanish Cloister' (stanza 4), 'Porphyria's Lover' (15–21), or 'The Bishop Orders His Tomb' (56–61). In terms of its eroticism 'The Laboratory' is an even more interesting example. Set within the world of repressive conservatism represented by eighteenth-century France, it draws us into sympathy with a would-be woman poisoner, small of stature, intent on murdering her husband's tall mistress with a lethal concoction she has purchased from a disgusting old chemist. The erotic frisson is all the stronger for the tawdry, louche circumstances: 'Now, take all my jewels, gorge gold to your fill, | You may kiss me, old man, on my mouth if you will!' (45–6). Here, directly, we are drawn into sympathy with what is illicit or perverse in a context in which what is respectable and legal may well be politically oppressive. It is from within the context of the rebellious spirit evoked in a context like this, a female poisoner striking a blow at the duplicitous civilities of the *ancien régime* (the poem's subtitle), that we can perhaps understand why the young Browning found the elderly Wordsworth so irritating.

(vi) 'The Lost Leader'

When Browning came to know Elizabeth Barrett he toned down his dislike of Wordsworth in the face of her obvious admiration. 'Browning shared the opinion of the second generation of Romantic writers (Shelley, Byron, Keats, Hazlitt, Leigh Hunt) that the first generation (Wordsworth, Coleridge, Southey: the 'Lake School') had committed political apostasy in their conversion to conservatism' (*Longman* ii. 177). Wordsworth's situation in the later half of his life is well described in one of the standard authorities: 'The great work of his early and middle years was now over, and Wordsworth slowly settled into the role of patriotic, conservative public man, abandoning the radical politics and idealism of his youth' (Drabble 2000: 1116). There was, however, a real edge to Browning's dislike of him. When asked by R. H. Horne to suggest an epigraph for the essay on Wordsworth in *A New Spirit of the*

Age (1844), Browning chose *Paradise Lost*, Book X, lines 441–54. This is the description of Satan making his entry to the council of the devils in Pandemonium. When Browning quoted the passage in his letter to Horne, he added his own italics and capitalization to convey the strength of his feeling against Wordsworth:

> At last, as from a cloud, his fulgent head
> And shape star-bright appeared, or brighter; *claid*
> *With what permissive glory* SINCE HIS FALL
> *Was left him, or false glitter.* All amazed
> At that so sudden blaze, the *Stygian throng*
> *Bent their aspect.*
>
> (Corr. viii. 219)

The vehemence of this choice – Horne, of course, felt unable to use it – connects back to the passionate intensity that seems to have been one aspect of Browning's personality **[42]**. Wordsworth, in his seventies, was a prominent figure in these years. In 1839 he received an honorary degree from the University of Oxford; in 1842 he published *Poems, Chiefly of Early and Late Years* and was granted a Civil List pension of £300 a year; in 1843 he succeeded Robert Southey as Poet Laureate, the event to which 'The Lost Leader' refers.

Wordsworth's late poetry, generally so little admired, is nonetheless the statement of a nuanced conservative religious humanism, delivered in language that is didactic and moral. 'Ecclesiastical Sonnets' (1832) shows a moving affiliation to the Anglican Church and seeks to demonstrate the centrality of the Anglican Church to national life. 'Sonnets dedicated to Liberty and Order' (1845) articulate with some aplomb an anti-revolutionary, anti-radical politics. Browning's 'The Lost Leader' (which was published in 1845) should be read in the context of texts like these. In theory it is spoken by a liberal poet resentful of the way in which the 'Leader' of the progressive political forces has betrayed his cause, but actually the dramatic mask is thin. It is really Browning's own indictment of Wordsworth, a poet who he believed had succumbed to the blandishments of the establishment:

> We that had loved him so, followed him, honoured him,
> Lived in his mild and magnificent eye,
> Learned his great language, caught his clear accents,
> Made him our pattern to live and to die!
> Shakespeare was of us, Milton was for us,
> Burns, Shelley, were with us, – they watch from their graves!

He alone breaks from the van and the freemen,
– He alone sinks to the rear and the slaves!
(9–16)

This is a poetry of direct statement, breaking out (like 'Count Gismond') from the involved ironic structures we analysed earlier, and for a moment (as it were) giving us a glimpse of a Browning whose politics might be a little more committed or overt. It is a hint of an intensity of political feeling that is usually smothered in the involved ironies that make up so much of his art.

Further reading

One of the best ways of furthering reading is again to look at the short introductions to each poem in either the *Oxford* or *Longman* editions: the poems of *Dramatic Lyrics* and *Dramatic Romances and Lyrics* are covered in *Oxford* vols iii and iv, and in *Longman* i and ii. Both these editions give a wealth of detailed contextual material.

In book-length studies, there are good close discussions in Tucker (1980) chapter 5, and in Ryals (1983) chapters 6 and 8. Bristow (1991) has detailed readings of 'Porphyria's Lover' pp. 47–51, 'My Last Duchess' pp. 53–62, and 'Pictor Ignotus' pp. 91–4. And Karlin (1993), one of the subtlest studies, has excellent readings of 'The Lost Leader' pp. 32–46, 'Soliloquy of the Spanish Cloister' pp. 74–9, 'Porphyria's Lover' pp. 208–16, and 'The Englishman in Italy' pp. 243–56. In older critical modes 'My Last Duchess' has a whole book devoted to it: Berman (1972). Other valuable individual accounts are McCusker (1983) on 'Soliloquy of the Spanish Cloister', Tucker (1984) and Bidney (1984) on 'Porphyria's Lover' and its paired poem 'Johannes Agricola in Meditation', and the discussion of 'The Englishman in Italy' in Miller (1985), pp. 180–228. There is a short, suggestive discussion of 'The Laboratory', a still neglected poem, in Wood (2001), chapter 3.

(d) *MEN AND WOMEN* AND *DRAMATIS PERSONAE*

The fifty-one poems of *Men and Women* were written in 1853–5, in a period of sometimes intense productivity, and published in two volumes in 1855. As the final poem 'One Word More' explains, each poem is in a different voice, 'my fifty men and women' (1): in effect, fifty dramatic monologues, either blank verse or stanzaic, in a variety of styles. They represent the heart of Browning's achievement.

In the Oxford edition Ian Jack gives notes on prosody because 'the remarkable variety of these poems is clearly a deliberate display of metrical virtuosity on Browning's part' (*Oxford* v. xxxvi). As with metre, so with mood: there are often violent juxtapositions, between for example the open rhythm and comic-grotesque mode of 'Up at a Villa– Down in the City' and the constrained pathos-laden stanza of 'A Woman's Last Word'. The range of subject-matter is equally striking. We have the burning of the Master of the Order of the Knights-Templar in 1314 ('The Heretic's Tragedy'), an account of one of the obscure emperors of the fifth century ('Protus'), the meditations of a bishop *circa* 1853 ('Bishop Blougram's Apology'), the quest of a medieval knight ('Childe Roland to the Dark Tower Came'), the thoughts of a nineteenth-century scientist about eighteenth-century Venice ('A Toccata of Galuppi's'), and so on. This kind of variety continues in *Dramatis Personae* (1864), where one speaker is a half-savage man-monster ('Caliban upon Setebos') while another is a dying saint ('A Death in the Desert').

The emotional range of these poems matches their versatility of metre and subject-matter. In Part II (c) we analysed the complex irony of the early monologues, and their condensed, enclosed effects. Now Browning's art opens out. This is partly a question of length: whereas 'My Last Duchess' and 'Soliloquy of the Spanish Cloister' are 56 and 72 lines respectively, 'Andrea del Sarto' and 'Bishop Blougram's Apology' – two of the longer monologues in *Men and Women* – are 267 and 1014 lines respectively. It is also a question of the workings of irony. In *Men and Women* the irony is far less stark, more relaxed, more generous and nuanced than in the earlier monologues. To the latter we applied the observation that irony 'risks disaster more aggressively than any other device' (Booth 1974: 41). Now this comment is less applicable. 'A Toccata of Galuppi's' and 'Bishop Blougram's Apology' both prove this point.

The range and variety of the monologues concerned with love in *Men and Women* can be related to the slow emotional deepening of the Brownings' marriage [29–30]. The vivid coloration of many poems, and the range of the poems about art, relate to the slow-working but profound impact of living in Florence after 1846 [25–8]. A third aspect of *Men and Women* now needs further investigation: its relative withdrawal from politics and the contemporary realm. For all its flamboyant, virtuoso shifts of metre and mood, *Men and Women* is striking for the way it explores a subjective, literary, inner world, focused on the intimacies of love.

Men and Women is written within the disillusioned aftermath of the 1848 revolutions, within the pessimism that a liberal like Browning naturally felt in the wake of those crucial eruptions and the conservative restorations that followed them. We saw in Part I **[26–8]** how he witnessed at first-hand the restoration of autocracy in Florence in 1849. In 1851–2, also, he had witnessed other aspects of the post-revolutionary phase in France.

When the July Monarchy of Louis-Philippe was overthrown in France in 1848, the Second Republic drifted briefly in a genuinely leftwards direction. This was halted by brutal class war. In the 'June days' of 1848 General Cavaignac's troops crushed the resistance of the workers, killing thousands. Thereafter politics drifted to the right, culminating in Louis Napoleon's *coup d'état* of 2 December 1851. As one historian puts it: 'within three years the French, who had thrown out their King, were saddled once more with an authoritarian Emperor' (Davies 1996: 805).

The Brownings were in Paris from late September 1851 to July 1852, and again in October 1852, and so witnessed the *coup d'état* of 2 December and its aftermath, and felt the reverberations of discontent within the intellectual circles in which they moved. In December 1851, in a plebiscite, Louis Napoleon got a democratic mandate for his unique version of populist absolutism, but the effects of his new rule were stark. Initially over 26,000 people were arrested. Some were sent to the prison colony of Devil's Island, almost 10,000 were deported to Algeria, 3,000 were imprisoned, and 5,000 placed under police surveillance. Parts of France were still under martial law in early 1852. From the first, Browning felt antipathy for Louis Napoleon, something that culminated in his *Prince Hohenstiel-Schwangau* (1871). In fact, being the kind of liberal he was, he had few real grounds on which to oppose the kind of politics Napoleon represented. On 16 October 1852 – a week before they left for Florence – the Brownings watched Napoleon's triumphal entry into Paris after an extended provincial tour. Shortly afterwards the Empire was restored and (after a plebiscite) Louis Napoleon proclaimed himself Emperor Napoleon III. The early phase of the Second Empire (1852–9) was authoritarian and repressive.

Men and Women works hard to seek out the truth in three related areas: art, religion, and love, and the intensity with which it explores these themes can be seen as the obverse of its disillusionment with politics. The first poem of the collection, 'Love Among the Ruins', signals this. It is, of course, spoken dramatically, by a young man or shepherd profoundly in love, but the central trope – the futility of history and politics as against the value of love – is nonetheless in some sense Browning's own. The monologue parodies and dismisses the self-important 'triumphs' and 'glories' of some ancient empire. This is presumably the Roman Empire, but it could as well be talking about the more recent pretensions of Louis Napoleon's Second Empire:

> Oh heart! oh blood that freezes, blood that burns!
>   Earth's returns
> For whole centuries of folly, noise and sin!
>   Shut them in,
> With their triumphs and their glories and the rest!
>   Love is best.
>
>   (79–84)

Other poems, like 'Respectability', 'How it Strikes a Contemporary' and 'The Heretic's Tragedy' could all be linked with this mood. More generally, as will become evident, Browning is focusing on questions like 'What makes good art?', on virtue and religious belief, and on the nature and perplexities of love. The restoration of conservative politics in Italy after 1848–9 is glimpsed negatively in 'The Patriot', in 'Up at a Villa–Down in the City' (stanza 9), and in 'De Gustibus–' (33–8), and, more hopefully, in 'Old Pictures in Florence'. But politics is a subsidiary theme compared to art, religion, and love. The public sphere is mainly difficult and other – as, for example, in one speaker's wonderfully dismissive allusion to the marriage of Napoleon III and the Empress Eugenie ('A Lovers' Quarrel', stanza 5). When Browning returned to Florence from Paris in October 1852, he went back to a quieter town, one where there were fewer potential distractions or social engagements. As he settled down to real writing in 1853, what he was producing was a sustained meditation on what now seemed to him the most important things in life.

(i) Poems about art

There is a range of poems in *Men and Women* focused on painting, poetry, and music, and, to a lesser extent, this vein continues in *Dramatis Personae*. The most obvious poems are 'Fra Lippo Lippi', 'How it Strikes a Contemporary', 'Master Hugues of Saxe-Gotha', 'Andrea del Sarto', 'Old Pictures in Florence', 'Popularity', and 'Transcendentalism'. ('A Toccata of Galuppi's', which is discussed under 'Poems of Religion', could just as well be placed here.) In *Dramatis Personae*, 'Abt Vogler' is the best instance. Various questions arise: What view of art emerges if we consider these poems together? Why at this time was Browning concerned to write so many self-reflexive poems examining the nature of art and creativity? 'Popularity' and 'Transcendentalism' are directly about poetry, but those poems that reflect on painting and music nonetheless discuss ideas that cross-refer to Browning's own poetic practice.

As a group these poems evoke and defend a distinct view of art. Browning seems to have felt that his times were antipathetic to true art, that true art was under threat. Here he defends art against some antagonistic positions. Some of these positions are materialistic – implicitly denying the value of art – others are sentimental or unreal in other ways. The overall idea of art that emerges is traditional, while also being inflected by Romanticism.

Browning's first assumption is that poetry is a skill or craft that – if it is worth anything – necessarily involves real work. The central metaphor of 'Popularity' implies this. Inferior or pretentious poets follow artistic fashion, avoiding effort and dedication. The true poet is like the dye-maker, taking the rough sea mussels, and then, gradually, skilfully, extracting the beautiful essence: he will 'pound and squeeze | And clarify' and so 'refine to proof | The liquor filtered by degrees' (52–4). Skill or craftsmanship must be animated by the artist's spiritual intensity. This is the related theme of 'Andrea del Sarto'. The Florentine painter, Andrea del Sarto (1486–1531), the monologist, displays a perfect technical facility but lacks spiritual fire: he cannot 'pour' out his 'soul' onto the canvas, he cannot reach through naturalism to supernaturalism. The monologue implies that the great artist (like Raphael or Michelangelo) is necessarily religious, and that to be such an artist is difficult.

'Transcendentalism' – whose full ironic title is 'Transcendentalism: A Poem in Twelve Books' – connects this necessary intensity with the genre of lyric. It contrasts lyric poetry, focused on physical reality, with a philosophical, didactic, or moralizing poetry, which attempts to tell the truth discursively. Lyric responds to and embodies the physical universe, the world of the senses. It incarnates the pleasure of the beautiful. Didactic poetry, on the other hand – and Browning may well have been thinking of Wordsworth – flounders in abstraction. It loses sensuous intensity, and so loses all power to seriously attract or move us (see Hawlin 1990a: 141–6).

'Fra Lippo Lippi' extends this idea of the necessarily worldly nature of art. It defends a sensuous, particular, and social art against an art that is purist or idealized. Art must engage with 'the shapes of things, their colours, lights and shades' (284), and also, implicitly, with God-given sexuality: 'the value and significance of flesh' (268). It must keep the Madonna and Saints in the real world. It has to enjoy depicting, for example, a murderer's girlfriend giving him her gold earrings so he can get money with which to escape (149–62). Browning's personal engagement seems particularly strong in this monologue, as though he feels keenly threatened by art that embodies an idealized vision, by any art that directs itself too readily towards moralism or easy uplift. As a post-Romantic or post-Enlightenment poet, working in an environment where a supernatural or theological view of humankind seems to be failing, he feels compelled to restate an incarnational idea of art in bold terms. Art must address the world as it is – beautiful, tragic, sensuous, ugly – *not* attempt, as it were, to go over its head. Browning insists that it is only through an art grounded in reality that there can be any possibility of religious vision.

'Fra Lippo Lippi' **[175–81]** has always seemed the central poem of *Men and Women*. In barely 400 lines the whole life and times of the Florentine painter Fra Filippo Lippi (1406–69) are vividly brought to life. The monologist is Fra Lippi himself, and the poem sets him in a lively situation. It is roughly 1440 in Florence, on a spring night during the Carnival. Lippi, monk and painter, has been caught by the *sbirri* (the Florence police) out late and near to a brothel. A constable actually has his hand gripping Lippi's throat (13). So, apprehended in a compromising place, the monk-artist initially threatens the constable with the influence of his wealthy patron, Cosimo de Medici, but then – feeling sure he is not going to be arrested – relaxes and gives an extended justification of his life and art.

Browning's source for this monologue, as also for 'Andrea del Sarto', was Giorgio Vasari's *Le Vita de' più eccellenti Pittori, Scultori, et Architettori* (1550, 2nd ed., 1568), the famous 'Lives of the Painters', the first great study of Italian Renaissance art, but – as the monologue itself bears witness – he supplemented this with his own study of the artist's works in the Uffizi, the Pitti Palace, various churches in Florence, and also at nearby Prato. The basic elements of the story are taken from Vasari: the account of how, as a poor orphan, Lippi was placed in the monastery without a true vocation, how subsequently he developed as an artist, and how – on one occasion – locked up by his patron Cosimo de Medici, he escaped from the room with a rope made of sheets.

The monologue is a brilliant impressionistic reconstruction of fifteenth-century Florence. If it is studied in one of the scholarly editions – *Penguin* or *Oxford*, for example – or in C. F. Thomas (1991), it is possible to see how much historical detail is pieced together in an apparently off-hand way in order to create the quiddity of history, its tactile reality. One example can serve. When Lippi describes how he escapes from the Medici-Riccardi Palace with his rope of sheets in order to chase after

young women, he says: 'Lord, it's fast holding by the rings in front – |
Those great rings serve more purposes than just | To plant a flag in, or
tie up a horse!' (228–30). Lippi uses the metal rings on the façade of the
palace to aid his escape and also to help him get back in. The rings can be
seen today, and Browning certainly looked at them as he contemplated
Vasari's account of this incident. Here, as so often, the turbulent energy
of the poetry is deceptive. This kind of impressionism is a product of
quiet thought. Each piece of historical reference is carefully placed against
another, as in a mosaic, to make up a vivid whole.

Historical reconstruction in 'Fra Lippo Lippi' is, however, not naive.
Browning is self-consciously resuscitating history in order to examine
nineteenth-century interpretations of the Renaissance, and, more
generally (as we have seen) his own ideas of his role as a poet. The
book that most fully lies behind the poem is *De la poésie chrétienne*
('The Poetry of Christian Art') by the French Catholic critic Alexis
François Rio. Rio gave a full reading of the development of the Renaissance. He favoured the early painters, particularly Giotto (1266–
1337) and Fra Angelico (1387–1455), in whose purity and idealism of
style he saw a corresponding religious zeal. Through the fifteenth
century he saw a developing decadence, in which, as art became more
technically skilled and more fully naturalistic, it lost religious intensity
and became worldly. Within this thesis, Rio identifies Masaccio (1401–
28) and Fra Filippo Lippi as two painters who particularly furthered
the introduction of naturalism. To him they were both decadent gen-
iuses, whose work turned art away from religion to its own Promethean
ends (see DeLaura 1980).

To properly understand Rio, and Browning's rebuttal of his ideas, it
is important to look closely at some of the art mentioned in the poem:
at Giotto and Fra Angelico – the heroes of Rio and of the Prior in the
poem – and at Masaccio and Fra Filippo Lippi – Browning's heroes.
Rio's thesis was the product of a particular kind of French conservative
Catholicism, though, in another sense, it was very 'unCatholic': in
lauding the purist style of Giotto and Fra Angelico, it had no time for
the fleshy splendours of the Counter-Reformation Baroque. Its
influence, however, was widespread, particularly on Protestant-trained
sensibilities: Anna Jameson (Browning's friend), Mary Shelley, and John
Ruskin all took over aspects of its argument. Browning opposed it
passionately, and in the monologue his artist-monk becomes a kind of
warts-and-all hero.

The monologue is firmly Protestant in the way it questions the value
of the celibate vocation, but actually this aspect is on the surface, and
– as so often in Browning – the real object of his attack is bourgeois

moralism. The opening is surely intended as a shock for certain kinds of sensibility. The painter of religious subjects is caught 'at an alley's end | Where sportive ladies leave their doors ajar' (5–6), i.e. near a brothel. Lippi implies that if the over-zealous police search his monastery they will find other monks with their mistresses in their cells (7–11). Yet it is this frail and faulty man who goes on to celebrate the beauty of the God-given creation and an art that responds to that beauty. 'You're my man', says Lippi to the head of the *sbirri*:

> you've seen the world
> – The beauty and the wonder and the power,
> The shapes of things, their colours, lights and shades,
> Changes, surprises, – and God made it all!
> – For what? Do you feel thankful, ay or no,
> For this fair town's face, yonder river's line,
> The mountain round it and the sky above,
> Much more the figures of man, woman, child,
> These are the frame to? What's it all about?
> To be passed over, despised? or dwelt upon,
> Wondered at? oh, this last of course! – you say.
>   (282–92)

This passage is full of the intensity of wonder, and its concern links in with the other poems in the group we are discussing.

In 'Andrea del Sarto', the later painter Andrea del Sarto (1486–1531) speaks aloud his thoughts on an autumn evening in 1525, at his house up on Fiesole overlooking Florence. Though still relatively young, he is exhausted both emotionally and artistically. With his tacit acquiescence, his wife has a lover, a man who gambles excessively, who they both euphemistically call her 'Cousin' (220, 239, 267). Her exquisite but 'soulless' beauty is a symbol of his art, which – while it is technically perfect – is empty of inspiration, energy, and religious vision.

'Andrea del Sarto' is an analysis of artistic failure. The poem's premise is that del Sarto had the same technical ability as Raphael or Michelangelo. Why then, Browning is asking, is he not a comparably great artist? Del Sarto seeks only a tame existential security, symbolized in the scene-setting near the monologue's opening: the monastery wall that del Sarto sees opposite 'Holds the trees safer, huddled more inside' (43). And del Sarto shies away from the vivid and necessarily sexual fullness of life, and the spirituality that is a part of that fullness. There are painters in Florence with less expertise than himself, he says, and they fail technically, but

There burns a truer light of God in them,
In their vexed beating stuffed and stopped-up brain,
Heart, or whate'er else, than goes on to prompt
This low-pulsed forthright craftman's hand of mine.
(79–82)

His own art, says Andrea, lacks intensity and wonder: 'All is silver-grey | Placid and perfect with my art' (98–9). In the drawing of an arm by Raphael he admires 'the play, the insight and the stretch' (116). The arm may be technically incorrect in terms of perspective, but its imaginative reach is completely beyond him.

These linked ideas of intensity and sensuousness can also be seen in 'Popularity' and 'Transcendentalism'. The central image of 'Popularity', in stanzas 9 and 10, is of King Solomon sitting in his hall of judgement. He is 'gold-robed' (43) but sits against a background of deep 'blue' or crimson wall-hangings (44). These are dyed with the precious purpura dye extracted from 'Tyrian shells' (26). In their raw state, the shells and the molluscs in them are completely uninteresting: they represent the simple quiddities of the world, the world untransformed by imagination. But the skilled dye-maker – like the true poet – knows exactly how to extract from them the precious crimson liquid (i.e. art, the distillation of imagination). This is the poem's central, unusual trope: the movement from 'live whelks' in their shells (38) to the sensuously splendid image of the crimson wall-hangings in Solomon's hall (42). How does something so apparently mundane in the end produce something so splendid? This image is then topped by another – a piling of image on image that enacts the intensity that is the poem's subject: the gold pistil in the centre of the blue-bell flower, at the time when the bee, like a drunken lover, goes to 'mate' with it – an image of 'gold-robed' King Solomon sitting against the backdrop of the gorgeous hangings (46–50).

'Transcendentalism: A Poem in Twelve Books' is governed by a directly similar image, again highly unusual: that of the magician, John of Halberstadt, chanting special magic spells, 'a brace of rhymes' (39), and so suddenly filling a room with roses, roses that twist in and out of the tables and chairs, and so amaze everyone with their loveliness (39–43). This magician or 'mage' is a figure of the lyric poet (in opposition to the philosophizing poet who is derided in the poem). The magician (or lyric poet) 'buries us with a glory' (44), i.e. overwhelms us with a sense of the intensity and beauty of the world. In this way he makes us 'young once more, | Pouring heaven into this shut house of life' (44–5). Sensuous lyric intensity is the true road to spiritual intuition.

(ii) Poems of religion

In the first part of the nineteenth century many intellectuals felt that the grounds for religious doubt had been growing. The discoveries of geology and related sciences, some aspects of philosophy and biblical criticism, seemed to be undermining revealed religion. Browning was aware of these trends, and first attempted to respond to them seriously in *Christmas-Eve and Easter-Day* (1850), particularly in the description of the German professor (781 ff), who could be any number of Hegelian thinkers, but was probably inspired by Ludwig Feuerbach or David Friedrich Strauss.

For the German philosopher Ludwig Feuerbach (1804–72), God was non-existent, only an imaginative projection of the human mind. For the German biblical scholar D. F. Strauss (1808–74) the biblical account of Jesus's life was a 'historical myth': the ancient Jews were a primitive, unscientific people who believed in miracles. Now, being scientific and 'modern' in consciousness, he assumed that the miracle-worker Jesus must have been no such thing, just an itinerant preacher sentenced to death by the authorities. Strauss's *Das Leben Jesu kritisch bearbeitet* (1835–6, 'The Life of Jesus, Critically Examined') was the work which, as she translated it in 1844–6, consolidated George Eliot's move away from her earlier evangelical faith.

Browning's response to these currents of thought was nuanced. As with the 'Science versus Religion' debate sparked by Darwin's *Origin of Species* (1859) a few years later, a debate that is far odder and more complicated than it is often made to appear, so this earlier debate over the so-called Higher Criticism is a complex affair. In Browning's case, his first response was to suspect that the new thinking did not simply invalidate older currents of religious thought and feeling. In the light of this insight, he wrote various monologues addressing these religious questions and asserting in different ways his ongoing commitment to the basic truth of Christianity.

The group of poems in *Men and Women* that might be considered under the heading 'Poems of Religion' could include 'A Toccata of Galuppi's', 'An Epistle … of Karshish', 'Childe Roland', 'The Statue and the Bust', 'Bishop Blougram's Apology', 'Saul', 'Holy-Cross Day', 'Cleon', 'The Heretic's Tragedy' and 'A Grammarian's Funeral'. In *Dramatis Personae* (1864) it could include 'A Death in the Desert', 'Caliban upon Setebos', 'Apparent Failure', and the 'Epilogue'. The following short analyses are intended to give the gist of these central poems and their interrelated themes.

'Bishop Blougram's Apology' is a comic-grotesque challenge to the new mood of religious doubt. The monologue has a contemporary setting. We are not being taken back to the fourteenth or fifteenth century, but are vividly in the 1850s. The speaker is a bishop – usually thought to be modelled on Cardinal Nicholas Wiseman (1802–65) – who is in extended conversation with a journalist, Mr Gigadibs, on the subject of religious faith. Before the monologue commences Gigadibs has given the bishop a piece of his mind, explained his religious doubts, and challenged the priest to explain how he – a sophisticated, learned man – can really still believe in Christianity within the modern, nineteenth-century world. The monologue is Bishop Blougram's complex, rolling self-defence, based partly on long-held beliefs and premises, partly improvised to rebut Gigadibs's claims. Blougram himself describes it as 'The Eccentric Confidence' (962), what we would now call 'an off-the-record briefing'. We hear a bishop speaking impromptu, in an unbuttoned, convivial style.

The poem has an interesting background in contemporary anti-Catholicism. In the nineteenth century England was still a strongly Protestant nation, and anti-Catholic feeling (from the most nuanced position through to the most brutal bigotry) was pervasive. 'Bishop Blougram' was written in 1854 or 1855, but it refers back to events of 1850–1, the furore over the so-called 'Papal Aggression'. Roman Catholics had only regained some basic civil rights in the 1820s; now the Pope decided to reinstate Catholic bishops in England for the small 80,000 body of the Roman Catholic faithful. (This is the 'novel hierarchy [of bishops]' referred to at lines 973–4.) Though this was a purely internal matter to the Roman Catholic Church, Protestant England felt threatened, and there was a huge storm of anti-Catholic feeling in the press and elsewhere. The Pope's mundane action was seen as highly controversial, some kind of interference in the national life of Britain. This outbreak of Protestant bigotry was in many ways an inverted and insecure definition of 'Britishness' (a little bit like 'Euro-scepticism' today).

Browning plays with these Protestant-Catholic tensions in the course of the monologue. In the opening paragraph he goes out of his way to emphasize that the wonderfully-named Sylvester Blougram is a *Roman Catholic* bishop. There are allusions to Augustus Pugin (the famous convert to Catholicism), to 'these hot long ceremonies of our church' (10) – the feast of Corpus Christi ('The Body of Christ') – and also (playfully) to the idea that Catholics might want to claim back Westminster Abbey from the Anglicans (3). In the opening, in other words, Browning seems deliberately to be provoking the anti-

Catholicism of many of his intended (Protestant) readers, and there are many later points in the monologue that seem to pander to this feeling further.

The bishop's arguments for religious faith have a casuistic and worldly air, seemingly in keeping with his larger character. One of his main arguments for belief seems to be, for example, that, by a fulsome profession of faith in Christianity he himself has done very well in the world, enjoying a lifestyle and status quite beyond that of the lowly Gigadibs. As a hack journalist Gigadibs can only ever hope to eke out a penurious living by writing for the Reviews.

If we take his arguments at face-value, this side of Blougram seems hypocritical and disreputable. But, from the start, he shows an ironic self-insight and self-deprecation. The more we engage with his monologue the harder it seems to make easy judgements of approval or condemnation. The mixture of good and bad seems impossible to peg down. And what is true for his character, can also seem true for the subject he discusses: agnosticism is shown up as a parasitic, simplifying discourse. Bishop Blougram is able to describe eloquently our fluctuating emotions in relation to the problem of God. Browning's (Protestant) readers would have found themselves drawn into an awkward alliance with a worldly Roman Catholic bishop in his defence of Christianity against the rantings of a journalist:

> how can we guard our unbelief,
> Make it bear fruit to us?—the problem here.
> Just when we are safest [in our religious doubt], there's a sunset-
> touch,
> A fancy from a flower-bell, some one's death,
> A chorus-ending from Euripides,–
> And that's enough for fifty hopes and fears
> As old and new at once as nature's self,
> To rap and knock and enter in our soul,
> Take hands and dance there, a fantastic ring,
> Round the ancient idol, on his base again, –
> The grand Perhaps! We look on helplessly.
>
> (180–90)

Other striking poems dealing with religious faith and doubt are 'An Epistle of Karshish' and its companion poem 'Cleon', and, in *Dramatis Personae*, 'A Death in the Desert'. Critics have striven to see exactly which contemporary works of rationalistic scripture criticism and religious doubt – what the Victorians sometimes called 'neologism' –

Browning was responding to in each poem, but Browning was well read and knew or had heard about most of these works, so characteristic of the period. The most obvious works that lie behind 'Karshish' and 'Cleon' are David Strauss's *Das Leben Jesu* (already mentioned) and Ludwig Feuerbach's *Das Wesen des Christentums* (1841; 'The Essence of Christianity'). These also feature in 'A Death in the Desert', as do *Essays and Reviews* (1860) and – as some critics maintain – Ernest Renan's *La Vie de Jésus* (1863; 'The Life of Jesus'), which Browning read in November 1863. As we might expect from someone who continued to find Christianity compelling, Browning found Renan's work 'weaker and less honest than I was led to expect' (McAleer 1951: 180).

'An Epistle of Karshish' is set in about AD 65 and describes a vivid encounter between a fictional Arab man of science (the speaker) and Lazarus, the man who Jesus miraculously brought back to life in the gospel of John, 11: 1–44. The poem is an open confrontation with the issue of whether the miraculous is possible. D. F. Strauss and others were denying the historical reality of Jesus's miracles. Browning suggests that miracles are possible, and again he is working less by direct argument than by the creation of character. Strauss, as we have seen, suggested that the 'primitive' Jewish consciousness could believe and accept the idea of miracles, could believe in the possibility of a 'wonder-worker' like Jesus, whereas the 'modern', 'scientific' mindset could not. Browning undermines this simplistic polarity by creating the character of Karshish, an eccentric but nonetheless rigorous man of science, who stumbles upon Lazarus during a tour of Palestine. Karshish, a sceptical, hard-headed empiricist, would like to conclude that Lazarus (a man claiming he has been 'raised from the dead') is mad, but the character of Lazarus himself – level-headed, straightforward, and saintly – gives him pause. Through his meeting with Lazarus, Karshish learns about Jesus, and at the end of the monologue he is coming near to wondering if Jesus's claims about himself might be true.

'A Death in the Desert' is set roughly in AD 100, when St John (the last surviving of Jesus's disciples and now well over ninety years of age) is dying somewhere near the town of Ephesus. Browning assumes, in accord with the traditions of his day, that the disciple John wrote the Gospel of his name, the Book of Revelations, and the three Epistles. Now he imagines another surviving piece of Scripture, John's deathbed speech reported by an early Christian named Pamphylax, and given to us by an unnamed narrator. In the framework of the monologue (1–12, 665–87), and through the monologue itself, Browning is confronting the new knowledge about the historicity of the Scriptures and also addressing the scholarly problems concerned with their authenticity and transmission. Browning's St John is allowed to reach out from his historical context in order to address issues of religious doubt in the nineteenth century.

The remaining space in this section will be devoted to three poems which, though they address 'religious' issues more tangentially, are some of the finest in the volume: 'The Statue and the Bust', 'A Toccata of Galuppi's', and 'Childe Roland to the Dark Tower Came'.

The outline of the story of 'The Statue and the Bust' can give us an insight into how Browning is teasing or worrying at a simplified bourgeois moralism, the idea of 'respectability', and what might be set in its place. The stanza form, an abbreviated version of *terza rima* – famously, of course, the form of Dante's *Divine Comedy* – is a clue to the intensity of religious feeling that lies behind the poem.

In sixteenth-century Florence a young aristocrat, just married to a man from the Riccardi family, falls really in love on her wedding day with her husband's master, the Grand Duke Ferdinand de' Medici, and he with her. Instead of running off together or consummating their passion, they spend a lifetime in suspended longing: she looks out of her palace window as the Duke each day rides past on his horse. Eventually, sensing some profound missed opportunity in their one-and-only lives, they ironically commemorate these poses by each separately commissioning an artist to replicate them: hence the title, 'The Statue and the Bust'. The poem has a crucial epilogue in which Browning directly addresses the worried bourgeois reader who is thinking 'But delay was best, | For their end was a crime' (226–7), i.e. 'Are you, Robert Browning, encouraging or condoning adultery?' Browning's answer is implied through the whole of the last section, but embodied, in miniature, in these lines:

Only they [the Grand Duke and the lady] see not God, I know,
Nor all that chivalry of his,
The soldier-saints who, row on row,

Burn upward each to his point of bliss ...

(220–3)

Virtue, for Browning, is a passionate love-affair with goodness and with the good God: it is *not* a false inhibition of the spirit, a playing safe with a set of rules. Had the couple run off together and committed adultery, they might – even through sin – have discovered something real about their lives. As it was, their ennui was a consequence of timidity and convention, bourgeois moralism and compromise – something very different from the integrity of real virtue. We may notice, here, how the ideal of the intensity of virtue matches Browning's ideas about intensity in art.

The monologist of 'A Toccata of Galuppi's' [170–5] is a nineteenth-century man of science who is struggling to make serious discoveries about nature – as he puts it, to 'triumph o'er a secret wrung from nature's close reserve' (32). He looks back on Venice in the eighteenth century, the last period of its decadence before it lost its independence, and – via the music of the eighteenth-century Venetian composer, Baldassaro Galuppi – fantasizes for himself a picture of a sensuous, frivolous city. Browning is undoubtedly on the side of the poem's speaker: his moral and intellectual seriousness is contrasted positively with the hedonism of the young Venetians. Here Browning's Protestant Christianity is crossed with his reading of Plato. The idea that the speaker expresses at lines 38–9, that, in the afterlife, his soul will pass to higher and better regions, while the souls of the hedonistic Venetians will simply 'die', is a version of the afterlife as found in Plato's *Phaedo*, one that we know Browning himself echoed in conversation.

The monologue, however, is complicated by irony. The speaker is not simply a source of wisdom. He has a grudging, unimaginative mindset, and a certain provincial narrowness: for example, he has never been 'out of England' (9). He thinks he can easily dismiss the hedonism of eighteenth-century Venice and yet he finds himself drawn into an erotic reverie about the city's young people. He realizes that, despite his serious view of life, he too is going to die just like the frivolous Venetians – 'I feel chilly and grown old' (45) – so that the truth and goodness implicit in his seriousness can never be a matter for simple moral superiority. 'According to him', Henry Adams wrote of Browning's conversation in 1863, 'the minds or souls that really did develop themselves and educate themselves in life, could alone expect to enter a future career for which this life was a preparatory course' (Levenson 1982: i. 355). Browning's speaker shares this perception, though he has to clear it first of egotistic moralizing. In the end, he views the Venetians with poignancy, even with a sense of tragedy: 'Dear dead women, with such hair, too – what's become of all the gold | Used to hang and brush their bosoms? I feel chilly and grown old' (44–5).

'Childe Roland to the Dark Tower Came' [181–7] has proved the single poem most resistant to criticism in *Men and Women*, partly because of the way in which it seems to imitate the myth-like intensity of some of the great Romantic poems. The monologue is spoken by a medieval knight who has passed through a desolate, blighted landscape on his way to 'the Dark Tower' (15), the destination of his long quest. Little in this monologue is explained. We never hear exactly what the knight's quest is, and the ending is both sinister and seemingly triumphant: Roland finds the tower for which he has been searching for years, and blows his 'slug-horn' to announce his arrival (203), or perhaps to challenge whoever is in the tower to come out and do battle. But at this point the monologue ends abruptly. Is Roland's quest to kill a dragon and rescue a lady? to kill a giant or some evil baron or knight? We are not told. Browning said that the monologue was inspired by a dream, and its ambiguities certainly enhance its nightmare-like quality.

Interpretation of the monologue has varied enormously. It has been read in relation to the subconscious recollection of fairytales like *Jack and the Bean-stalk* (Golder 1924); as a symbolic account of the journey towards death; as (implicitly) about Browning's response to the ugliness and suffering generated by industrialism (Erdman 1957); and as being about Browning's 'creative negation' of Shelley – in other words, a kind of grotesque reworking of a romantic quest poem like Shelley's *Alastor* (Bloom 1974). Ian Jack suggests that Browning 'simply recorded "a kind of dream" inspired by his deepest fears of failure and spiritual inadequacy' (Jack 1973: 194). The fecundity of possible suggestion has left some critics annoyed: 'The poem has attracted a great deal of discussion, most of it worthless' (Drew 1990: 60).

One of the most obvious things that can be said is that Roland travels alone, and that this loneliness is an issue within the poem, certainly a strong element in its nightmare quality. Roland had set out with 'The Band' (39), a group of knights dedicated to the quest for the Dark Tower, but gradually these knights have either proved traitorous or fallen off from the quest in some other way. In this sense, there is a strong echo of the marching army of progressive poets in 'The Lost Leader', where 'the van and the freemen' (15) are deserted by Wordsworth, 'the lost leader'. And, in relation to the suggestions made at the beginning of this section, it is tempting to read the monologue as covertly political, about the alienated liberal imagination questing on through the wasteland of politics created in the wake of the conservative reaction to 1848.

Browning's contemporaries, of course, were equally puzzled. John Chadwick asked the poet whether the poem's meaning could be expressed in the biblical phrase 'He that endureth to the end shall be saved' (Matt. 10: 22), and Browning is reported to have replied 'Yes, just about that' (*Oxford* v. 137). Of course, the rich verbal texture and description of the poem cannot simply be reduced to this phrase, and Browning's demur 'just about that' makes this clear. 'Childe Roland' is, however, about a lonely individual just managing to hold together his spirits as he travels through a landscape of alienation and despair, a landscape that continually saps his hope and will-power. One question we can ask of it is: what, imaginatively, is creating the resonance of that desolate and sometimes surreal landscape? To relate it to the political realm – the one element of human experience largely excluded from *Men and Women* as a whole – might not be so far from the mark as it initially appears.

(iii) Poems of love

At the heart of *Men and Women* lies a series of lyrics concerned with love. Under this heading we could include poems as various as 'Love Among the Ruins', 'A Lovers' Quarrel', 'A Woman's Last Word', 'By the Fire-Side', 'Any Wife to Any Husband', 'A Serenade at the Villa', 'A Pretty Woman', 'Respectability', 'A Light Woman', 'Love in a Life', 'Life in a Love', 'In a Year', 'Two in the Campagna', and 'One Word More'. Love is in many ways the central theme of the volume, a fact sometimes obscured by the fame of monologues like 'Fra Lippo Lippi' and 'Andrea del Sarto'. This vein continues on into *Dramatis Personae* in, for example, 'James Lee's Wife', 'Dîs Aliter Visum', and 'Youth and Art'.

These lyrics are largely unconcerned with marriage or relationships as a public or social fact. They do not look outwards to the social or communitarian implications of marriage, nor even to the liberal view of marriage as 'a building block of society'. To put it baldly, the way in which relationships feature here is very different from the way in which they generally feature in nineteenth-century novels, where, of necessity, they are treated within a wider social context. These poems are focused on the *inside* of relationships, their privacy. At times, there is an anti-social pull implicit in them because of the way in which they focus in on the details of intimacy.

Some critics, particularly Karlin, have shown the autobiographical aspects of some poems (Karlin 1989). There can be no doubt that the intimacy and isolation of the Brownings' own marriage as it worked itself out in Italy – far from family and English society – contributed to this aspect of the love lyrics. But there is also a political aspect to be taken into account here. As the public sphere seemed recalcitrant and unreformable, so Browning looked within towards a private realm of love as a source of compensation. Two matching factors consequently come to the fore: the intensities of love and, correspondingly, its perplexities. Browning is putting the private realm under such pressure of compensatory meaning, asking so much of it, that, while success here literally saves the soul, failure is ever present as a danger.

'Love' is a cliché, and we can easily miss the radical nature of the intensity that is being described here. In 'Respectability', for example, the public realm is meaningless: the conservative politician François Guizot hypocritically greets his opponent, Charles-Forbes-René, comte de Montalembert, at the Institut de France – an event Browning actually witnessed in February 1852. But this public glad-handing (with Louis Napoleon now as Emperor) has no real significance at all. In the poem, 'the world' (17) means conventionality, social acceptability, and the sterility of contemporary politics; and this world 'fears' the sincerity of passion and eroticism because (even though these take place in the private sphere) they are implicitly an exposé of its own meaninglessness. The lovers of the poem, one of whom is the speaker, enjoy the intimacies of their evening walks along the Seine, and a passion and physical frankness which 'the world' would like to curtail:

> I know! the world proscribes not love;
>   Allows my finger to caress
>   Your lips' contour and downiness,
> Provided it supply a glove.
>
>   (17–20)

In 'By the Fire-Side' the middle-aged speaker looks both backwards, to the start of his marriage, and forwards to old age and heaven, and it is love that gives shape and meaning to his existence both in time and beyond it. When 'the great Word' (Jesus Christ) returns to the earth at the end of time, 'when earth breaks up and heaven expands' (132–3), his wife Leonor must lead him into Heaven: 'See and make me see, for your part, | New depths of the divine!' (139–40).

These operatic intensities are all the more striking because of the generally nuanced tone and mood of the verse. The monologue begins, for instance, with a bitter-sweet, witty picture of the speaker in semi-dotage, the 'poetry' of his life turned to 'prose', reading 'a great wise book as beseemeth age' (6–10). From this self-deprecating opening the speaker proceeds to look back to the extreme of youthful intensity, a moment in Italy, near a deserted chapel, high up an Alpine valley, when he and Leonor experienced nakedness of soul, a total intimacy: 'Oh moment, one and infinite!' (181)

What leads us into this intensity of emotion is a passage embodying intensity of vision, a heightened act of seeing that acts metaphorically to draw us into the world of heightened passion. The 'thorny balls' of the sweet-chestnuts strew the mountain path (53), as do the creeper's leaves, their gold streaked with 'crimson' or deadness, like blood on a shield (56–8). These dead leaves are in turn seen next to the 'rose-flesh' and 'coral nipple' of newly 'bulged' mushrooms (61–3). In this autumnal scene images of life and death jostle together in accord with the larger meaning of the poem: that the moment of love in autumn that is described gives meaning to a whole life, salving the inevitable 'autumn' of age and diminishment:

> Oh the sense of the yellow mountain-flowers,
>   And thorny balls, each three in one,
> The chestnuts throw on our path in showers!
>   For the drop of the woodland fruit's begun,
> These early November hours,
>
> That crimson the creeper's leaf across
>   Like a splash of blood, intense, abrupt,
> O'er a shield else gold from rim to boss,
>   And lay it for show on the fairy-cupped
> Elf-needled mat of moss,
>
> By the rose-flesh mushrooms, undivulged
>   Last evening – nay, in today's first dew
> Yon sudden coral nipple bulged,
>   Where a freaked fawn-coloured flaky crew
> Of toadstools peep indulged.
>   (51–65)

The toadstools 'peep' sexually at the newly 'bulged' nipple of fungus!

Against the pleasure and playfulness of this passage we can begin to set, by way of contrast, those poems concerned with the perplexities of love. In the poems where love is fulfilled – like 'Love Among the Ruins', 'Respectability', and 'By the Fire-Side' – its effects are rich and transforming. Its intensity is such, however – like a high note in opera – that it is necessarily rare: such intensity cannot be the subject of poem after poem. And in this respect it seems unsurprising that the vein of poems concerned with less fulfilled or failing aspects of love is much more extensive. That 'moment, one and infinite' (181) of 'By the Fire-Side' is hard to get inside, so that more poems record the arguments, frustrations, and dissatisfactions of love than go to record this romantic intensity.

'A Woman's Last Word' is a good example of how the metrical virtuosity we noted earlier can enhance meaning. The small stanza, eloquent as it is, nonetheless beautifully captures the faltering voice of the woman speaker, on the edge of tears, as she attempts to recover her composure in the wake of a quarrel. The title is ironic. The 'last word' is not a satisfying final rebuttal, a word of violence, but an attempt by the woman at total submission to her partner, an attempt to heal or simply conceal from view all the difficult issues and emotions stirred up during the argument. The woman paints herself as a faulty 'Eve' potentially ruining the Eden of the relationship (13–20), and tries to characterize herself and her partner as two squabbling birds, fighting over nothing, while a great 'hawk on bough' waits to swoop and kill them (5–8). This image is unusual, but it brilliantly depicts the potential ending of love – a kind of death – which the woman has sensed.

'A Lovers' Quarrel' deals with similar territory. It is a beautiful spring day but the male speaker is desolate, having been deserted by his partner. The poem seems to hinge on the quotation from Proverbs 'Death and life are in the power of the tongue' (18: 21): 'a moment's spite' (104), 'a hasty word' (106), which he now regrets, has undermined the speaker's relationship. Before, the relationship was wonderful and sexually intense: his partner would teach him how 'to flirt a fan | As the Spanish ladies can' (64–5), and he would draw moustaches on her lip with charcoal, so turning her 'into such a man' (68). Now this intimacy is ruined.

The culmination of this vein of poetry is 'Two in the Campagna'. The speaker is again a man in search of the 'moment, one and infinite', and again he is shut out of it. The scene is set in the Campagna, the lovely countryside around Rome 'with its endless fleece | Of feathery grasses everywhere' (21–2). As in 'Love Among the Ruins' this is seemingly the ideal scene in which to appreciate and realize the absolute value of love. Landscape is again enactive of meaning. Here it seems to suggest exactly what the speaker is searching for – a spiritual and emotional 'nakedness', a sexual freedom and intimacy that has heaven's sanction:

> Such life here, through such lengths of hours,
>   Such miracles performed in play,
> Such primal naked forms of flowers,
>   Such letting nature have her way
> While heaven looks from its towers!
>
>   (26–30)

The male speaker seeks an intensity of physical and spiritual communion, and he speaks about it with eloquence: he wants to 'drink my fill [a physical image] | At your soul's springs [a spiritual image]' (43–4), and, similarly: 'I kiss your cheek, | Catch your soul's warmth' (47–8). The speaker gets tantalizingly near to this fulfilment, but 'then the good minute goes' (50). He is left with his dissatisfaction and the knowledge of a contradiction: 'Infinite passion, and the pain | Of finite hearts that yearn' (59–60). Love in *Men and Women* is a transcendent reality, but it is hard to scale its heights.

Further reading

The simplest way to go further with individual poems in *Men and Women* and *Dramatis Personae* is to look at the head-notes in *Penguin* i. 1107–70 and the brief introductions in *Oxford* vol. v. Of older critical accounts, the most useful and straightforward is probably Jack (1973), chapters 12 and 13. There are good readings of 'A Toccata of Galuppi's', 'Andrea del Sarto', 'Fra Lippo Lippi', and 'Cleon' in Tucker (1980), chapters 6 and 7. There is an excellent account of some of the central poems in Woolford (1988) chapter 5, which deals with Browning's redistribution and rearrangement of the *Men and Women* poems in *Poetical Works* (1863). Hawlin (1990a) looks at the relationship between some of the major poems and Browning's 'Essay on Shelley'. In Bristow (1991) there are excellent accounts of 'Fra Lippo Lippi' (pp. 95–102), 'Andrea del Sarto' (pp. 102–9), and 'Two in the Campagna' (pp. 134–8). Ryals (1993) has succinct sections on the two volumes, chapters 7 and 9. Armstrong (1993), chapter 11, presents a complex 'post-Hegelian reading' which is nonetheless suggestive and useful. Karlin (1993), chapter 11, has excellent inter-related accounts of 'Childe Roland' and 'By the Fire-Side', and his chapter 3 is one of the definitive pieces on 'Mr Sludge, "The Medium"'. In Woolford and Karlin (1996) there is a good chapter on 'Love and Marriage' discussing the love poems. Hair (1999) has good readings of a number of poems, particularly of 'Childe Roland' (pp. 103–9). For further suggestions on reading, see also Drew (1990), pp. 57–72.

(e) *THE RING AND THE BOOK*

Browning purchased the source book for *The Ring and the Book* **[191–200]** in 1860 or possibly 1859, and for the next four years he had ample time to meditate its contents, to dream over the story that he would eventually turn into his most ambitious work. He began serious writing in October 1864, and worked on the poem (with some periods of inactivity) for four years, until it reached over 21,000 lines in length – twice the length of *Paradise Lost*. Henry James called it 'a great living thing', 'a proportioned monstrous magnificence', and was particularly attracted by its 'complexity of suggestion' (James 1914: 309, 321). Some critics who want clear definitions would demur at calling it an epic, but this seems the simplest description.

Most critics have seen *The Ring and the Book* as central to Browning's canon – in a way that, for instance, the poetry after 1869 is not – and parts of it are now usually included in selections of his work. Yet such is its scale, and such its many challenges, that it is sometimes sidelined in more cursory studies. Those who know it well often see it – though it is far less well known – as on a par with other masterpieces of the Victorian period, with Brontë's *Wuthering Heights* (1847) or Dickens's *Great Expectations* (1861) or Hardy's *Tess of the D'Urbervilles* (1891).

Browning's source was a unique collection of legal documents from a murder-trial of 1698 in Rome, which he called familiarly the 'old yellow Book' (i. 33), the name that has been used for it ever since. This description is exaggerated and deceptive. These Latin law documents (now held in Balliol College Library, Oxford) are actually rather neat in appearance, clearly printed, not particularly aged, and well-bound in white-grey vellum. The designation 'old yellow Book' is part of Browning's imaginative purpose: he wants to stress how he is resuscitating something very old, going back into the details and particularities of the past in order to bring alive events of over a hundred and fifty years before. For Browning, as for a Romantic writer like Sir Walter Scott (1771–1832), the past is exciting because it is different. Browning wants to emphasize how the world of seventeenth-century Rome is foreign in manners and mores, in social structure and in legal system, to the world of nineteenth-century England.

The murder took place in January 1698, and in the poem the events leading up to the murder and then its aftermath are seen through the eyes of nine different characters. Three of them are representative Romans, having their say on the latest sensation (Books II to IV). Three are characters at the heart of events – the murderer Guido Franceschini (who speaks twice, in Books V and XI), his victim, his wife Pompilia (Book VII), and a priest Giuseppe Caponsacchi who tries to prevent the murder (Book VI). Two are lawyers, for the defence and prosecution (Books VIII and IX), and (at the climax) there is Pope Innocent XII (Book X), who has to act as the final arbiter on the lawsuit. Books I and XII act as introduction and coda. All these different views of the events interact and cross-refer, producing an extraordinary kaleidoscopic effect, within which, nonetheless, Browning expects us to pick out the truth of the murder-case.

The form of *The Ring and the Book* is experimental. Browning is still using the dramatic monologue, but he is deploying it in a new way. Prior to this his longest monologues were 'Bishop Blougram's Apology' (1014 lines) and 'Mr Sludge, "The Medium"' (1525 lines), but these were exceptions rather than the rule. All the monologues in *The Ring and the Book* are longer, three of them over 2,000 lines in length. In other words, Browning is here using the monologue in a much more extended way. In addition he has taken the crucial decision to focus all the monologues – all the different monologists' voices – on one unique series of events.

Even though the monologists are telling basically the same narrative, the effect is not simply one of repetition. In each case the story is being told through a new pair of eyes, but – more than this – different characters know different parts of the story or are inclined to emphasize different elements within it. In this way, as we proceed through the twelve books, we are continually adding new details to our knowledge of the story, being struck by the contrasting ways in which the characters see the same events, and cross-referring these versions against each other. Individual images or phrases recur, altered by the new character who speaks them and by their new context, altered especially by each character's moral formation. With such an involved ironic construction, it is best to begin with a clear grasp of the plot.

The story of *The Ring and the Book* begins in December 1693 with the hasty marriage of a 13-year-old, middle-class girl, Pompilia Comparini, to a 45-year-old aristocrat, Count Guido Franceschini. For both families it was a marriage of convenience. From Count Franceschini's perspective, he was marrying a fairly wealthy girl, with a good dowry, to breed and continue his name, and to repair his family's poverty. The family's fortunes had been going downhill and he had failed to win any significant patronage during a long period living in Rome. Pompilia's mother, Violante Comparini, was the main mover on the Comparini side: her aim was to marry her daughter into the aristocracy, and so to move her family up the social scale. In addition to a hefty dowry, the Comparini seem to have made over most of their money into the hands of their son-in-law: on completion of the financial arrangements, they accompanied their newly-married daughter to Arezzo, about 120 miles north of Rome, the site of Franceschini's palace, where they intended to live out their old age.

Here the marriage of convenience unravelled. The Comparini discovered that Count Franceschini was not as wealthy as they had been led to believe. The palace was crumbling, the food mean, and the social environment – in a small town – narrower than that they had been used to in Rome. Worse than this, their new son-in-law set out to humiliate and ill-treat them. Later, of course, he denied this, but they felt so threatened that after three months they decamped back to Rome.

Now, in 1694, the events leading to the murder really begin to get going. The aggrieved Comparini were determined to try and withhold the dowry from their son-in-law, and to retain as much of their wealth as possible. Violante Comparini revealed, first to a priest in confession, and then to the authorities, that Pompilia was not her real daughter: she had bought her as a baby from a prostitute in order to give her husband happiness, and also to secure income from government bonds that – in the absence of an heir – would have passed into other hands. Together the Comparini published a pamphlet detailing how they had been duped (as they saw it) into the marriage, and mocking Franceschini's miserable lifestyle.

Most probably Pompilia was a prostitute's child, but now this fact seemed only a convenience: if Pompilia was really not the Comparini's daughter, how could she really be their heir? Could the dowry and other moneys still be payable to Franceschini since, in theory, Pompilia was not someone for whom her parents were responsible? Franceschini claimed that the suggestion of illegitimacy was a slur on his ancient aristocratic name, and simply a ruse to keep parts of the dowry from him. Witnesses and evidence began to be compiled, and the whole farrago went into a complicated series of lawsuits that simmered away in Rome in the following years. Meanwhile, back in Arezzo, Pompilia, still only 14 and 15 years of age, was left in a difficult situation, without her parents' moral support.

What now happened is again a matter of dispute. It seems most likely that Pompilia developed a relationship with a handsome priest, Giuseppe Caponsacchi, found herself pregnant by him, and that – stealing clothes and possessions – they eloped together early on the morning of 29 April 1697. They headed out of Tuscany, across the border into the Papal States, though what exactly they intended to do there is uncertain. This is the version of events maintained by Count Franceschini: a priest had cuckolded him, and his wife's expected baby was probably not his.

During the lawsuits, however, another version of events emerged. In this scenario, Franceschini had mistreated and violently abused his wife. The lawsuits mounted against him by the Comparini had annoyed an already malevolent man, and he had revenged himself on his isolated wife with the connivance of his family. Eventually, pregnant by her husband but fearful for her life, Pompilia had arranged to escape to her parents in Rome with the first person she could get to accompany her, Giuseppe Caponsacchi, an honourable, true priest. This is the version of events that Browning followed, though the possibilities of the other version are well aired in the poem.

On the night of the elopement in April 1697, Franceschini claimed that he and his household had been drugged. When he eventually awoke the next morning he set out in pursuit of his runaway wife and her lover, tracking them, via each staging inn, down through Tuscany and .Umbria. This is one dramatic climax of the poem (described most fully in Books VI and VII). The couple had a head start, but they had to go by *vettura* (carriage). Franceschini, on horseback, was six to ten hours behind. Through Monday and Tuesday he chased them on the 120-mile journey southwards and eventually, because they had stopped for the night at a small inn at Castelnuovo (only 15 miles from Rome), caught up with them.

The so-called 'Secondary Source' gives the best account of what happened next. This was another contemporary Italian pamphlet that came into Browning's possession, via friends in Florence, in 1863. The following translation is from *Oxford*:

> And so, on the following Tuesday [actually Wednesday], at the posthouse inn in Castelnuovo, he overtook her in the company of Caponsacchi. The young woman was unabashed at the sight of her husband; her spirits roused, she blamed him for all the cruelties that had forced her to flee. Franceschini was speechless, and confused as to what course of action to take, so he thought best to turn to the authorities: the runaways were arrested by the District Governor, escorted to Rome, put in the New Prisons, and charged with adultery for eloping together. The evidence to establish the case consisted of love-letters that had turned up, and a deposition taken from the coach-driver; but the adultery was not successfully proved, and the Canon was sentenced to three years at Civitavecchia [a form of 'relegation' or 'exile' 20 miles from Rome], and the lady was imprisoned at the Convent of the Scalette on the Via della Lungara.
>
> (*Oxford* vii. 311)

Now there was a brief respite: Pompilia was in a convent for 'fallen women'; the priest Caponsacchi was out of the way at Civitavecchia;

Count Franceschini returned to Arezzo alone. The lawsuits continued, with little prospect of resolution. Pompilia was remitted by the courts to the Comparini's house, since it would be inappropriate for her to give birth in a convent. In Arezzo, Count Franceschini became progressively more exasperated by the fact that he no longer really had a wife, that her money was eluding him, and that his 'honour' was stained. At the end of 1697, only two weeks after the birth of Pompilia's child – which he probably considered the priest's bastard – he took action. Gathering together four workers from his vineyards, and arming them, Franceschini headed for Rome. Arriving just outside the city on Christmas Eve, he then stayed for a week at his brother's house. On 2 January 1698 he struck:

> Biagio Agostinelli and Domenico Gambasini remained on guard at the street door, while Franceschini commanded one of the others to knock and pretend he was carrying a letter from the Canon Caponsacchi at Civitavecchia. The door was opened. Instantly the villainous Franceschini – shoulder to shoulder with two of his henchmen – leapt at Violante Comparini ... killed her outright, and threw her body to the ground ... [Pompilia] hid under a bed, but was dragged out and ... murdered in the most brutal way by her own husband, with twenty-two stab wounds.
>
> (*Oxford* vii. 313)

Her foster-father, Pietro Comparini, was also killed. Though Franceschini and his accomplices managed to escape some distance from Rome, they were arrested and imprisoned. Pompilia survived for four days despite the extent of her wounds.

Now began the court case that provided the actual source material that had chanced into Browning's hands. Browning himself seems to have regarded the two sets of lawyers with something like contempt: to him their legal method seemed nit-picking and obscurantist, 'professional' in the sense of self-serving, and too dispassionate, not sufficiently alive to the tragedy of the events. In fact, it could be argued that the legal process was exemplary. The defence case was that the murder should be seen as a crime of passion, and that therefore the death penalty should be remitted: Franceschini was inflamed with jealousy, his honour was insulted, and wrongly – but pardonably – he had taken the law into his own hands. The subtitle of the legal documents gives an indication of this argument: 'It is disputed if and when a husband may kill an adulterous wife without incurring the regular death penalty' (*Oxford* vii. ix). The prosecution case was equally clear. It questioned whether the adultery was self-evident, or whether indeed it had happened at all. It questioned why, if this was really a crime of passion, Franceschini had failed to kill his wife and her supposed lover at the first opportunity, when he overtook them at Castelnuovo. The prosecution case stressed the evident premeditation of the murder and the illegal circumstances attending it. Franceschini and his fellow assassins were found guilty, and after an unsuccessful appeal for clemency to the Pope, they were executed on 22 February 1698.

(i) Basic considerations

The Ring and the Book is crucial to the Browning canon because of its own intrinsic merit, but also because of the way in which it epitomizes so many of the critical debates over postmodernism in the last twenty years. As a work that consciously reconstructs a piece of history, interprets that piece of history, but then – seemingly – relativizes it by telling the events from different viewpoints, it could be seen as the embodiment of contemporary debates in criticism, historiography, and epistemology. How can we reconstruct the past? How can we find the truth when (as so often) the truth is conflicted, fought over by different interpretations, different moral agendas? Was Count Franceschini a betrayed husband, blinded by passion? Or was he a calculating sadist, who punished an innocent but unsubmissive wife?

From a postmodern viewpoint, Browning could be accused of 'naive realism' in the way he addresses the historical past. He enters imaginatively into a series of events from the 1690s, but, both in the poem (in Book I) and in his recorded comments concerning the poem, he seems convinced that – though the documents appear open to a multiplicity of interpretations – actually he has seen through to *the truth*, and to that truth's prophetic meaning. In Browning's interpretation Count Franceschini (however well he disguises himself) is ultimately a nearly Satanic figure, a dragon of evil, Pompilia is a saint of suffering and forbearance, and Caponsacchi is a heroic figure, a St George-like, knightly rescuer (see Book I, 501–678). Those whose thinking is informed by postmodernism may be sceptical of the possibility of seeing into history in this way, and sceptical of one-and-true interpretations, and they may baulk both at what Browning implies he is doing and at the boldness of the interpretation he advances.

When Browning told friends and acquaintances the story's outline they sometimes thought he had invented it, and in these circumstances he wanted to stress its objectivity. However, in Book I, he is open about the ways in which he is recreating the past. He insists that he is fusing his 'live soul', his alert imagination, with the 'inert stuff' of history (469). He is like a skilled jeweller mixing the 'alloy' of imagination with the soft 'gold' of historical fact in order to create his 'Ring', the past shaped into a work of art (1–32). He sees himself as a prophet-poet who – like Elisha in the Second Book of Kings – lays his inner vitality on the corpse of the past, and so makes its dead flesh 'wax warm' (i. 760–72). The corpse of the past comes back to life. This open-ness about the way he is bringing his own subjectivity into his dealings with the past bears some resemblance to the procedures of postmodern history. In this respect, *The Ring and the Book* can be compared to the work of a historian like Natalie Zemon Davis. In the introduction to her *The Return of Martin Guerre* (1983) – the work that followed her collaboration on the film – she openly declares 'What I offer you here is in part my invention, but held tightly in check by the voices of the past' (Davis 1983: 5).

Though he is nearer to realism and objectivity than to postmodern scepticism and nuance, really Browning's historical approach is grounded in his religious awareness. The realist or objective historian will still be offended by the way he discounts the evidence that Pompilia and Caponsacchi may really have been having an affair – the evidence, that is, that Count Franceschini had grounds for outrage. The postmodernist historian, on the other hand, will be offended at his conviction that his interpretation is the one-and-only true one.

Browning's reading of history is conditioned by Bible history – history in the Old Testament, where events, however terrible and confused, are part of a meaningful pattern – and also (and relatedly) by his reading of Milton's *Paradise Lost*. Partly like Milton, he is seeking to 'assert eternal providence, | And justify the ways of God to men' (*Paradise Lost*, i. 25–6). He has chosen a tragic piece of history and is trying to see how it can make sense from a providential viewpoint, how the darkness of history can make sense if there is a good God. This is why Book X – Pope Innocent XII's monologue – deals so extensively with religious faith. The ultimate issue in the poem is a staple of the philosophy of religion: Why does a good God allow evil to dominate history to the extent it does? Browning takes a hard case and nonetheless seeks to assert a religious vision.

The religious 'answers' that he provides in Book X are probably now not the aspect of the work that most interests us. The philosophy of religion and modern theology provide more intellectually nuanced discussions of such fundamental questions as why the good God 'allows' evil. The imaginative richness and significance of *The Ring and the Book* could be said to reside much more fully in its villains and half-villains than in its overt philosophical discussions, and it is to this aspect of the poem that we should now turn.

(ii) Characters and moral formations

The Pope in Book X is the only commentator in the poem who Browning allows to get near to his own interpretation of events, to see the prophetic truth in the history before him. Excluding for the moment the characters directly involved in the drama, the other commentators of the poem all fail to do so. Their interpretations are skewed by their moral formations.

Half-Rome, the speaker of Book II, is a character representative of the half of the Roman population who – as they gossip over the murder-case – conclude that Franceschini was within his rights to murder his wife. Half-Rome represents patriarchy run mad: a husband must be in firm control of his wife; Pompilia must be presumed to have been having an affair; Franceschini, in killing her, was striking a blow for family values and social order. Other Half-Rome, the speaker of Book III, is a kind of sentimental would-be feminist: Pompilia is a lovely 'flower' of a woman who could do no wrong, so that her husband must be the villain. Tertium Quid, the speaker of Book IV, is a would-be post-modernist: he playfully upholds two contradictory interpretations: Franceschini is both injured aristocrat and excessive villain, Pompilia is both injured innocence and unfaithful wife. Tertium Quid regards 'truth' as of little consequence, because he regards himself as remote, humanly speaking, from the events. Tertium Quid speaks to the aristocrats of society, and his main concern in discussing the murder-case is to establish the fact of his own critical acumen, and also his superiority to 'plebs' and 'cits', the working-class and the bourgeoisie, both of whom he despises. The two lawyers, Dominus Hyacinthus de Archangelis for the defence (Book VIII) and Johannes-Baptista Bottinius for the prosecution (Book IX), show similar kinds of lack of insight as a result of professional egotism and self-regard.

These summaries do little justice either to the flexibility and nuance of the writing or to the interest and subtlety of Browning's epistemology. Epistemology is the philosophical discipline that tries to understand how we know some things to be true and others to be false; it considers the nature, basis, and limits of knowledge. Browning was not a formal philosopher, but his work does take up a definable position. Where a given issue or political happening, or, as here, a piece of history, is fought over by conflicting interpretations – where there is no consensus – how do we find out the truth about it? This problem fascinated Browning.

Browning's implicit answer to the problem bears comparison with the views of his very different contemporary John Henry Newman (1801–90) in *Sermons preached before the University of Oxford* (1843). For Browning, as for Newman, moral and spiritual dispositions enter into intellectual analysis. We all bring to any intellectual question premises, presumptions, first principles, 'antecedent probabilities', and these things affect what we will consider more or less likely to be true. Such moral presuppositions or antecedent states of mind are related to and can be shaped by our moral character: to put it baldly (and of course moral distinctions are rarely so simple) a good person will be inclined to think some things likely or probable which a bad person will not, and that person's total analysis of a situation is therefore likely to be different from the bad person's. These presuppositions or presumptions become what could be thought of as the lenses through which we examine the evidence. They precondition the contours of our likely analysis of a given argument or issue. People wearing red-tinted moral lenses (as it were) will be unlikely to see the moral green or yellow in the scene before them.

Half-Rome, for example, is a jealous husband, worried that his wife may be about to begin an affair. There are no grounds for thinking that his wife really is on the verge of adultery, and every ground for thinking that this is part of Half-Rome's characteristic mindset. Half-Rome regards it as his husbandly duty to dominate his wife: woman, the feminine generally, is that which is intrinsically uncontrollable, flexible, and loose, and in these circumstances masculinity, order, and control become imperative. It is with these moral lenses that he sets out to interpret the murder-case, and from the start he identifies with Count Franceschini who (as he sees it) is another husband who has had to deal with an unfaithful wife and taken just and appropriate corrective action against her. The violence implicit in this position interacts with and contributes to its sexism, to form a frame of mind that is deeply if subtly repellent (see Buckler 1985: 67–74).

Browning's epistemology interacts with interesting questions about styles of language. Each monologist has a different and appropriate style of speech and argument – that is to say, each moral perspective on the events is enacted through its own style of language. Each monologist is made real by a different series of metaphors and images, speech rhythms, characteristic phrases and exclamations, different argumentative procedures. In her book *Browning's Voices in The Ring and the Book* (1969), Mary Rose Sullivan gave one of the first descriptions of this, but (as later critics have shown) she did not fully take on board the interest of Browning's method. A character's perspective on events, affected by his or her moral formation, is embodied in a particular style of language, but – in turn – the style of language conditions what that character is capable of seeing and perceiving. So, for example, a state of mind is embodied in vicious or degraded language, but this language, and the moral presumptions implicit in it, then feeds back into the state of mind.

Here are two examples. First, from the monologue of Half-Rome (Book II, 17–37):

> Sir, do you see,
> They laid both bodies in the church, this morn
> The first thing, on the chancel two steps up,
> Behind the little marble balustrade;
> Disposed them, Pietro the old murdered fool
> To the right of the altar, and his wretched wife
> On the other side. In trying to count stabs,
> People supposed Violante showed the most,
> Till somebody explained us that mistake;
> His wounds had been dealt out indifferent where,
> But she took all her stabbings in the face,
> Since punished thus solely for honour's sake,
> *Honoris causâ*, that's the proper term.
> A delicacy there is, our gallants hold,
> When you avenge your honour and only then,
> That you disfigure the subject, fray the face,
> Not just take life and end, in clownish guise.
> It was Violante gave the first offence,
> Got therefore the conspicuous punishment:
> While Pietro, who helped merely, his mere death
> Answered the purpose, so his face went free.
>
> (ii. 17–37)

Browning imagines this monologue as being spoken on 3 January 1698. This passage tells us about the aftermath of the murder: prior to their funeral Mass and burial, the bodies of Violante and Pietro Comparini have been laid on the altar in their parish church of San Lorenzo. Half-Rome vividly creates the scene for us: the shocked crowds from the local community have come to see the bodies and discuss the terrible murder of the previous day.

But his observation is not neutral. Half-Rome describes this scene but he is also part of it: for us, as readers, he is both observer and observed. He has chosen to mill around the church all day because he is enthralled by the details of the murder. His engagement with the scene is voyeuristic. At line 30 he aligns himself with the views of the 'gallants' (i.e. young aristocrats, men of pleasure) and the 'delicate' or discriminating code of revenge that is fashionable in their social circles. If you feel that your 'honour' has been threatened – as for instance by being married to a prostitute's daughter – then simple murder would be poor revenge, it would be 'clownish' (33), i.e. peasant-like. Rather you need to deliberately mutilate the face of your enemy with stab-wounds. Half-Rome chooses his words punctiliously: his first phrase is chillingly remote or objective: 'you disfigure the subject' (32). Then he chooses a slightly franker, but the nonetheless elegant formula: you 'fray the face' (32). Here both phrasing and speech rhythm enact a particular mindset: superior, aloof, narcissistic, and cruel. Half-Rome supports Franceschini's revenge for its control and exactness, its subtly appropriate form, and is oblivious to the sadism implicit in his own viewpoint.

The Other Half-Rome, the monologist of Book III, is very different. Take, for example, this passage at III. 1–28:

> Another day that finds her living yet,
> Little Pompilia, with the patient brow
> And lamentable smile on those poor lips,
> And, under the white hospital-array,
> A flower-like body, to frighten at a bruise
> You'd think, yet now, stabbed through and through again,
> Alive i' the ruins. 'T is a miracle.
> It seems that, when her husband struck her first,
> She prayed Madonna just that she might live
> So long as to confess and be absolved;
> And whether it was that, all her sad life long,
> Never before successful in a prayer,
> This prayer rose with authority too dread, –
> Or whether, because earth was hell to her,
> By compensation, when the blackness broke
> She got one glimpse of quiet and the cool blue,
> To show her for a moment such things were, –
> Or else, – as the Augustinian Brother thinks,
> The friar who took confession from her lip, –
> When a probationary soul that moves
> From nobleness to nobleness, as she,
> Over the rough way of the world, succumbs,

Bloodies its last thorn with unflinching foot,
The angels love to do their work betimes,
Staunch some wounds here nor leave so much for God.
Who knows? However it be, confessed, absolved,
She lies, with overplus of life beside
To speak and right herself from first to last, ...

(iii. 1–28)

This is the opening of Book III, and it also carries forward our knowledge of the story: it is probably spoken on 4 January, two days after Franceschini's attack. The wounded and dying Pompilia has been taken to St Anna's hospital, where she has confessed her sins to an Augustinian friar. The speaker of the passage, the character Other Half-Rome – again an individual, who is representative of half of Rome's gossiping population – seems to have been lurking around the hospital, hoping to be admitted to view the death-bed. The passage serves the function of advancing the story, but again what is really fascinating is how language acts as an index of character and moral insight.

Other Half-Rome's sadness at Pompilia's death-bed is appropriate, yet we already sense his sentimentality and religiosity. The tug of pathos in his adjectives is obvious: '*Little* Pompilia' (2), the '*lamentable* [pitiable] smile' (3), the '*flower-like* body' (5). But the subtler indication of these things is the rhetorical heightening of lines 11–25, which gives the overplus of three possible explanations for Pompilia's survival, each more elaborate than the preceding one. The third explanation is ornate and baroque, almost like a sculpture by Gianlorenzo Bernini: Pompilia is imagined being tended by invisible angels, who minister to her wounds and so stop her bleeding to death (18–25). Other Half-Rome's sentimental moral lenses limit his view of reality. They allow him to indulge pathos while inhibiting him from exercising intellectual rigour. He assimilates Pompilia into his own world of kitsch piety, worshipping her as his idea of a saint.

The characters of Books IV, VIII, and IX work in a roughly similar manner, though in each case the moral formation and the intricacies of character are different.

(iii) Pompilia and Caponsacchi

The Ring and the Book is such a rich and, initially, confusing work that at first it is hard to locate its emotional centre. Critics have often noted, however, its biographical resonance, and this, at least for the first-time reader, can give some purchase on 21,000 lines of poetry.

Pompilia Comparini (Book VII) is the poem's central character, a profoundly good young woman who has won her understanding of virtue against terrible odds. Pompilia's character may seem an idealized creation, slightly kitschy and sentimental in a characteristically Victorian vein, but Browning's depiction is grounded in a certain kind of realism. Pompilia describes, painfully, for example, how she sought to avoid marital rape and fled to the Archbishop of Arezzo for help, only to be thrown back into the arms of her husband, who proceeded to take her virginity in violent fashion (vii. 721–859). Material like this gives her monologue edge, and makes some Victorian readings of it sound sentimental, rather on the lines of the sentimentality that is exposed in the character of Other Half-Rome (Book III).

A number of sources and influences helped Browning in creating Pompilia and her story. One striking and obvious influence is the character of Marian Erle in Barrett's *Aurora Leigh* (1856). Marian Erle is a working-class girl who comes near to marrying the upper-class Romney Leigh, is then raped by an unnamed man, and has to endure social stigma as she struggles to bring up on her own the child that results from the rape. Barrett (as a middle-class gentlewoman) was conscious of exploring bold subject-matter in the story of Erle's rape, and she was initially worried about showing this part of *Aurora Leigh* to Browning (Reynolds 1996: 333). He responded positively from the first, and certainly learned from it. Marian Erle is a model of real virtue in spite of how society casts aspersions on her. In a similar manner Pompilia also has to suffer a weight of parody and innuendo: she is variously viewed as a wanton and an adulteress. In fact, she is a 15-year-old girl who chooses to stand up for herself, against the power and prestige of her husband and a society that readily backs up his right to authoritarian control.

The most obvious single source for Pompilia is Barrett herself. Of course, this statement needs to be hedged about with qualifications. This is no simple one-to-one correspondence, and autobiography has been transmuted into the world of the poem in complex ways.

G. K. Chesterton pointed out the biographical resonance as long ago as 1903, and many different kinds of critics – including those with a consciously feminist orientation – have endorsed the basic parallel. Caponsacchi (the St George figure) rescues Pompilia (the maiden or Andromeda figure) from Count Franceschini (the dragon) in a way that parallels how Robert Browning carried away Elizabeth Barrett from the house of her dominating father in 1846. Some scholars believe it is important to stress (seeing things from Barrett's viewpoint) that there was no impropriety in the Brownings' secret marriage: all but one of the proper social forms (informing her father) was carried out to the letter. In keeping with this spirit, Ian Jack, for example, uses the term 'near-elopement' of the events of 1846 (*Oxford* v. x). Nonetheless, it seems obvious that the Brownings' marriage was a bold move under the circumstances, not a flouting of society and convention, but cert-ainly a down-grading of its powers and forms. Browning felt it was the action that made him into a true man, that saved his soul, and echoes of its impact can be found in many different places in his work.

So, for example, in 'The Statue and the Bust' in *Men and Women*: before the Duke falls in love with the bride of the Riccardi he is only 'Empty and fine like a swordless sheath' (15). At the moment when he falls in love 'a blade for a knight's emprise | Filled the fine empty sheath of a man, – | The Duke grew straightway brave and wise' (25–7). The fact that the Duke does not act on this love (even against convention, even against morality) is roundly castigated in the poem.

In *The Ring and the Book* Caponsacchi and Pompilia are not 'in love' in an overt sense: they are in fact chaste, in spite of the fact that Franceschini and other characters accuse them of having a sexual affair. But both Caponsacchi and Pompilia sense that, under different circumstances, they might have made a true marriage, wholly different from the parody of marriage that Pompilia suffers at the hands of Franceschini. In this sense the poem hinges on what Henry James calls 'the great constringent relation of man and woman', the 'relation most worth while in life for either party' (James 1914: 409).

Pompilia seeks to be rescued – she is not, in the end, a passive victim – and Caponsacchi eventually summons the courage to rescue her. By these actions they contest the patriarchy implicit in their society, and also the even more pervasive sense of hierarchy and deference implicit in the absolutist social structures that the poem so vividly brings to life. The society of Rome and Tuscany at the end of the seventeenth century – as Browning portrays it – is one ruthlessly stratified in class terms, filled with corrupt aristocrats and their hangers-on, with self-serving and worldly bishops and archbishops. It is a society where 'birth and breeding' are everything, and women are traded in marriage. In these circumstances Pompilia and Caponsacchi's actions, normal as they are in moral terms, enact a kind of revolution, a brilliant and moving recovery of emotional and spiritual norms.

Further reading

The most comprehensive of older book-length studies are Altick and Loucks (1968) and Sullivan (1969). There is also a straightforward account in Jack (1973), chapter 14. Volumes vii (1998) and viii (2001) of the *Oxford* edition have useful introductions to the individual books drawing on contemporary scholarship and criticism. Ryals (1993), chapter 10, is succinct and informative. All of these accounts present easy points of access to critical material on the poem.

Browning's source book, 'the Old Yellow Book' – the original of which is now in the library of Balliol College, Oxford – is photographically reproduced, with a translation, in Hodell (1908). There is another translation by Gest (1927) in which the legal material is arranged thematically. Hodell's translation on its own (without the original Latin) is also available in the Everyman edition, Hodell (1911; reprinted).

In the last twenty years there have been three book-length studies: Buckler (1985), Brady (1988), and Rigg (1999). Buckler's reading has been accused of being relentlessly in a New Critical mode, but it is full of valuable insights into the poem's characters. Brady's feminist approach has been described as crudely ahistorical in its presuppositions, but again, if her critical framework has weaknesses, her actual reading of Pompilia's monologue is compelling. Rigg's study is the least controversial, reading Browning as a sophisticated ironist (in the tradition of the German Romanticist Friedrich Schlegel). Slinn (1991), chapters 5 and 6, is a very determined deconstructive reading: the aim is to show that 'truth' is lost in the poem's webs of irony. Karlin (1993), chapter 10, looks in detail at Guido Franceschini. Other valuable recent accounts are Woolford (1988), chapter 7; Petch (1989), a detailed study of the lawyers; Matthew Reynolds (1998); and Hair (1999), chapter 6. There is a select bibliography of older material in Drew (1990), pp. 72–6.

(f) THE LATE POETRY

It has become almost traditional to separate Browning's work after 1870 from the rest of his writing. The fourth and last instalment of *The Ring and the Book* was published in February 1869. In the next twenty years he published fifteen volumes of new poetry, most of them long or very long, forming a prolific close to his career. The issue has always been how much of this work deserves serious attention and to what extent it represents a decline from his earlier achievement.

The older view is clear enough. 'One can get on very well in life without having read all the later poetry of Browning or Swinburne' (T. S. Eliot 1957: 48). Ian Jack's one-volume edition of *Browning: Poetical Works* (1970) only went up to *Dramatis Personae* (1864). His related study *Browning's Major Poetry* (1973) covers the same poetry but adds in *The Ring and the Book*; however, it does not have a single chapter on the later work. For Jack *The Ring and the Book* itself shows a lessening of Browning's powers, and he comments in lowering terms: 'one is driven to the conclusion that the complexity of its technique is more apparent than real, and that the poem is inspired by a vision of life that is simpler and more naive than that which informs the great short poems of the 1840s and 1850s' (Jack 1973: 298).

Other critics find this view too drastic, too simple a condemnation of a vast body of work – over a thousand pages in the *Penguin* edition. Daniel Karlin, Donald S. Hair, and others have championed aspects of the later work, but two critics in particular have given it more sustained attention. Clyde de L. Ryals' *Browning's Later Poetry, 1871–1889* (1975) was the first attempt at a sustained reappraisal, and Adam Roberts's *Robert Browning Revisited* (1996) paid particular attention to the later work. Roberts begins with this clarion call:

> Critics acknowledge that the great man went on writing, of course, but the consensus remains that the result was nothing but acres of barren verbiage. Of all misrepresentations of Browning, this most enduring one is surely the least defensible. Far from stopping experimenting and engaging in poetry with *The Ring and the Book*, Browning went on to produce some of his most powerful and challenging work in his later life.
>
> (Roberts 1996: 108)

There is a some waning of Browning's powers in the late work viewed as a whole, and some of it is genuinely inferior to anything else he wrote: *Ferishtah's Fancies* (1884) for example. Also it is clear that the late work becomes less truly dramatic, and is more often overtly didactic or philosophical. To some critics this in itself marks a falling off. But Adam Roberts and others are broadly right: this phase should not be considered simply as 'acres of barren verbiage'. Even considering the late poetry as a unit – a division often used, and used here for convenience – has limitations. To some extent it distorts a fuller understanding of Browning's work. The late poetry requires, above all, to be sifted. What follows is therefore a small selection from this body of work, the best of some of the different kinds within it. It will provide some signposts for the first-time reader, even if it will not satisfy every expert.

(i) *Red Cotton Night-Cap Country*

Red Cotton Night-Cap Country (1873), in four long sections or verse chapters, is the most immediately accessible of the longer late poems.

It is set in Normandy, near St Aubin-sur-Mer, Calvados, where Browning had been on holiday in 1870, where he first heard from his friend Milsand the true story of the suicide of the Paris jeweller Antoine Mellerio (1827–70). On subsequent visits to Normandy, with Milsand's help, he investigated the case further, visiting Mellerio's chateau, talking to local people about the events, and getting copies of the legal documents relating to the case. As Thomas Collins points out, one reason the material may have fascinated him was because it formed a parallel to the genesis of *The Ring and the Book* (see *Penguin* ii. 986). For that work he had acquired legal documents relating to events in 1698. Now he was working with legal and other material relating to an extraordinary series of events that had only just run their course.

The subject-matter of the poem was taken directly from life, so much so that, at proof stage, the publisher George Smith became worried about the possibility of a libel suit and asked Browning to fictionalize all the names: Antoine Mellerio became Léonce Miranda. His mistress, whose false name was originally Anna de Beaupré, became Clara de Millefleurs.

The biggest influence on Browning's style of story-telling here is his love of the novels of Balzac: Balzac-like realism saturates the text. Part I, addressed by the poet to Anne Thackeray – his companion on a walk to visit the scenes of the story – may seem circuitous, but really it draws us into the story, creating the sights and sounds of the area of France where the events occur. The poem as a whole proceeds in this 'Conradian spiralling motion downward from the surface to the heart of the matter' (Ryals 1993: 193).

The story, commencing in Part II, is violent and extraordinary. The young Léonce Miranda inherits from his father the wealthy jewellery firm 'Miranda' (actually Brothers Mellerio) and leads a dissipated life. Eventually he falls in love with the apparently genteel Clara de Millefleurs, and is deeply committed to her before he discovers that her name is false and that she is in fact already married (though separated). Clara gets a civil divorce, but within the strong ethos of French Roman Catholicism she cannot marry again: Léonce decides to live with her outside marriage, and retreats from Paris society to his father's old house in the country, which he renovates and remodels.

Now Léonce gradually falls apart. He is a good Roman Catholic and finds it difficult to live with a woman outside the bonds of marriage. His mother and relatives see his liaison as scandalous and sinful, yet he feels quite unable to dismiss the woman he loves. So he is torn – in the poem's terms – between earth and heaven, 'turf' and 'towers', the senses and the soul, – between his mistress Clara, and his devotion to the Virgin Mary (as represented in her local shrine at the church of La Ravissante). After a devastating confrontation with his mother he tries to commit suicide. In another fit of remorse and confusion, attempting to separate from Clara, he burns off his hands in a fire (2556–91). Finally, in April 1870, he commits suicide by throwing himself from the tower of his mansion (3234–603).

Into this raw, tragic material Browning – we may feel – rushed in where angels fear to tread. To us today, at least, it is clear that the real-life Antoine Mellerio was psychologically disturbed, perhaps mentally ill, and that the kind of help he needed was simply not available to him within his particular class and social situation. A straightforward reading of the suicide, in other words, would presuppose mental illness and depression. Browning suggests that the suicide was not as it appeared, that the jump from the tower was a rational way of resolving an agony of religious doubt. Torn between worldly and spiritual visions of life, Miranda leapt on purpose as a test of religious faith, expecting that the Virgin Mary would send angels to uphold him and carry him to her shrine at La Ravissante.

This reading of the story makes no sense whatever. If we judge Browning by real standards of psychology or emotional insight we would have to say that he failed. He works within a caricatured psychological framework, a kind of cartoon version of genuine psychology. His reading of the life in terms of the opposition between 'turf' and 'towers', the senses and the soul, is too pat and schematic, convenient in terms of his own religious outlook, but too little engaged with a painful situation in which more complicated emotional and psychological factors must have played a part. This limited psychology is all the more striking because of the naturalistic scene-setting that contrasts with it. The poem vividly describes particular aspects of life in Normandy and Paris, and is particularly good at evoking the Roman Catholic middle-class milieu in which Mellerio lived. This accounts for the split satisfactions of the poem itself. Like the best of the early work, it brilliantly describes particular times and places, certain kinds of setting and event, but the analysis of the meaning of the story, the probing into the inner reality of Mellerio's life, is compromised by too simple an assertion of Browning's own religious faith.

(ii) 'Ivàn Ivànovitch'

Our second selection from the late work, the short verse story 'Ivàn Ivànovitch' from *Dramatic Idyls: First Series* (1879), is more fully achieved. It is a vivid retelling of a Russian folktale. A woman, coming back to her village on a sledge, through the great wild tracks of the Russian forest, is attacked by a pack of wolves. The wolves manage to grab each of her three children who are with her on the sledge, but she herself (though unconscious and wounded) arrives at her home village alive. When Ivàn Ivànovitch (one of her neighbours) hears her tragic account of what has happened, he simply chops off her head, an instant execution, a just, godly (if utterly surprising) judgement – so the poem maintains.

The village authorities, after much debate, also conclude that this extra-judicial killing is just: in this case 'law protects | Murder, for once' (402–3). The woman should have sacrificed her life for her children: their death and her survival, when motherly self-sacrifice was imperative, is implicitly a betrayal. She deserved to die.

Clearly this outcome represents an extraordinary, exaggerated morality on Browning's part, lacking both nuance and compassion. The woman herself, in her account of what happened, hints at her own terrible self-knowledge that she could have done something more to save her children's lives: had she let her own body be taken by the wolf-pack, the pack might have been slowed or delayed, and the horse would have continued on automatically taking her children back to the safety of the village. Faced with the obligation of sacrificing her life, she balked, and she now suffers terribly through self-knowledge. But Ivàn Ivànovitch's personally-authorized death penalty simply overrides this nuanced awareness with a black and white morality.

We could say that the moral awareness is simplifying, brutal, and unforgiving, and so find the poem unsatisfying. But it is in the ending that Browning twists the poem around to a different awareness. At this point, the village authorities, after much debate, have finally decided (on the advice of the priest) that the murder is in this case somehow religiously justified. They assume that Ivàn must be skulking in his house, expecting the charge of murder, and that it would be charitable to let him know his reprieve. But they find him wholly relaxed, playing with his own children. After the tortuous and shocking story of the woman losing her three children to the wolves, the following passage, with its opposite but parallel description of domestic bliss and intense fatherly love, is genuinely unsettling:

> Ivàn Ivànovitch
> Knelt, building on the floor that Kremlin rare and rich
> He deftly cut and carved on lazy winter nights.
> Some five young faces watched, breathlessly, as, to rights,

Piece upon piece, he reared the fabric nigh complete.
Stèscha, Iwàn's old mother, sat spinning by the heat
Of the oven where his wife Kàtia stood baking bread.
Iwàn's self, as he turned his honey-coloured head,
Was just in act to drop, 'twixt fir-cones, – each a dome, –
The scooped-out yellow gourd presumably the home
Of Kolokol the Big: the bell, therein to hitch,
– An acorn-cup – was ready: Iwàn Iwànovitch
Turned with it in his mouth.

              They told him he was free
As air to walk abroad. 'How otherwise?' asked he.
                            (411–24)

Where so many of the early monologues create both a certain historical and dramatic verisimilitude and a strong ironic sense, here the aggressive irony – the attack on the reader – seems to have become all in all. Yet the unbalancing effect of the ending is so sure and so deft as to be successful in its own limited terms.

(iii)'The Parleying with Gerard de Lairesse'

The final two works of this selection can be treated more briefly. The parleying 'With Gerard de Lairesse' is one of a series published together as *Parleyings with Certain People of Importance in Their Day* (1887). In this form of poem Browning has clearly moved away from drama to a more teacherly, didactic mode. He interrogates a series of historical figures – the writer Bernard de Mandeville, the Jesuit historian Daniel Bartoli, the poet Christopher Smart, etc. – but he does all the talking, talking *at* his characters, expressing directly a number of his own ideas. Of this group of poems the 'parleying' with Gerard de Lairesse is the most successful. De Lairesse (1641–1711) was a Dutch artist who went blind, and then wrote *Het Groot Schilderbeck* ('The Art of Painting'), a translation of which had been one of Browning's favourite childhood books. The 'parleying' evokes the qualities of de Lairesse's work as a neoclassical painter, celebrating what is good and vivid in that mode, and then censuring its limitations.

Sections VIII to XII present a series of vivid sketches of imagined works by de Lairesse, beautiful landscapes set at different times of day, with classical figures lodged within them giving each painting its notional subject: Prometheus bound to the rock, Artemis with her bow and arrows, and so forth. Having evoked these neoclassical landscapes,

Browning then dismisses them, seeing such art as backward-looking, a clinging to old forms, a failure to be modern. Look to the future: 'Earth's young significance is all to learn: | The dead Greek lore lies buried in the urn | Where who seeks fire finds ashes' (391–3).

The parleying is interesting in two respects. First, in dismissing seventeenth-century neoclassicism in art, Browning is also taking an implied sweep at neoclassicism in nineteenth-century literature. In particular, he was probably thinking of Matthew Arnold's neoclassical leanings. Thomas Collins describes this well:

> Browning saw himself among his contemporary poets as the one who had been most ruthlessly 'modern', and Matthew Arnold, whose 'Preface' of 1853 had urged writers to use materials and principles from the past, and who had himself used them, is the poet for whom de Lairesse acts as surrogate – Browning had quoted from the 'Preface' with approval perhaps more apparent than real in his preface to the *Agamemnon of Aeschylus*.
>
> (*Penguin* ii. 1113)

Second, Browning associates the act of being modern, of adventuring into new artistic modes and styles, with the groundwork of Christianity. The ancient Greek mindset embodies a certain quality of closure, based ultimately on its view of death: the Greek poet greets the spring sadly: 'Spring for the tree and herb – no Spring for us!' (424). The idea of venturing into new forms of art, the idea of modernity, is predicated on the Resurrection, the profoundest faith in the future, the belief in eternal life. To enact this complex idea the parleying ends with a short lyric celebrating springtime, with death no longer a final reality:

> Dance, yellows and whites and reds,–
> Lead your gay orgy, leaves, stalks, heads
> Astir with the wind in the tulip-beds!
>
> There's sunshine; scarcely a wind at all
> Disturbs starved grass and daisies small
> On a certain mound by a churchyard wall.
>
> Daisies and grass be my heart's bedfellows
> On the mound wind spares and sunshine mellows:
> Dance you, reds and whites and yellows!
>
> (426–34)

(iv) 'Beatrice Signorini'

The last poem of this selection is 'Beatrice Signorini', generally regarded as the best poem of Browning's final volume, *Asolando* (1889). The partial draft autograph manuscript of the poem (now at the Eton College Library) shows that it was at least begun as early as 1853. In other words 'Beatrice Signorini' is a poem about art and painting that somehow did not quite make it into *Men and Women* (1855) and, given its subject-matter, it is also a poem with a potentially interesting biographical resonance.

The anecdote on which the poem is based comes from Filippo Baldinucci's *Notizie de' professori del disegno* and concerns the minor baroque painter Francesco Romanelli (1617–62). In early manhood Romanelli had a sustained platonic relationship with the greatest woman painter of the seventeenth century, Artemisia Gentileschi (1593–1652), older than him and at the height of her powers. The poem hinges on the difference between this heightened relationship between artist and artist and Romanelli's relationship with Beatrice Signorini, his 'placid-perfect wife' (247).

Romanelli is disconcerted by his relationship with Artemisia Gentileschi. He would like to patronize her, or have her within his power in some way, but she is confident, both emotionally and artistically. He half likes the idea of worshipping her, but – with sexist aplomb – thinks this impossible because 'Male is the master' (96). Eventually, thwarted, he decides to curtail the relationship altogether and return to his wife in Viterbo. As a parting gift Gentileschi paints him a perfect rondel of flowers, flowers 'festooned | About an empty space' (164–5), and urges him to paint within this rondel the woman he likes best. In a 'sudden glow | Of soul' (242–3) – within which he rises above his relative mediocrity – Romanelli paints an impassioned portrait of Gentileschi herself.

The scene shifts from Rome to Viterbo. Romanelli has left behind Gentileschi, the woman who is larger-souled than he, and returned, as he thinks (in highly sexist terms) to his tame wife. All the time we see these two women partly through Romanelli's eyes, and the contrast he creates between them is almost a version of the whore / Madonna complex: Gentileschi is 'strong' and 'confident', while Beatrice Signorini is 'My gentle consort with the milk for blood!' (266), the 'placid' stay-at-home. Romanelli is so confident of this opposition that he decides to show his wife his portrait of Gentileschi, confident that she will demurely praise it, that if she gleans any of its emotional significance it will be something she will accept or tolerate. To his shock (and delight), while praising the flower-frame, she savages the portrait of Gentileschi with her hair-pin in a fantastic display of passion at her rival. At this moment Romanelli suddenly awakens to the reality of his love for his wife, and bursts out laughing:

> And out judgement burst
> With frank unloading of love's laughter, first
> Freed from its unsuspected source. Some throe
> Must needs unlock love's prison-bars, let flow
> The joyance.
>
> (321–5)

A summary neither does justice to the subtle irony of Browning's story-telling in this great poem, nor to the rich implications of its theme. In many respects it is a reworking of 'My Last Duchess' [67–70], and could almost be seen as that poem's companion piece. Romanelli, with his philosophy of 'Male is the master', is a distinct (if amiable and unthreatening) reprise of the Duke. He is deeply attracted to Gentileschi and knows there is much he could learn from her, but she is too full of life, too confident, too emotionally ranging for him to feel at ease with her. So he paints her portrait and takes it back to Viterbo, where – in a strong echo of 'My Last Duchess' – he sets it behind a 'veil' and reserves it for his 'private delectation' (292–3).

If the poem ended at this point we would have only a repetition of 'My Last Duchess'. Its conclusion, however, proves a vivid rewriting of the earlier work. Beatrice Signorini does not prove to be the tame, 'placid' wife the painter expects. In fact she is more like Gentileschi than Romanelli ever thought possible. In destroying the portrait of her spiritual rival, Beatrice Signorini breaks out of the role in which Romanelli would cast her, and so is able to draw him into a real, loving, and equal relationship. It is as if the Duke in 'My Last Duchess', having married the Count's daughter (as the poem predicts), were to have his second wife overpower his previous sexist, dominating mindset and free him from his whole mediocre obsession with his own self-importance. In 'My Last Duchess' it is impossible to imagine such a future for the Duke, only that he will repeat his mistakes. The Duke is forever imprisoned in his particular way of viewing things, his wife tamed down into a painting he can fully control. In 'Beatrice Signorini' Romanelli (in less overtly murderous terms) is also on his way to reducing the idea of woman to something static and passionless, when his actual wife's behaviour shatters his 'object' and forces him to break out of his previous way of thinking.

Further reading

Relatively speaking, the late poetry is still the least explored part of Browning's work. The only full study is by Ryals (1975). Two more recent books, however, do make a point of dealing more fully with the late work: Roberts (1996) and Hair (1999). There is an excellent essay on *Aristophanes' Apology* in Karlin (1993), chapter 7. Of the three main scholarly editions of Browning, only *Ohio* has yet reached into the later work. Its vols x, xiii, and xvi have invaluable material on the works they cover.

For other discussions of the late work, one needs to go back to earlier criticism. DeVane (1927) is the fullest study of *Parleyings with Certain People of Importance in Their Day*. King (1968) has discussions of *Fifine at the Fair* and *Parleyings*, Drew (1970) of *Prince Hohenstiel-Schwangau, Fifine at the Fair, Red Cotton Night-Cap Country, The Inn Album*, and *La Saisiaz*, and Hassett (1982) of *Prince Hohenstiel-Schwangau, Fifine at the Fair*, and *Red Cotton Night-Cap Country*. Siegchrist (1981) presents the legal sources that Browning used for *Red Cotton Night-Cap Country*.

PART III

CRITICISM

All major writers now provoke a mass of critical literature, partly simply because of the size of academe and the university systems across America, Britain, and other countries that study English literature. Yet in the last twenty years, Browning still seems to have inspired an overplus of critical commentary and view, as much interest as we would expect of a major writer and then more. There have been three journals devoted to him: *Browning Society Notes*, *Studies in Browning and His Circle*, and *Browning Institute Studies*; at the same time there have been three major on-going editions, *Oxford*, *Ohio*, and *Longman*, each with a slightly different rationale. It is noteworthy that Browning has inspired three editions aiming at comprehensive, scholarly presentation of his work in a period when Shelley, for example, has only finally, in the Longman edition, begun to achieve one authoritative text. Browning has been inspiring many scholars and critics to a great deal of appreciation and thought, a fact all the more striking given the way in which his reputation suffered a significant decline in the first part of the twentieth century **[129–36]**.

Generalization is always hazardous, but in giving an overview one thing that is striking in the criticism is the persistence of traditional, 'humanist', aesthetic orientated points of view. Left-radical/Marxist, deconstructive, psychoanalytic, feminist, and other critical orientations have all – as with other writers in the last twenty years – made their mark, but less so than with some other major writers. This is not necessarily because Browning criticism is 'reactionary'. One might say the opposite: that major strands within Browning criticism have kept faith with ideas of biography, context, and the category of the aesthetic in ways that anticipate the present turning of the critical tide. Some kinds of deconstructive criticism now look beleaguered in the wake of attacks from both left-radical and religious-minded critics – Nicholas Boyle's *Who Are We Now?* (1998), for example, is a telling attack on Jacques Derrida and deconstruction – while in Isobel Armstrong's *The Radical Aesthetic* the category of the aesthetic itself is importantly rehabilitated; as she declares:

> Over the past two decades, the category of the aesthetic has been for the most part either ignored or attacked by cultural and literary theory. Marxists, cultural materialists, post-structuralists and deconstructive psychoanalysts have largely retreated from asking aesthetic questions of texts and the field of cultural production.
>
> (Armstrong 2000: 1–2)

Armstrong herself is one of the most notable critics of Browning and of Victorian poetry generally in this period, and perhaps there are connections between her wider perspective and her detailed studies of Browning's work.

The profile of criticism around Browning is interestingly skewed in other words. There has been a significant vein of deconstructive criticism, represented in the following sections by reference to the work of Herbert Tucker and Warwick Slinn. But, relatively speaking, left-radical and Marxist criticism has not had much to say about Browning, at least in any concentrated way. One significant book-length study employing this approach is Loy Martin's *Browning's Dramatic Monologues and the Post-Romantic Subject* (1985) which has been influential, but which has not had any obvious successor **[161–5]**. There are parallel gaps in the biography. As we saw in Part I, Browning's half-uncles William and Reuben worked for Rothschild's bank in Paris and London respectively, but the potential significance of this kind of background has not been explored; as Tucker remarks, 'Browning's familial and imaginative relationship to the banking and legal trades, and thus to corporate capitalism, must be one of the great untold stories of Browning studies' (Woolford 1998: 22).

In the following sections feminist approaches are represented by interesting readings of 'Porphyria's Lover' and 'My Last Duchess' **[155–61]**, but generally such approaches have been less developed around Browning than around some other major writers. This is perhaps because feminist-orientated critics have often focused on Barrett, with Browning as a relatively subsidiary part of their interest. Browning criticism generally has also been very eclectic in its procedures, often not aligned with one determining point of view. And perhaps, more than some groups of critics, Browning specialists have learnt a lot from each other in direct and indirect debate: the cross-overs and influences within the criticism are very marked.

In these circumstances, I have chosen to give an overview of the criticism through a series of case studies, looking at the works again in roughly chronological order and selecting the most interesting critics and the most exciting viewpoints. I have avoided critical jargon and specialist vocabulary as much as possible, and have shown particular kinds of approach in action in a way that should be accessible to most readers. The examples are not chosen at random, but are designed through their different emphases and contradictions, to give a sense of Browning criticism as a whole. The basic vocabulary of criticism over the last twenty years – terms like 'deconstruction', 'feminist', 'historicist', and so forth – has often been defined, and the reader who is hesitant about these terms might like to look in the first instance at the excellent definitions in Margaret Drabble's *Oxford Companion to*

English Literature (6th edn, 2000 – p. 245 **criticism**) or at the fuller account in Peter Barry's *Beginning Theory* (1995).

Before coming to detailed study of the recent criticism, it is important to have some sense of perspective by looking at the sharp fluctuation in Browning's reputation in the century after his death.

(a) IN AND OUT OF THE CANON: 1889–1979

Browning achieved wide recognition in the late 1860s, and for the last two decades of his life his reputation remained high. His burial in Poets' Corner, Westminster Abbey, was a major public event attended by people as diverse as the Archbishop of Canterbury, the novelist Margaret Oliphant, the French and Italian ambassadors, and the adventure novelist Rider Haggard. *The Times* contained a moving account: 'Such was the interment in the place of highest honour of one of the most illustrious of the sons of literature' (1 Jan. 1890).

At this point 'the whole machinery of Browning's canonization was already in place' (O'Neill 1995: 1). In England the Browning Society was devoted to the explication of his work, and in America – where critics were proud that appreciation seemed to have been carried further than in England – Browning clubs arose in many towns (Greer 1952). The story of Browning's subsequent reputation in the century following his death has been a complicated one, though it could be characterized simply as 'fame, decline, and fame again'.

In the 1890s and 1900s Browning's reputation ran high as a poet *and* as a thinker, and discussions of the poetry were often bound up with moral, philosophical, and religious debates. Many of his poems deal directly or indirectly with major issues – Is a historically-based Christianity true? Why is there evil and disaster in the world? What is it to live a good life? – and so his poems became important sites for argument and thought.

The very fact that Browning's poems were sometimes 'difficult' in terms of language, theme, and presentation increased their appeal in this respect. Poems like 'Bishop Blougram's Apology', 'The Statue and the Bust', 'A Death in the Desert', and pre-eminently of course *The Ring and the Book*, do require explication for all but the most experienced readers, and so explication led to philosophizing, and then the generation (from out of the body of the poems) of ideas about life and its meaning.

After the upsurge of literary theory in the 1980s and 1990s, it is easy to look down in a patronizing way at this kind of reading. Many critics now hold sophisticated views about the relationship between poetry and ideas, and are wary of simply extracting ideas from poems and treating them separately from the poems in which they inhere. But not all discussion in the late nineteenth and early twentieth century was naive in this respect, and professional philosophers of the age took time to consider Browning's work. As O'Neill notes, in the 1890s several members of Harvard University's Department of Philosophy had things to say about Browning, and the distinguished philosopher George Santayana's famous attack on Browning and Whitman, 'The Poetry of Barbarism' (1900), though negative in its conclusions, nonetheless indicates the extent to which discussion of the work was bound up with serious philosophical and aesthetic debate. In England, Sir Henry Jones's *Browning as a Philosophical and Religious Teacher* (1891) is, in its title, an epitome of one of the ways in which the poet was regarded at this time.

The decline in Browning's reputation took place in the 1920s through the influence of Modernism and within the wider reaction against things Victorian. Having been described as a 'positive' or 'optimistic' thinker, Browning's reputation necessarily suffered at a time when difficult questions were being posed in the wake of the national trauma of the First World War. O'Neill puts this more emphatically:

> In this period of adjustment [the 1920s] to a widely felt 'modern' condition, consisting of both alienation and the need to remake the foundations of civilization, Browning's reputation as an optimist diminished his value for a post-war generation.
>
> (O'Neill 1995: 55)

Also, of course, the great writers of Modernism were all consciously breaking new ground, reacting against or developing away from the aesthetics of the previous century, and Browning's reputation declined along with the reputations of many Victorian writers.

The impact of T. S. Eliot's *The Waste Land* (1922), and the influence of the literary criticism that he wrote in the 1910s and 1920s were a catalyst in this respect. T. S. Eliot was consciously revising literary tradition and the canon of English poetry, bringing forward the metaphysical poets (Donne, Herbert, Marvell, etc.) and other seventeenth-century literature, and downgrading some Romantic literature and particularly some Victorian literature. According to Eliot there had been a 'dissociation of sensibility' within English poetry some time in the seventeenth century. Before that point, thought and emotion in poetry were beautifully melded and interlinked: a sprightly intellectualism entwined itself with feeling and emotion to produce vital poetry. After that, in the eighteenth century, decline set in, and, on the rare occasions when Eliot quoted Browning, he did so to show what he regarded as the weakness of his style. In the essay 'The Metaphysical Poets' (1921) Eliot cites the work of George Chapman (1559–1634) as showing qualities he thinks exemplary: 'a direct sensuous apprehension of thought, or a recreation of thought into feeling, which is exactly what we find in Donne'. He goes on to quote various contrasting extracts, including lines 693–7 of 'Bishop Blougram's Apology', and then proceeds to this almost notorious passage:

> The difference [between the extracts] is not a simple difference of degree between poets. It is something which had happened to the mind of England between the time of Donne or Lord Herbert of Cherbury and the time of Tennyson and Browning; it is the difference between the intellectual poet and the reflective poet. Tennyson and Browning are poets, and they think; but they do not feel their thought as immediately as the odour of a rose.... while [in the best of eighteenth-century poetry] the language became more refined, the feeling became more crude. The feeling, the sensibility, expressed in the *Country Churchyard* (to say nothing of Tennyson and Browning) is cruder than that in the *Coy Mistress*.
>
> (1921; Eliot 1969: 286–8)

This famous essay, and the aesthetic generated through Eliot's other essays, was crucial to what happened to views of Browning from the 1920s through to at least the 1950s. To put it simply, T. S. Eliot was one of the major figures of the age, and as critics and a wider readership struggled to come to terms with his masterpiece *The Waste Land* (1922) so they read his critical essays in order to understand the change in sensibility he believed he was pioneering. They took on board, then, not only this particular essay, but the wider view of literature implied in the other essays, and all this moved Browning down in any ranking of poets.

There is an irony here. While one of the major modernist poets, T. S. Eliot, was using Browning as an instance of what is relatively 'crude' in terms of 'feeling' and 'sensibility', one of the other major modernist poets – arguably, the most important – Ezra Pound (1885–1972), himself an influence on Eliot, was taking Browning's work as a source of inspiration and example in terms of genre, style and diction, organisation and allusion, and the deployment of historical materials.

Ezra Pound felt that Browning was one of his most important and positive literary influences. In 1907, in his private student journal, he wrote: 'As grass blade in its sheathe, so are we like in tendency, thou Robert Browning and myself. And so I take no shame to grow from thee' (Bornstein 1985: 106). How Pound 'grew from' Browning can be seen in his early poems that often take over aspects of form and language from Browning's dramatic monologues – poems like 'Mesmerism', 'Fifine Answers', and 'Scriptor Ignotus', for example – and also in poems like 'Near Perigord' in the Sordello-like way in which Pound resuscitates history. Consequently, one of Pound's descriptions of parts of his early work comes very close to being a description of the technique of Browning's monologues:

> To me the short so-called dramatic lyric – at any rate the sort of thing I do – is the poetic part of a drama the rest of which (to me the prose part) is left to the reader's imagination or implied or set in a short note. I catch the character I happen to be interested in at the moment he interests me, usually a moment of song, self-analysis, or sudden understanding or revelation ... I paint my man as I *conceive* him
> (letter to W. C. Williams, 1908)(Paige 1971: 3–4)

This description could well be applied to Browning's 'Pictor Ignotus', 'A Toccata of Galuppi's', or 'Andrea del Sarto'. The deeper, less obvious, influence on Pound came from *Sordello*.

Pound profoundly admired *Sordello* and it helped him in the whole formulation of the structure of *The Cantos*, their use of allusion, and their handling of history. To some extent this is obscured by the way in which he rewrote the opening Cantos. The *Three Cantos*, which he published separately in 1917, show much more fully the ways in which *Sordello* was a kind of starting-place for his own epic. The opening is striking:

> Hang it all, there can be but one *Sordello*!
> But say I want to, say I take your whole bag of tricks,
> Let in your quirks and tweeks, and say the thing's an art-form,
> Your *Sordello*, and that the modern world
> Needs such a rag-bag to stuff all its thought in
> (Pound 1917; quoted from Bornstein 1985: 120)

Pound affectionately parodies Browning's manner, even as he considers in joking terms what precedent of form *Sordello* might be. In a letter to Eliot's father of 1915, Pound sets both his own early work and that of Eliot himself in the context of Browning's. He mentions Browning positively in his critical prose again and again. For example, reviewing Eliot's *Prufrock and Other Observations* in 1917, Browning provided the natural point of comparison:

> The most interesting poems in Victorian English are Browning's *Men and Women*, or, if that statement is too absolute, let me contend that the form of these poems is the most vital form of that period in English, and that the poems written in that form are the least like each other in content.... Since Browning there have been very few good poems of this sort. Mr Eliot has made two notable additions to the list ['Prufrock' and 'Portrait of a Lady'].
>
> (Pound 1963: 419–20)

Aspects of this poetic relationship have been mapped by Bornstein (1985), Gibson (1987) and Brown (1998), but if one puts these three excellent accounts together one might think that there was still more to do in defining exactly the extent of this influence. Pound treasured Browning as someone whose colloquialisms, abruptness and elisions gave poetry new freshness and vigour, and whose experiments in form (particularly *Sordello*) and use of history might offer ways of structuring that elusive thing, his own modern epic.

Despite the Browning-Pound relationship, it was Eliot's views and his downgrading of Browning that predominated in the first half of the twentieth century. Behind Eliot lies the view of his teacher at Harvard, George Santayana, who thought that Browning was simply too full of a rumbustious, chaotic energy, that he disdained a Dante-like search for ethical and aesthetic perfection, so that as a consequence his verse was often 'obscure, affected, and grotesque' (1900; quoted from 1916: 209). And this view is reiterated in one of the most influential works of criticism between the wars, F. R. Leavis's *New Bearings in English Poetry* (1932):

> [Browning] did indeed bring his living interests into his poetry, but it is too plain that they are not the interests of an adult sensitive mind.... When he is a poet he is concerned merely with simple emotions and sentiments.... so inferior a mind and spirit as Browning's could not provide the impulse needed to bring back into poetry the adult intelligence.
>
> (Leavis 1932: 20).

In highlighting the views of Eliot and Leavis we are being selective, for, as O'Neill remarks, 'Hostility to the nineteenth century, and to Browning in particular, is apparent in almost any anthology or account of literary history published in the years between the wars' (O'Neill 1995: 56). These views are worth emphasizing, nonetheless, because they were so influential. Most people seriously interested in modern literature in the first part of the twentieth century had read and imbibed these ideas. Older critics, in the 1980s and 1990s, could still rehearse the way in which they had been put off nineteenth-century poetry by the force of such pronouncements. In this simple sense, sensibilities trained in and attuned to Eliot's aesthetic – witty, pure, classical, religiously aspiring, and with a keen sense of decorum and inner control – found it difficult to turn to Browning's robust, colloquial, abrupt, prolix, tortuously lyrical manner and find some real meaning in it.

It was only as the aesthetic of poetic Modernism itself began to fade, to be subjected to critical scrutiny and objection, to itself be examined as a phase of literary history, that the strictures of T. S. Eliot and others came to seem less obvious. Then, from the 1950s, and more clearly in the 1960s, interest in Browning (and in all nineteenth-century poetry) gradually got going again. This draws a simple line through a complex matter, but it is not much of a distortion.

During the period when Browning's wider reputation was in eclipse, in America and Canada much scholarly work was done by W. C. DeVane (1927) (1955) and W. O. Raymond (1965) to establish basic contexts for the poems' subject-matter and also the poet's biography. So, when revaluations of Browning came to be made, they had behind them a wealth of basic scholarship and explication on which they could draw. Robert Langbaum's *The Poetry of Experience* (1957) began to break down the apparently simple divide between Victorian poetry and the works of Modernism, and to open up more sophisticated ways of reading Browning. The work of Roma A. King, Jr. (1957), Park Honan (1961), Isobel Armstrong (1969) (1974), and Philip Drew (1970) (to name a selection of critics) followed suit in different ways, establishing *not* Browning 'the philosophical and religious teacher', but rather Browning the poet, skilled at creating characters, in deploying ironic modes, in responding in complex ways to the ideas of his time.

As we move into the second half of the twentieth century, one critic dominates: the variously ingenious and idiosyncratic Harold Bloom. Bloom originally stated his idea of poetic influence, of how one major poet grows out of a reaction to another – a theory now widely contested – in *The Anxiety of Influence* (1973), but as he went on to develop it, it was Browning who came more and more to occupy a central place in his thinking. Bloom's Browning was a 'strong' poet engaged in an oedipal struggle to free himself from the influence of Shelley – Browning was mythic, deep, and self-knowing, anything but the tame poet who dressed up religious ideas in simple dramas. From roughly *The Ringers in the Tower* (1971) onwards, Bloom developed his views in connection with the poem which he saw as central to Browning's work and central to a wider understanding of the relationships between Romantic, Victorian, and Modernist poetry: 'Childe Roland to the Dark Tower Came'. Bloom confessed to something like an obsession with its strange power, and his readings of 'Childe Roland', and the view of Browning they inspired, were widely influential.

To Bloom, Browning was quite simply 'the most considerable poet in English since the major Romantics, surpassing his great contemporary rival Tennyson, and the principal twentieth-century poets, including even Yeats, Hardy, and Wallace Stevens, let alone the various fashionable modernists whose reputations are now rightly in rapid decline' (Bloom and Trilling 1973: 493). This statement needs to be considered in context before it is dismissed as hyperbole. Bloom commenced his career with studies of Romantic poetry (Blake, Wordsworth, Coleridge, Keats, Shelley, and Byron), and he was a devoted admirer of Yeats, Hardy, and Wallace Stevens. This is, in other words, a knowledgeable appraisal, and one which an opponent should take seriously. We do not have to accept Bloom's quasi-Nietzschean view of 'strong' poets, or his ideas of tradition, psychoanalysis, and intertextuality, to accept his evaluation of Browning. We should, though, have some sense of the weight of implication that he attaches to the idea of the 'strong' poet:

> Canon-formation is not an arbitrary process, and is not, for more than a generation or two, socially or politically determined, even by the most intense of literary politics. Poets survive because of inherent strength; this strength is manifested through their influence upon other strong poets, and influence that goes through more than two generations of strong poets tends to become part of tradition, even to become tradition itself. Poems stay alive when they engender live poems, even through resistance, resentment, misinterpretation; and poems become immortal when their descendants in turn engender vital poems. Out of the strong comes forth strength, even if not sweetness, and when strength has imposed itself long enough, then we learn to call it tradition, whether we like it or not.
>
> (Bloom 1975: 200)

Bloom (though he has had and still has many opponents and objectors) reappraised Browning's status quite as confidently as T. S. Eliot, and came to very different conclusions. In this way, we could say, Browning survived the onslaught of Modernism and had his reputation gradually rehabilitated in the second half of the twentieth century.

(b) RESPONSES TO THE EARLY LONG POEMS

What difference has the last twenty years' criticism made to the appreciation and understanding of the early long works, *Pauline*, *Paracelsus*, and *Sordello*? Broadly speaking the early long works have attracted more significant attention in the last two decades than they did previously, and have come to be seen as more sophisticated, ironic, and experimental.

The obvious case is *Sordello*, the most ambitious of these poems, and the one on which Browning worked hardest. Older criticism was sometimes happier repeating the jokes about its unintelligibility than in trying to address it on anything like its own terms. To go right back, almost a century, Chesterton could write: '*Sordello*, with all its load of learning, and almost more oppressive load of beauty, has never had a very important influence even upon Browningites, and with the rest of the world has passed into a jest' (Chesterton 1903: 42). This attitude, even in a milder form, is now unsustainable.

Sordello, like *Pauline* and *Paracelsus*, has attracted serious critical attention, and also been carefully annotated in both the *Oxford* and *Longman* editions. The commentary is excellent even in the less elaborate *Penguin* edition, but both *Oxford* and *Longman* address all questions of ambiguity in their annotations, giving paraphrases of the most obscure passages. This difficult work is now more accessible to more readers than ever before, provided that they are prepared to do some work to come to terms with it.

Browning's early works have attracted recent attention for a number of reasons. First, of course, any great artist had difficulty 'getting going', starting their career as a maker of art or poetry, and this initial phase can be revealing for an understanding of their later career. In Browning's case this interest is compounded by the decade in which he started to write, the 1830s, which, in the history of poetry at least, looks like a terrible in-between time. The Romantic poets had flared and passed away: Keats died in 1821, Shelley in 1822, Byron in 1824, Coleridge (whose work Browning cared much less for) in 1834. Only Wordsworth lived on to 1850, and – as we have seen – Browning was antagonistic to his political conservatism **[78–80]**.

This sense of an aftermath is not simply a matter of later construction, but was something that contemporaries felt. Byron, in particular, had enjoyed huge sales, reaching a wide audience. Now that the popular market he had generated had faded, poetry seemed a less appealing commodity to publishers. In 1835, after Browning had gone to see the publisher John Murray, jun., he reported the latter's opinion 'that "King Pandion he is dead: & all his Peers wrapped up in lead." i.e. Lord Byron is "no mo" & Poetry "no go"' (*Corr.* iii. 133).

Not all critics feel as strongly as Harold Bloom that Shelley was the decisive influence on the young Browning, but all agree that he was significant. Shelley is a strong and vital poet, and Browning was saturated with his readings of Shelley's work. In these early years he had to find his own way of making poetry, he had to learn from, but grow beyond, Shelley's example, and this – given the relatively low status of poetry in the 1830s – must have been a difficult thing to do. *Pauline*, *Paracelsus*, and *Sordello*, then, are the record of Browning's struggle to make himself a poet, to find his own means of expression, and to make a reputation. They are complicated and ambitious works written into the post-Romantic moment.

Taking the criticism of these works in the period 1980–2000, and looking back to criticism earlier in the century, we could say simply that recent criticism tends to approach these works in a more thoughtful way. Earlier criticism often tends (if only implicitly) to see them as 'apprentice' works in a negative sense, as unfulfilled, as covertly or semi-autobiographical in a relatively naive mode. In different ways, recent criticism sees them as more sophisticated, more self-conscious about their procedures, more self-knowing about themselves as innovative in terms of genre and manner. Rather than seeing the young Browning as gradually bungling his way, struggling through these unsuccessful works until he hit on his successful form, the dramatic monologue, the tendency now is to see the early phase as brave and experimental, consciously adaptive in terms of genre, and searching and self-conscious in its deployment of irony as one of its major features.

(i) *Pauline*

Critical responses to *Pauline* provide a good illustration of this. Older criticism tends to treat the confessional aspect here as autobiographical or semi-autobiographical. Browning is wearing a dramatic mask, perhaps quite a thin one, and presenting in fictional guise his own thoughts and feelings as a confused 20-year-old. One of Browning's friends, Joseph Arnould, described the poem to another of Browning's friends, Alfred Domett, in ways that suggest this reading: *Pauline*, he said, was 'a strange, wild (in parts singularly magnificent) poet-biography: his own early life as it presented itself to his own soul viewed poetically: in fact, psychologically speaking, his "Sartor Resartus" [the famous autobiographical work by Carlyle]' (Kenyon 1906: 141). Criticism in the late twentieth century does not necessarily overturn this view, but it tends either to be more tentative or more sceptical about it, shifting emphasis onto the ways in which Browning is distancing himself from the poem's speaker. How much distancing is there? With older criticism, as it were, Browning is looking at himself in a mirror. In more recent criticism, he is looking at himself in a mirror reflecting his image from another mirror. In deconstructive criticism, which is always more sceptical in the widest sense, *Pauline* becomes not at all autobiographical, but rather a poem only pretending to be confessional, really being an exploration of the dramatic mode itself and its ironies.

Much critical attention has been given to the poem's framework, the first motto from Clément Marot, the epigraph from Heinrich Cornelius Agrippa, the footnote in French signed by Pauline at line 811, and the different dates fixed to the poem, one after the epigraph (*London: January 1833*), the other at the end of the whole text (*Richmond: 22 October 1832*). Here is a game on top of a game. Browning is pretending to be the speaker of the poem (who is different from himself), and then he is also pretending that this speaker's poem has been edited and issued by Pauline (the imaginary Frenchwoman who is its dedicatee). In other words the poem is an edition of itself, not simply issued directly from the imaginary speaker:

Not only did [Browning] insist on the dramatic nature of his speaker's utterance, he also supplied a kind of editorial apparatus to suggest that the confession was not his own. The note in French signed by Pauline at line 811, the Latin headnote from Agrippa, the motto from Marot in French, the affixed dates at the beginning and end – all these are signals that the work should be regarded as a fictional edition ... Editing is a way of distancing experience, of setting the fictional persona at a further remove from the author ...

(Ryals 1993: 17–18)

It is worth spending some time on the details of the exotic and mischievous nature of this framework. The motto or epigraph from the French Renaissance poet Clément Marot (1496–1544) reads in translation: 'I am no more that which I have been, and shall never be able to be it'. Marot was a first-generation Protestant who, amidst the confusions of his life and times, aspired to a pure and simple religious faith – a hint to us, perhaps, of one way of reading *Pauline*. The second epigraph is taken from the Renaissance alchemist and occultist Heinrich Cornelius Agrippa (1486–1535), from *De occulta philosophia* (1531), a work that Browning had met in his father's book collection. Here Browning deploys a long extract, the beginning of which reads in translation:

> I have no doubt that the title of our book may by its unusual character entice very many to read it, and that among them some of biased opinions, with weak minds – many even hostile and churlish – will attack our genius, who in the rashness of their ignorance will cry out, almost before they have read the title, that we are teaching forbidden things, are scattering the seeds of heresies, that we are an annoyance to righteous ears, to enlightened minds an object of offence ...
>
> (*Penguin* i. 1023)

The footnote in French at line 811, begins (in translation):

> I am very much afraid that my poor friend is not always to be perfectly understood in what remains to be read of this strange fragment, but he is less fitted than anyone else to clarify what from its nature can ever be only dream and confusion. Besides I am not sure whether in seeking better to integrate certain parts, one would not risk damaging the only merit to which so singular a production can pretend, that of giving a precise enough idea of the kind that has only been sketched.
>
> (*Penguin* i. 1027)

Browning is not only pretending to be the suffering young man who speaks the poem, he is also pretending to be that speaker's beloved girlfriend, the Frenchwoman Pauline, and so engaging in literary criticism on his own work, describing it as no more than an 'ébauche' (a sketch).

Herbert Tucker is the critic who has written most interestingly about what he calls these 'paratexts', i.e. texts lying beside or in parallel with the main text. He adds to them Browning's later comments on the poem in the Prefaces of 1867 and 1888, where Browning calls *Pauline* 'this crude preliminary sketch' and 'an eyesore' written in 'juvenile haste and heat' (*Penguin* i. 3). Tucker argues that these later prose apologies actually draw attention to the work which superficially they attempt to hide from view, and that they are in effect 'further fragments of [the poem's] confession, chips from the same workshop, tricks from the same bag' (Tucker 1998: 7). His argument essentially is that the poem presents us with nested boxes of apologies: an apology within an apology within an apology. The poem itself says:

> Sad confession first,
> Remorse and pardon and old claims renewed,
> Ere I can be – as I shall be no more.
>
> (25–7)

In other words, the speaker within the poem keeps telling us that he is looking back at an earlier and inadequate self: he has grown up and moved away from that earlier self. This apology is then reinforced and repeated again in the device of the mock edition, in the words of the motto from Marot 'I am no more that which I have been, and shall never be able to be it'. And this same point is made again, in different terms, by Browning's later Prefaces of 1867 and 1888, where he himself (in his own person) distances himself from his own early poem and earlier self. We have, says Tucker, a 'quasi-infinite regress' generated by 'the multiple, sedimented editorial mediation that Browning has staged'. The 'real' self that the poem is supposedly about keeps disappearing, so that really the poem becomes about the whole act of being a dramatic writer, about how one disappears or 'escapes' from one's own text: 'The fashioned self that denies its name, and repudiates its own characteristics, nevertheless does so in a characteristic fashion' (Tucker 1998: 6, 10). This is deconstructive reading with a vengeance, and typical of the essential scepticism of such readings in the way it renders the work 'unstable, equivocal, wavering, groundless' (Miller 1992: 19). But can one really escape from the felt emotional pressure of autobiography so completely in *Pauline*? The poem may be sophisticated and even playful in the way it distances the poem from the poet, in the way in which it puts material with some kind of autobiographical resonance at several removes from the author. But can we ever completely give up its autobiographical basis? It is on these issues that future criticism may turn.

(ii) *Paracelsus*

Paracelsus has also become a more sophisticated, daring and original work under the eye of recent criticism. This appreciation of it has been grounded first in Browning's own self-consciousness about its genre.

Paracelsus is a closet-drama, or poetic drama, having some of the appearance of a play, but actually written directly for private one-on-one reading. It has one main protagonist, Paracelsus himself, who is the central speaker throughout, with, around him, only the minor roles of Festus, Michal, and Aprile. From one point of view, this way of writing, particularly when so dominated by the speech of the main protagonist, can look as though it is neither one thing nor another. It neither has the open emotional complexity generated when different characters have to talk and interact with each other as in a stage play, nor does it have (completely) the dramatic directness and the density of ironic implication of the dramatic monologue. Is it not – at least as practised here – a kind of failed, in-between genre? Isn't Browning only on his way towards the dramatic monologue, writing a play that is not really a play, or (alternatively) writing five long dramatic monologues, stuck end to end, which are not (in the best sense) dramatic monologues?

The original preface, dated 15 March 1835, while being elliptical and initially difficult to understand, shows Browning's own awareness that he was doing something new, and that he was handling genre in ways that readers might find difficult. The preface stresses that *Paracelsus* is not a play, and not intended as a play, but also that it is not 'what is called a Dramatic Poem', i.e. Browning has not simply abandoned the idea of a play in order to still reproduce many of the conventions and characteristics of something written for live performance. It is a *consciously* non-dramatic work –

> an attempt ... to reverse the method usually adopted by writers whose aim it is to set forth any phenomenon of the mind or the passions, by the operation of persons and events; and that, instead of having recourse to an external machinery of incidents to create and evolve the crisis I desire to produce, I have ventured to display somewhat minutely the mood itself in its rise and progress, and have suffered the agency by which it is influenced and determined, to be generally discernible in its effects alone, and subordinate throughout, if not altogether excluded ...
>
> (*Penguin* i. 1029)

Most critics see this handling of genre as developing out of the aesthetics and acting styles of the theatre in the early nineteenth century. Ryals puts the matter succinctly: '[In the early nineteenth century] stressing character over action, the actor reserved his talents and energies for the big scenes when motive was disclosed, so that a play like *Richard III, Hamlet,* and *Macbeth* became, in the hands of Sarah Siddons or Edmund Kean, a series of "moments"' (Ryals 1983: 32). Lyrical intensity was being prioritized over larger issues to do with the overall rhythm and movement of the dramatic action, the total shape of the play, and emphases like these might naturally lead towards the form of *Paracelsus.*

The whole of Paracelsus's life from 1493 to 1541 is being treated through the consideration of five intense or lyrical points in time, five tableaux; Browning is careful to give an exact setting by date to each of the five parts of the poem: 1512, 1521, 1526, 1528, and 1541. A whole life comes burningly alive in five 'moments' of crisis and revelation. The apparent dross of less intense dramatic or narrative writing falls away, leaving the reader to connect together the five epiphanic or lyrical moments into a more coherent or reasoned pattern – or, as Browning puts it: 'were my scenes stars it must be his [the reader's] co-operating fancy which, supplying all chasms, shall connect the scattered lights into one constellation – a Lyre or a Crown' (*Penguin* i. 1030).

In Part II **[50–3]** we looked at Paracelsus as a Promethean quester who goes wrong. He sets out to capture the whole of human knowledge, to make himself a god, to stand on an eminence, and is then gradually disillusioned and dragged back to earth, and in this way made to understand the true nature of his humanity. Paracelsus fails in his formal aims, but he 'attains' in coming to really understand more truly the nature of his own life within the context of failure. To put it simply, we characterized Paracelsus in line with the speaker of *Pauline* and in line with Sordello, as essentially undergoing a journey of growing up, a process of maturation. All three characters set off as egotists, thinking they are completely original in their ideals and aims, considering themselves as self-originating. Gradually they have to discover their connectedness to other people, the tradition that lies behind all they would achieve, and the community of other human beings (both those around them and those who precede them in history). These poems can be characterized as being about the end of adolescence. Each character is forced to move beyond simple egotism and self-assertion, to understand the necessity of love, to understand their ties to other people, to community, history, and tradition.

Clyde de L. Ryals makes this point in similar terms when he describes the character of Aprile in Part II as Paracelsus's double:

> Like Paracelsus, Aprile has adopted an all-or-nothing attitude. He too would reach the Absolute directly, without mediation, which means that, asserting his priority, he rejects tradition. Yet now, near death [in Part II], he perceives that no one can overleap time to eternity but each must work with present rude, limited tools in approaching the Absolute. What he learns, in other words, is what Browning, whose goal had been to be an entirely new kind of poet owing little or nothing to poetic tradition, was beginning to learn: his secondariness and dependency.
>
> (Ryals 1993: 27)

The phrasing here is influenced by what still remains the best single reading of *Paracelsus*, that by Herbert Tucker in *Browning's Beginnings* (1980: 53–79). It is not possible to summarize here the full subtlety of that reading in a short space, but some outline is essential.

Tucker sees *Paracelsus* as a sophisticated, ironic, self-reflexive work in which Browning is thinking about his own situation as a writer, thinking about what it means to be 'original' or great. Paracelsus sets off to achieve the ultimate in science and philosophy, to understand the whole world, and in doing so (though he does not realize it) to achieve utopia, to bring time to a stop. All his predecessors in science and philosophy have failed completely. Now he will succeed completely.

Tucker sees mirrored in this Browning's aspirations as a writer: he will be the true Shelley (as it were), he will write the final, definitive, history-transcending poetry. Gradually, through the trials of false self-exaltation and false despair, Paracelsus-Browning has to discover a different awareness that understands the importance of 'the lively community of tradition'. Paracelsus struggles to outdo earlier scientists and philosophers, to be wholly new and original, but in the end he discovers that he is just like them: he is part of a community of failure that is nonetheless part of the ongoing progress of humankind as a whole. (The crucial passage describing this idea of progress is in Part V, 653–786). In arguing this, Tucker draws both on Harold Bloom's ideas of poetic influence as outlined in *The Anxiety of Influence* (1973), and also on T. S. Eliot's famous essay 'Tradition and the Individual Talent' (1919), a work that lies behind Bloom's ideas.

One thing that Tucker really adds to an understanding of the poem is a sense of Browning's self-consciousness about the irony he deploys both in the details and in the overall structure of *Paracelsus*. In this

passage in Part I, for example, the conventionally-minded but unheroic
Festus is urging Paracelsus to take some account of the work of previous
scientists and philosophers. 'At least accept the light they lend', he
pleads:

PARACELSUS: Their light! the sum of all is briefly this:
They laboured and grew famous, and the fruits
Are best seen in a dark and groaning earth
Given over to a blind and endless strife
With evils, what of all their lore abates?
No; I reject and spurn them utterly
And all they teach. Shall I still sit beside
Their dry wells, with a white lip and filmed eye,
While in the distance heaven is blue above
Mountains where sleep the unsunned tarns?

FESTUS: And yet
As strong delusions have prevailed ere now.
Men have set out as gallantly to seek
Their ruin. I have heard of such: yourself
Avow all hitherto have failed and fallen.

MICHAL: Nay, Festus, when but as the pilgrims faint
Through the drear way, do you expect to see
Their city dawn amid the clouds afar?

PARACELSUS: Ay, sounds it not like some old well-known tale?
For me, I estimate their works and them
So rightly, that *at times I almost dream*
I too have spent a life the sages' way,
And tread once more familiar paths.

                                              (i. 574–95)

The ironies of this passage – signalled here with added italics – make
the whole poem circular. Paracelsus is, in fact, just another of the sages,
just another quester setting out gallantly to seek his ruin. He is going
to tread 'once more familiar paths' even though now he thinks he is
setting out on a completely new one. Beginnings and endings,
originality and tradition, assertion and dependency, are being melted
into each other in rich spiralling figures of irony: '[Paracelsus] must fall
hard and for a long time before he appreciates the wisdom of choosing
second place as the only place from which he or anyone else may begin.

The poem is the story of his fortunate fall from isolated self-assertion into an intermediate niche in human time and its renewing traditions' (Tucker 1980: 54).

(iii) *Sordello*

The last of the early long works is *Sordello*, and by now it should not be necessary to alert the reader any more to its reputed obscurity. The fact is that, as outlined above, this obscurity has now been breaking down under a battery of exegesis and commentary, and the reader who is prepared for some hard work, who is willing to work through the poem in either the *Oxford* or the *Longman* edition, can get at least some purchase on its basic meaning. In this climate, criticism no longer leaves *Sordello* out of the total pattern of Browning's works, and all full accounts of his career and development give it space. Recent criticism has looked at four main aspects: the question of genre, the deployment of irony, the way in which history is treated, and – last but not least – the question of obscurity itself. Was *Sordello*'s obscurity in some sense intended?

Though all this criticism approaches the poem in different ways, with different kinds of preoccupation and vocabularies, as a whole it has shifted the general perception of *Sordello*. In the Chesterton comment quoted earlier one can sense a once generally prevalent view: that *Sordello* was simply a work that had gone wrong; that Browning was (at this stage) an incomplete poet; that the work was internally chaotic in its narrative structure as well as in the opacity of individual sentences – quite simply, the work was an out-and-out failure on all counts. There were perhaps some takers for this view in the period 1900 to 1970, but in the last two decades no critics who specialize in Browning would accept it, or would use anything like these terms. There has been a growing sense that, while *Sordello* may be flawed, it is a considerable work, one that failed through its ambition and sophistication rather than through bungling or naivety. Maybe the reader is still sceptical. Isn't this just specialists defending their own? Or don't perhaps specialists rather enjoy decoding the poem's hieroglyphics, hieroglyphics for which most people have no time? In the end the only answer to these questions lies in testing out the poem for yourself; as Ezra Pound told his father: 'I began to get it on about the 6th reading' (Ward 1985: 11).

As *Sordello* emerges in the criticism of the last two decades it is a bold, ambitious historical poem, trying to represent vividly a pageant of thirteenth-century Italian history. More specifically, it is an experimental narrative trying to focus all its energy on a tiny space of time: the final minutes in the life of the troubadour poet Sordello in 1224, as he struggles with the last remains of his egotism and solipsism, and tries to commit himself more fully to 'the people', to the world, history, and the future. The political subtlety of the ending reflects in many ways the dilemmas of a liberal like Browning in the 1830s and 1840s.

In Book V Sordello discovers that he is the son of Taurello Salin-guerra, one of the most powerful warriors of the age. Taurello offers him political power, the opportunity that he, Sordello, should become head of the Ghibellines and a dominant ruler. In Book VI Sordello has to choose between taking up this offer in the spirit in which it has been made – i.e. becoming a powerful ruler on the unprogressive side of history – or taking up this power in a different spirit and trying to use it for good, or (and this is the third, unspoken option) remaining only himself, remaining only a poet. In Books I and II of *Sordello* poetic art is closely associated with the inward gaze, with solipsism: Sordello's emotional life is isolated from the wider needs of society. As Sordello gradually becomes aware, the world needs reforming, but political action seems difficult or tainted. How can the world really be improved? Is their any point in the poet really engaging with the sufferings of 'the people', the ongoing tragedy of history? Sordello dies partly at least because he finds these questions unanswerable. Stating the poem's subject-matter in these simple terms gives some sense of its literary, historical, and political interest.

The new considerations of *Sordello* have often been grounded in an awareness of genre. Most commentators agree that the poem grows out of the tradition of narrative romance as practised by Scott and Byron, but if this is the genre within which *Sordello* is best considered it is immediately clear that Browning complicates it in a number of ways. The most obvious of these are his deployment of the narrator-commentator device and the poem's time-sequencing:

> Browning deliberately slows the narrative, so that instead of the conventional velocity and gusto that carry the reader rapidly through the course of the story, there are elaborately developed patterns that force the reader to consider the significance of each part in relation to the whole.
>
> (Hair 1972: 31–2)

Ryals sees Browning's deployment of the narrator-commentator figure as the device which complicates the poem in interesting ways and which helps to achieve its full ironic resonance. Ryals's reading stresses the real Browning who wrote the poem, then within the poem the narrator-commentator figure (a fashioned version of Browning), and then, again, the ways in which this narrator-commentator speaks to the protagonist Sordello and also – in the long digression at the end of Book III – speaks about himself. Ryals compares the narrator-commentator device to the harlequin figure in *commedia dell'arte*, who is in charge of the plot and yet mocks the play, and to the device of parabasis in Greek comedy, the device by which 'the author's spokesman interrupts the action of the play to address the audience directly on matters of concern to the author': 'The poet bears the same relation to his poem as God does to his creation. Each may be said to be both *in* and *out* of creation, immanent *and* transcendent' (Ryals 1983: 67).

From this perspective Ryals sees the poem as within the tradition of 'Romantic Irony', a tradition he describes in complicated terms with reference to the theorizing of the German Romantic critic Friedrich Schlegel (1772–1829). It is not necessary, however, to follow him fully into this material to understand his basic point. Browning has put himself, or rather a version of himself, within the poem, talking about what he is doing, commenting on it, engaging intimately with the developments of the story, and so – as later in *The Ring and the Book* – making the telling of the story a part of the story.

A second aspect of the poem's complexity concerns its use of history. An interesting perspective here is that of Mary Ellis Gibson, who describes Browning's treatment of history as 'contextualist': that is to say, Browning is less interested in the centrality of his hero, as in romantic historiography, than in the spirit of an historical era and how his hero fits within it: 'The vivid particularity, the freshness of language, the historical ironies, and above all the sense of intricate connections between the individual and a historical moment give Browning's poetry its special quality of making the past immediate in the present' (Gibson 1987: 22).

From this observation Gibson goes on to an interesting discussion of what she calls the 'simultaneity' of history in *Sordello*. This is not a particularly difficult idea to grasp. One way of writing history, or of telling the story of Sordello's life, would be to do it in a straightforward linear fashion, starting at the beginning and going through to the end: one event following another, one cause leading to an effect. Of course our actual experience of our own lives is more complicated. There are millions of connections backwards and forwards in time that are obscured in a simple linear historical narrative, and in one sense a linear narrative makes quite a limited pattern out of the thousands of events, speeches, etc. that make up the flow of time. Carlyle poses this dilemma well in his saying 'Narrative is linear; Action is solid'. Gibson sees Browning's time-sequencing in *Sordello* as a deliberate attempt to get away from the limitations of the one-thing-follows-another style of narrative, to enter us more fully into the complexity, immediacy, and confusion of history as it happens, and also to help us (with him) see into the real meanings of events.

Straightforward chronology is less important than the context and meaning of events: 'As the poet himself suggests, his procedure in *Sordello* is to make circles out of linear chronologies and to focus our attention on moments that in themselves are much like tableaux' (Gibson 1987: 124). This may look initially a rather dubious argument. Isn't it just an elaborate way of explaining away the confused handling of narrative? Actually it does go some way to explaining what Browning might have thought he was achieving through the complex arrangement of his narrative.

The main events of the story are focused in 1224. When we first see Sordello, just after his interview with Palma, in Book I, lines 327–30, he is roughly thirty years old and at a crucial turning-point in his life. From this moment, the poem takes us backwards to Sordello's childhood, forwards through his early manhood, and then only returns fully to the opening scene of 1224 at Book III, line 273 onwards. From this point the main action is focused on just three days: the actual day of the fateful interview with Palma; the next day as Sordello and Palma journey to Ferrara and Sordello meets Salinguerra; and the final day, when Salinguerra and Sordello recognize each other as father and son, Sordello is offered the leadership of the Ghibelline faction, and he dies under the conflicting emotions that the offer provokes.

This pattern of events is not the only 'circle' in the poem. Events like the Ghibellines expulsion from Vicenza in 1194, the siege of Ferrara and its causes, and Ecelin's withdrawal to Oliero are treated again and again in different ways: 'Browning does not develop these events as sequential narrative; instead, accounts of them appear over and over with some variation in detail. Again, the reader is virtually required to conceive the poem as a simultaneous whole.' The sequence of events 'is blurred by variation and repetition; sequence is subordinated to historical situation developed by accretion' (Gibson 1987: 126).

One simple way of expressing Gibson's argument would be to say (as above) that *Sordello* is 'an experimental narrative trying to focus all its energy on the final minutes of the troubadour's life'. Another way of expressing it, would be to see Book VI as (in effect) a dramatic monologue spoken by Sordello as he nears death, and all the rest of the poem as background, context, and commentary on this one crucial speech. *Sordello*, in other words, shows distinct leanings towards the dramatic monologue as we know it in the simpler forms of 'My Last Duchess' and 'The Bishop Orders his Tomb'.

The third major aspect of criticism on *Sordello* is undoubtedly the most contentious. Did Browning intend to write a difficult poem? Is its notorious obscurity not inadvertent, but actually part of its actual design and meaning? The crucial study here is David E. Latané's *Browning's Sordello and the Aesthetics of Difficulty* (1987), which argues this case:

> One of the reasons the poem has been considered monstrous, I think, is that it has been from the start judged by a standard of 'articulate clearness' when its poetic aim – its deliberate choice of aesthetics – has been towards difficulty. When a critic states that 'the language of the poem is often incomprehensible' and that there are 'numerous lines which mean nothing,' we should remember that if these statements reflect an aesthetics of clarity, nothing of the sort was intended.
>
> (Latané 1987: 10)

This may sound a thoroughly question-begging statement, but actually Latané brings forward convincing evidence to show how Browning might have thought that it was better to aim at a 'fit audience ... though few' (this phrase is originally from Milton's *Paradise Lost*, vii. 31). Browning may have thought that in a historical poem he should aim at something much more than was achieved, for example, in the popular poems of Sir Walter Scott, poems which fulfilled very easily their readers' expectations. Latané argues that Browning deliberately built a measure of difficulty into his poem in order to encourage reader participation and response, for the true poet's aim should be 'the stimulation of the imagination, not the immediate and clear apprehension of determinate meaning' (here he is paraphrasing Friedrich Schlegel). Latané expresses this point later in his own terms when he says that Browning wanted to make the reading of the poem 'into an interaction rather than a straightforward relationship of power between teller and told' (Latané 1987: 34, 121).

Some have dismissed these arguments. So, Adam Roberts: 'It may seem implausible, but Browning simply did not anticipate his readership (which he acknowledges to be a small one) having any difficulties reading his epic – indeed, he talked about his work as "rather of a more popular nature" (*Corr.* iii. 134) than his earlier publications' (Roberts 1996: 25). Such a straightforward view has much on its side, but Latané is at his most convincing when he draws parallels, for example, with the complex works of the historian Thomas Carlyle, *Sartor Resartus* (1833–34) and *The French Revolution* (1837), which were successful in the 1830s. Both these works by Carlyle demanded quite complicated skill and participation on their readers' part, and yet they had found a real audience. Does Browning, though in poetry, really demand that much more of his readers?

Latané makes his argument in definite terms, postulating a self-conscious 'aesthetics of difficulty' in the 1830s, one that may not really have existed. But in a much simpler sense we can think of Browning as a brilliant young poet showing off his brilliance, writing his work at a sophisticated level, giving a kind of bravura performance, with much play of irony, much apparent air of improvisation, much complex but nonetheless enjoyable time-sequencing. Perhaps the image of the virtuoso – 'one who excels in, or devotes special attention to, technique in playing or singing' (*OED*) – is a useful one in trying to understand *Sordello*. Whereas the virtuoso in music was a respected and venerated figure in the nineteenth century (Chopin, Paganini, Liszt, etc.) and could make nineteenth-century ladies swoon, a virtuosic piece of poetry – demanding that the reader participate in creating every passage – might quite easily fail to impress.

(c) THE EARLY MONOLOGUES: A VARIETY OF APPROACHES

The dramatic monologues of *Dramatic Lyrics* (1842) and *Dramatic Romances and Lyrics* (1845) are at the centre of Browning's achievement. These are his most irreducible poems, much anthologized and much discussed. Though *Men and Women* (1855) and *Dramatis Personae* (1864) show wider inventiveness and a broader emotional range, it may be that these early monologues are in the end more impressive, the combination of their brevity, sparkling freshness of description, and involved irony being in some sense unrepeatable, even by Browning himself.

This section looks at criticism on five of these poems: 'Soliloquy of the Spanish Cloister', 'Porphyria's Lover', 'My Last Duchess' – Browning's best-known poem – 'Pictor Ignotus', and 'Count Gismond'. Different critics might concentrate on different poems, but most would consider this selection as central to any worthwhile appraisal. We have already tackled these poems briefly in II (c). The aim now is to discuss the criticism, and in particular to think about the variety of approaches. Different critics approach the monologues with different kinds of preoccupation – deconstructive, psychoanalytical, feminist, and so forth. Here we will take individual monologues and pair them with the work of one or more critics, to give a sense of the wider movements in Browning criticism as a whole.

(i) 'Soliloquy of the Spanish Cloister': 'Indeterminacy of Interpretation'

'Soliloquy of the Spanish Cloister' **[75]** looks like one of Browning's simplest and most direct uses of the monologue form. The poem is set in a monastery in Spain, in some unspecified historical time; it could be a contemporary nineteenth-century setting, but just as easily it could be set in a previous century. The monologue's speaker is an unnamed Spanish monk who has a profound hatred for one of his fellow monks, the seemingly saintly Brother Lawrence.

This is the initial, ironic (and partly Protestant) joke on which the monologue is based. People are supposed to go to monasteries to learn to love God and to love one another. This particular Spanish monastery, however, has become the seedbed for hatred of a vicious, if energetic and amusing, kind. There is a disjuncture between the title and the poem. 'Soliloquy' might suggest to us that we are about to read an inner rumination in the manner of Hamlet or Macbeth. Instead this soliloquy has a strong air of the comic-grotesque, a rollicking, humorous atmosphere. From the inarticulate growl of disgust with which it begins – 'Gr-r-r' (1) – to the even more angry and frustrated 'Gr-r-r – you swine!' (72) with which it ends, we follow with repugnant fascination the speaker's hate-filled thoughts about his fellow monk.

Why was Browning so interested in this kind of psychological portraiture, in presenting individuals who are 'mad or bad' or both, warped in some profound way? This question is one of the starting-points for Daniel Karlin's study of this poem, and for his wider view of Browning in *Browning's Hatreds* (1993). In other poems, of course, Browning is a celebrator of the power and goodness of human love: love is a transcendent value, infinitely enriching the individual human life, and connecting that life with Heaven: 'Love Among the Ruins', 'By the Fire-Side', and 'One Word More', among others, could be cited to prove this point. But Browning himself was capable of significant personal hostility against individuals – against Wordsworth, for instance, in 'The Lost Leader', against D. D. Home, the spiritualist, whom he regarded as a fraudster, in 'Mr Sludge, "The Medium"'– and he was also the creator of a series of great haters in purely dramatic terms. The energy of hatred as an emotion lies behind works like 'The Laboratory', 'Caliban upon Setebos', and the two monologues of Guido

Franceschini in *The Ring and the Book*. (Karlin gives many more examples.) So what, here, of the hatred of monk for monk? What is Browning really up to?

Karlin suggests that we read the poem in two ways simultaneously. The first is a straightforward moral reading, or what he calls the conventional reading:

> The conventional reading of 'Soliloquy of the Spanish Cloister' ... takes this poem to be using the technique of dramatic monologue as a means of ironically revealing the speaker's warped passion and prejudice. The poem offers a critique of hatred, an insight into its workings which functions both as moral exemplum and as satire. A key part of the lesson would be that hatred defeats its own object: the speaker appears not only to be giving us an unintentional and unflattering self-portrait, but to be painting the very opposite picture of Brother Lawrence which his pettiness, malice, and jealousy imagine ... Looking through the poem's distorted lens we 'correct' the image and see Brother Lawrence as kindly, good-humoured, [and] unaffected.
>
> (Karlin 1993: 74–5)

In other words, the irony works a reversal of values and images. The speaker presents himself as good and Brother Lawrence as bad, but – using the framework of irony that Browning instils into the monologue – readers reverse these judgements and see the speaker himself as bad and Brother Lawrence as nearly saintly.

So far so good, but at this point Karlin reverses this conventional ironic reading. If we read the poem aesthetically (rather than simply morally), he says, we may be struck by, for instance, the vitality of the speaker's artist-like vision, his vivid evocations of the sensuous loveliness of women (in 25–32), and his witty mimicry of his fellow-monks' inane conversation at the monastery's meal-times (in 9–16):

> The conflict between Brother Lawrence and his hater may be thought of in moral terms as a conflict between good and evil, or in aesthetic terms ... as one between the art of obedience and the art of rebellion. Behind Brother Lawrence stands the unfallen Adam, gardening in Paradise; behind his hater (much reduced from his grand original, admittedly) stands Milton's Satan – like the speaker of the 'Soliloquy' a leering, jealous voyeur, but also (for Shelley, Blake, and others) an embodiment of radical energy.
>
> (Karlin 1993: 78)

We could put this in another way by saying that the speaker is decadent but vital of consciousness, whereas Brother Lawrence is virtuous but dull. Even expressing it as simply as this begins to open out some of the ways in which this fine poem works on us.

John Woolford speaks of the 'indeterminacy of interpretation' that haunts many of the dramatic monologues (Woolford 1988: 71), and 'Soliloquy of the Spanish Cloister' is a case in point. Just as we might feel that we can settle into this reading of the poem – that the speaker is a decadent but vital in his perceptions – other emphases suggest themselves. So, take stanza 4, one of the stanzas that Karlin uses to demonstrate his reading:

> *Saint*, forsooth! While brown Dolores
> Squats outside the Convent bank
> With Sanchicha, telling stories,
> Steeping tresses in the tank,
> Blue-black, lustrous, thick like horsehairs,
> – Can't I see his dead eye glow,
> Bright as 'twere a Barbary corsair's?
> (That is, if he'd let it show!)
> (25–32)

Karlin brilliantly says that 'the speaker is an artist, … his eye is "alive", noticing in a way that Brother Lawrence's is not' (Karlin 1993: 76). But what *exactly* is the speaker seeing, we might ask? Women are not allowed into the monastery and these two Spanish peasant girls, Dolores and Sanchicha, are therefore just outside, near a bank that acts as some kind of separation from the outside world. They are near a water-tank. Perhaps they are supposed to be doing some job for the monastery, washing clothes or peeling vegetables, but instead they are squatted down, gossiping together, enjoying a break from their work. In Dolores's case, she is so animated by her conversation, that without her knowing it, part of her black hair has draped itself into the water-tank, creating for the speaker an erotically charged image.

It is a vivid scene, perfectly evoked in a few words, painterly in its intensity. Yet, do we have to agree with Karlin's reading of it? Other critics create different emphases.

The speaker undoubtedly does have a fine eye, but it is also a lecherous eye, the controlling 'male gaze' acting with a vengeance. In this stanza we see both a scene beautiful and simple in itself, like a painting by Gustave Courbet perhaps – two dark-skinned peasant girls chatting by a water-tank, in a moment of relaxation from their work –

but we also see how the speaker takes it over, captures and controls it for his own purposes. If we imagined – as we easily can – that the speaker is in his sixties and that Dolores and Sanchicha are teenagers, then we may be more wary about the exact way in which the speaker's eye is 'alive'.

Just as the speaker attempts to control the innocence of the young girls through his sexually-charged gaze, so he attempts to control, to diminish (to psychologically kill) the innocent Brother Lawrence. (We can already see parallels between the speaker's treatment of Lawrence, and the Duke's treatment of his Duchess in 'My Last Duchess'.) An important but initially difficult element in the monologue is the extent of the religious allusion, which can cause problems for the first-time reader. These allusions are obviously entirely appropriate for creating the atmosphere of a Spanish monastery, but they also serve a much wider function.

The speaker refers to the Christian doctrine of the Trinity (37), to the Arian heresy (39), to St Paul's Letter to the Galatians (49–52), to the Manichean heresy (56), and ends up singing a garbled version of the prayer *Hail Mary*: *'Plena gratia | Ave, Virgo!'* ('full of grace, Hail, Virgin!') (71–2). The implications of these references are probably not deep or complex, but it does help to know something about them. Arius (*c.* 250–*c.* 336) – the man who originated the Arian heresy – taught that Jesus was *not* fully man and fully God at the same time, as Christian tradition asserted. A 'Manichee' is someone following the teachings of Manes (*c.* 216–*c.* 276), who believed (again contrary to the tradition of Christian belief) that the world was ruled by two equal and opposing principles, one Good, the other Evil, and that the world of matter was irredeemably in the control of the principle of Evil. The difference in the poem, in other words, is between orthodox or traditional Christian belief, and belief that is judged to be wrong, unorthodox, or (in other words) heretical by the mainstream of Christian believers.

Through his religious allusions the speaker characterizes himself as orthodox and traditional in religion, while he wants to see Brother Lawrence as a heretic, a man with a false understanding of religion. The faultlines between orthodoxy and heresy have always been complicated and involved, and Browning was sensitive to this fact. (See, for example, poems like 'The Heretic's Tragedy' and 'Holy-Cross Day'.) There is something sinister about the way in which the speaker takes on himself the power and authority of orthodoxy in order to characterize the wholly innocent Lawrence as a heretic. (We perhaps might recall the martyrdom of St Lawrence in this context.) In a different, but parallel context, the Duke in 'My Last Duchess' calls up the authority of his 'nine-hundred-years-old name' and all it implies (aristocracy, a hierarchical social order, patrilineal descent) in order to assert his authority over his wife. The comic-grotesque mode of the 'Soliloquy' means that it never gets in any way as sinister as this, but it does give a certain edge to the comedy of the poem.

(ii) Towards feminist readings of 'Porphyria's Lover' and 'My Last Duchess'

Both 'Porphyria's Lover' and 'My Last Duchess' – early masterpieces of Browning's art – received a first treatment in Part II **[73–4, 67–70]**. Now we can go further with them in the context of the criticism, focusing in the end on feminist readings of 'My Last Duchess'.

Both these poems, like 'Soliloquy of the Spanish Cloister', are studies of disturbed, alienated mindsets. In both cases the male speakers murderously transform a live woman into a dead object. The speaker in 'Porphyria's Lover' does this quite literally by strangling his lover and keeping her corpse beside him, and the Duke of 'My Last Duchess' does it by giving orders for the murder of his first wife (his 'last duchess'), and then, having ensured her physical death, by paradoxically celebrating her 'living' presence in the portrait he commissioned from Frà Pandolf. Both poems involve men staring at women, and then sadistically controlling those women, so it is small wonder that they have attracted psychoanalytic and feminist readings.

Earl Ingersoll – inspired by the work of the influential psychoanalyst Jacques Lacan (1901–81) – sees both speakers as profound narcissists whose lives are controlled by the fear of death and meaninglessness. Human love must take place in time, must develop and change through time, and is vulnerable to diminishment and death: it is founded upon trust, intimacy, spontaneity, and physical warmth. But the Lover and the Duke are so afraid of loss or abandonment, so afraid at a deeper level of the fullness and warmth of love, that they actually kill the women who might love them, reduce them to objects, and so (apparently) hold at bay their own overwhelming fears of emptiness.

In 'Porphyria's Lover' the speaker lives in a cottage, perhaps somewhere on a big estate. His lover, Porphyria, who has the air of a lady with her graceful manners and white gloves, comes to him from a higher social world and seems to be prevented from marrying him by differences of class. At the start of the monologue he sits looking out on the park-land as the trees are rocked by an oncoming storm, and the violence and energy of the storm enact the passions and confusions (at this stage held in check) of his own mind (1–5). The social situation reverses what, for the nineteenth century, might be considered the usual relations of power between men and women. This is not a selfish aristocrat visiting and sexually exploiting a working-class girl, rather it is a middle-class or upper-class woman visiting, when she decides, a lower-class lover. (The poem's final title, 'Porphyria's Lover', aptly describes this imbalance: Porphyria, the woman, is named, in a rich-sounding, exotic way, while the male speaker is anonymous.) And this inversion really nags at the speaker, and, interacting with his narcissism, produces dire consequences.

Ingersoll wonders how exactly we should interpret Porphyria's 'darling one wish' (57). Of course, this wish is something that the speaker imposes on Porphyria after her death. He may just be fantasizing it, but it does seem legitimate to see it as growing out of the 'romantic' scene in the first part of the poem. The beautiful woman has broken away from 'tonight's gay feast' (27) and come to visit her lover and set his cottage in order (6–21). Perhaps, says Ingersoll, we should assume that her 'one wish' was something like: 'I wish I could stay here with you forever':

> In his own mad fashion, the Lover has (mis)read that text in order to escape being positioned as 'feminine,' i.e. a loved object to be abandoned again as she may have many times before. He reaffirms her 'feminine' position as one too weak to break those 'vainer ties' to a world in which he can have no presence. Torn between moments of passionate possession of her and inevitable abandonment or 'loss,' he has murdered her in order to turn her into a fetishistic object which can never leave.
>
> The fear of object loss, Lacan would suggest, is a metaphor of a repressed fear of a greater loss, the loss of life itself. It may well have been the Lover's fear of death – the ultimate menace to the self – which urged him to sacrifice her to his own uncontrolled desire to stave off extinction.
>
> (Ingersoll 1990: 154)

We have already analysed the basic story of 'My Last Duchess' in Part II [67–70]. What Ingersoll sees in the Duke's character is not, of course, his dominating strength of will and purpose, but rather his narcissistic and insecure need to construct a self-important image of himself – his 'nine-hundred-years-old name' (33). The Duke's egotistic self-assertion comes from a deep inner emptiness and fear, which means that he reads the duchess's love of life as constituting something close to sexual promiscuity. Since within himself the Duke fears death so profoundly, therefore he has to murder desire in his Duchess:

Fearful that her indiscriminate 'looks' might deprive him of the 'regard' he deems appropriate to his position at the centre of their world, he has reduced her to the beautiful object which, like the sacrificed Porphyria, can never be lost. By the end of the monologue, it is clear that the Duke is a fragile shell of prestige and the accoutrements of power concealing a hollow core, very like a cast bronze statue. It is ironically appropriate, then, that he has made her what he fears he himself is, one of the living dead, absent yet also there, 'as if alive.'

(Ingersoll 1990: 156)

This perception of the Duke's weakness of character is typical of the shift in readings of 'My Last Duchess' over the last twenty years. In older interpretations, attention was focused by and large on the Duke's character, and usually on his strength and power. A much-discussed critical issue was whether the Duke was 'witless' or 'shrewd' in telling the envoy about the murder of his first wife. One group of critics saw the Duke as witless, in the sense that he was so wrapped up in his own ego and his own selfish concerns that he was quite oblivious to the fact that he was exposing himself as a murderer. (The envoy was simply an underling who could not possibly make any use of this information to the Duke's discredit.) Another group of critics saw the Duke as 'shrewd'. They argued that there was method in his apparent madness: he was casually but knowingly informing the envoy of the fate of his first wife, so that the envoy could inform the Count – or indeed the Count's daughter (the Duke's prospective second wife) – of the kind of submissive behaviour that would be expected of her.

Of course, there is no real way of arbitrating between these two viewpoints from within the text, and this kind of criticism is essentially involved in building up an idea of the Duke's character separate from the text – in other words, in writing another text to set beside the text of the poem. For Tucker (1980), formally a critic allied to deconstruction, and hence strongly interested in rhetorical structures, any satisfactory reading has to stay much closer to the actual movements, gaps, and nuances of the Duke's speech. Constructions of character that too quickly lose touch with the poem's actual rhetorical pattern should be abandoned. Most subsequent views of the poem owe something to Tucker's perceptions about it, even when they take up different critical positions.

In Tucker we see the beginning of a sense that the Duchess (though dead) is quite as important a presence in the poem as the Duke himself. The monologue is not just about the Duke's character, but about how the Duke tries to interpret the duchess, or – as later critics would insist

– it is about a whole series of interpretations or readings: 'the Duke of the painting; the painter of the Duchess; the Duke of the painter; and so on' (Bristow 1991: 57–8). One of Tucker's insights has been often repeated: his emphasis on the Duke's hesitations and demurs. The relevant lines are these:

A heart – how shall I say? – too soon made glad (22)

Somehow – I know not how – as if she ranked (32)

In speech – (which I have not) – to make your will (36)

In formal terms these are expressions of modesty, but, at a less obvious level, they are also expressions of insecurity and discomfort. Why so many apologies for his lack of skill in speech? As Tucker says: 'when a skilled rhetorician [like the Duke] reaches three times in the space of fifteen lines for the same commonplace, especially for this one, the commonplace is no longer common but the expression of a private struggle' (Tucker 1980: 178).

The Duke has a definite interpretation of himself, of his prestige, of his aristocratic status, and of how the world should function around him, and the Duchess never fitted into this interpretation. Now, in death, she still challenges it. Quoting the beautiful lines 25–9, which (despite themselves) give us a real insight into the lively, loving character of the Duchess, Tucker goes on:

> these lines [are] a kind of vista … Despite the Duke's efforts to contain the Duchess, her joyful energy breaks into his discourse and charges these eventful lines with a mystery to which everything in the surrounding poem defers. Their mystery is hers: the mystery of a meaning withheld.
>
> (Tucker 1980: 179–80)

The Duke is like a beginning-reader of poetry aiming at closure, that is to say, trying to impose one and only one meaning, a trite formula, a reductive summary, on his Duchess's life and portrait. But she has precisely the qualities of good poetry and good art generally, 'the power of untamed meaning … the potential energy of a meaning that persistently eludes formulation' (Tucker 1980: 180–1). At the end of his monologue the Duke wants to characterize himself as an all-powerful Neptune 'taming a sea-horse' (55), but this is a dream, a wish-fulfilment, for he has still not really 'tamed' his duchess into the kind of one-dimensional, reductive interpretation that he desires.

Later critics take up these insights in different ways. For Catherine Maxwell, for example, a critic writing from a nuanced feminist perspective, it is important to notice that what resists the Duke's powers of interpretation is precisely a painting, a work of art. The painting is in some sense a figure for what Browning really thought art (including poetic art) was about:

> [The Duke] tries to reduce the Duchess to a picture because he perceives art objects as being more manipulable and yet he is still obviously threatened by the latent charm of the woman which emanates from her portrait. The personification of the painting occurs not just as the result of the Duke's insensitivity, but also as his subliminal troubled acknowledgement of the power of art and representation. A person may be reduced to a painting in the hope of greater control, but a painting, in its ability to arouse the strong emotions of its viewers, can out-manoeuvre the desire and wishes of its artist or owner ... The Duchess becomes complicit with the power of art, and it is through the appeal of her painted image that she stages a return which undermines her husband's position.
> (Maxwell 1992: 323)

In a later article Maxwell develops this argument further from a slightly different perspective. Again her concern is with the male mind's desire to control and appropriate a female presence, and the resistance provided by the feminine (a resistance which is essentially that of art itself). Now she reads 'My Last Duchess' and other poems including 'Porphyria's Lover', as deep responses to and critiques of the Greek Pygmalion myth. In Greek mythology, and then in literary treatments like that of Ovid, King Pygmalion, unsatisfied by the women he sees around him, sculpts his image of an ideal woman. He falls in love with the statue that he himself has created, and subsequently Venus, in answer to his prayer, brings the statue alive as the girl Galatea. The myth is deeply misogynistic and narcissistic. Maxwell sees Browning's poem as entering into the deeper implications of the myth and then overturning them:

> Although critics have spoken of Browning's obsession with the myth of Andromeda's rescue by Perseus, this story seems to me to be a reaction to a larger mythic influence and one in which the poet shows that preservation by the male is not necessarily synonymous with rescue and liberation. For Browning's real compulsion is Ovid's story of Pygmalion who, disgusted by the

women he sees about him, sculpts his ideal woman, and then falls hopelessly in love with the statue he has created. The goddess Venus at last takes pity on him and animates the statue so that it can become his flesh and blood bride. Browning lays bare the misogyny of Ovid's Pygmalion, for whom no living woman is good enough. His poems show how male subjects [like the Duke], threatened by woman's independent spirit, replace her with statues, pictures, prostheses, corpses, which seem to them more than acceptable substitutes for the real thing. Browning's male speakers typically invert Ovid's myth, reducing a woman, even through her death, to a composition of their own creating. They desire feminine simulacra, static art-objects, whose fixed value will reflect their self-estimation. Yet these attempts are always equivocally presented as, time and time again, Browning shows us their fatuity. We see exposed the confusion of values that allows these speakers their justifications. But not only is the error of judgment made plain; increasingly, as he explores the myth, Browning reveals how the speaker's plan goes askew. The female subject consistently eludes her captor, unmasks the poverty of his suppositions, or returns to haunt him ... 'My Last Duchess' stages a confrontation in which the dead returns to challenge the living, and thereby empties and renders null the gesture of appropriation.

(Maxwell 1993: 990, 994)

Perceptions like this connect with perhaps the most overtly feminist reading of the poem, that by Shifra Hochberg. Her title indicates her wider argument: 'Male authority and Female Subversion in Browning's "My Last Duchess"' (1991). For Hochberg the Duchess's portrait is a female-authorized 'countertext' to the male-authorized text of the Duke's dramatic monologue, and we have to read this countertext with care. The Duchess is not the passive victim of the Duke's male gaze. She stares out of the painting through the 'depth and passion' of her 'earnest glance' or gaze (8): she outstares the Duke, as it were. The Duke, sensing the extent to which the portrait displays the otherness of female sexuality and desire, has to veil it with a curtain (10), desperately (as it were) trying to control its subversive power. The portrait itself is full of pinkish hues: the repeated 'spot of joy' (14–15, 21) and 'the faint | Half-flush' that 'dies' along the Duchess's throat (18–19), a lovely coloration which Frà Pandolf has partly failed to capture. Outside the context of the portrait the Duchess is also associated with the erotically charged colour of red: in the sunset, the cherries, and the 'blush' of lines 26–31. All these things are synecdochal representations of female sexuality and pleasure, which elude the Duke's will to imaginatively control them, which elude the authority of his nine-hundred-years-old name 'handed down patrilineally from father to son'. And then, also, there is 'the positionality of power':

> Throughout the poem, standing and the authority to command others to sit is associated with the exercise of male control and dominance: the Duke demands that the envoy sit while contemplating the portrait of the Duchess (5); the Duke chooses 'Never to stoop' (43); and at the end of the monologue he enjoins the envoy to 'rise' and 'go | Together down' (53–54) to join the others. This discourse of the positionality of power extends to the portrait itself. It is significant that we are told twice, in lines 4 and 46, that the Duchess stands – not that her *portrait* stands, but that *she* does ... [T]he Duchess' erect stance, associated with the phallocentric power of the Duke, helps to thematize the erotic strength of the Duchess as well as the poem's central paradox of the intersection of power with seeming powerlessness.
>
> (Hochberg 1991: 80)

In this way 'Browning ... links the creative powers of woman with the creative powers of the poet and his feminized artistic sensibility' (Hochberg 1991: 79).

It is almost as though the Duchess is becoming a symbol for Browning's muse, his idea of what poetic art really is, and certainly these kinds of considerations are backed up by more obviously historical facts. John Lucas and Joseph Bristow, among others, have pointed out that Browning would have been aware – at least to some extent – of the feminist writing in the *Monthly Repository*, the liberal-radical journal where some of his early poems were published: 'Women contributors to the journal were explicitly feminist [following in the tradition of Mary Wollstonecraft], and traces of their critique can surely be felt in this poem' (Bristow 1991: 62). From this perspective the monologue is an exposure of an ultimately macho figure.

(iii) Artist in the marketplace: a Marxist view of 'Pictor Ignotus'

When we move away from the monologues above, from Browning's world of haters and murderers, we can initially feel that we are in a blander world. And certainly the two monologues we are going to consider next, 'Pictor Ignotus' and 'Count Gismond', have provoked less critical attention. As we shall see, however, they are nonetheless interesting and crucial poems, and the emerging criticism on them is gradually bringing them into sharper relief. Some of the potential ways of reading 'Pictor Ignotus' are already indicated in Part II **[70–2]**. Now we can take our thoughts further in relation to the criticism.

The first thing to notice about the critical literature on 'Pictor Ignotus' is the way in which older readings of the poem are remarkably consistent. There used to be a general sense that 'Pictor Ignotus' could only be read in one way. The speaker of the poem was a failed painter, a spiritual coward, a man who, having ducked out of the advances in painting in the sixteenth century, was engaged in a tortuous but ultimately futile self-justification. In other words, the monologue was ironic. The speaker hopes we will look favourably on his withdrawal from the spirit of his times, while what he really reveals to us is his sterile, undaring, unimpassioned imagination. 'Pictor Ignotus' seemed only to prefigure the greater and more significant poem 'Andrea del Sarto', which – such readings maintained – presented a similar figure. This is the starting-point for Loy D. Martin's analysis. As he puts it simply, 'All these [previous] critics, whether friendly or hostile, read "Pictor Ignotus" as a transparent rationalization of a pitiable or contemptible personal failure' (1985: 269). Martin is almost the only serious Marxist critic of Browning, and his study opens up ways of thinking about the poet that have been drawn upon by later critics.

Martin notices two things about the monologue, which in his view might relate it more immediately to Browning himself. One of the primary issues within the monologue – the speaker's essential problem – is how and on what terms an artist can relate to his audience. This was, of course, an important issue for Browning, finding most obvious expression in his concerns about 'popularity'. Martin's second intuition relates to the paradox of the title, 'Pictor Ignotus' ('Painter Unknown'). The sixteenth-century person speaking to us is 'unknown', his character is a blank. Yet how, exactly, within the terms suggested by the poem, could he become better known to us? This is the speaker's dilemma. If the speaker *did* follow the fashion and become a realist painter he would only become 'known' or 'famous' in a very particular sense: his name (and his artistic works) would become 'famous', a commodity, a brand, as it were – Raphael, Michelangelo, McDonalds, Ford – and his 'real' self would be alienated from this produced self. The realistic mode of painting demands 'originality', the unique signature or style of the artist – in one sense, apparently, a revelation of character. But when the artist has succeeded, and become a 'name' in the competitive market-place, his 'real' self has become a kind of blank, an unknown. He is split, between the famous commodity (his public name and work) and his 'private' self:

> ... the cost is intolerable; he becomes like a slave, a commodity that can be bought and sold, judged capriciously or coldly cast aside. [See ll. 50–6 in the poem.] Rather than elevating his painting to the level of the human, the realist painter in vogue degrades the human to the level of reified ornament, casually procured.
>
> (Martin 1985: 43)

But, on the other hand, if the painter declines to take up the new style of painting, declines the cult of personality and commodity that goes with it, then he ends up practising a dated style which communicates less and less effectively. He ceases to be part of the world in another sense, and so ends up as formally anonymous and totally unknown. He chooses to avoid the 'capricious' and 'cold' art market, but he chooses also 'to abandon the only pictorial language in which he can participate in human community. He returns to the symbolic "series, Virgin, Babe and Saint," a dead language that can only be repeated endlessly without hope of response' (Martin 1985: 45).

For Loy Martin, in other words, the speaker's dilemma is much more deep-seated than the traditional reading would suggest, and is in fact insoluble in the terms that the monologue presents us with. If the speaker plunges into the art market he risks profound alienation; if he chooses to stay out of it, he risks artistic death. 'The painter may either risk his total identity in the innovative style that the community demands or he must "stand apart" with his pictures and thus lose his identity altogether'. Underlying this impossible choice are 'the bourgeois myths of progress and personal ambition' (Martin 1985: 45).

This takes us a long way in a short space, and I want to backtrack onto a simpler but important part of Martin's argument: his concern to emphasize the historical moment of the poem in the early sixteenth century. The speaker finds himself caught between two main styles of painting, the symbolic and the realistic (or 'semiotic'). (To get some simple sense of the two styles, you might look at a painting by Fra Angelico and then at a painting by Raphael.) On the one hand, the painter has the code of symbolic religious painting, the language which he calls 'the same series, Virgin, Babe and Saint' (60). On the other hand, there are the emerging realist conventions, to which the speaker is partly attracted, and which he describes vividly at lines 15–22. These different artistic styles are not just intrinsic matters in themselves. They relate to the whole way in which art is produced and consumed.

Martin sees the speaker as poised on the brink of the highly commercial way of seeing art which we now all know, but which is not something we should really take for granted:

> In the Quattrocento [the fifteenth century], the 'consumer' for a painter's work was indeed relatively individual and homogeneous in nature. Paintings were produced on commission, and the contracts that set the painters to work typically stipulated in advance much of what the painting was to depict and even exactly what materials were to be used ... By contrast, the code of emerging realist conventions, while still perhaps allegorical or abstract, is nevertheless relatively indeterminate ... This is the form of the modern or bourgeois market, where an artisan like a painter must risk his own appraisal of what the public wants by completing his work previous to any commitment to purchase it.... he invests his talents, both internal and external, on the gamble that his appraisal of public demand will be accurate and his audacity will be rewarded. His success will depend on his correctly predicting the relations between signifier and signified that will strike his public as natural.
> (Martin 1985: 41–2)

This is the capitalist market in which, as Browning's speaker vividly says, the 'merchant' (the art dealer, connoisseur, publisher, record-dealer, or whoever) 'traffics in my heart' (62). Since Martin wrote these lines in the 1980s, the ways in which art can function as a commodity have become even clearer. For the speaker it is intolerable that the deepest reaches of personality, brought into expression in a work of art, are then bought and sold like any other product: that the human should be given a price-tag. But what is the solution? What is he to do? The speaker of 'Pictor Ignotus' chooses a kind of artistic death rather than submit. Browning, Martin suggests, invents the dramatic monologue to survive the same dilemma. The 'merchant' (the publisher, critic, reader) cannot 'traffic' in Browning's 'heart' because in a dramatic monologue that heart is not on display. It is apparently nowhere to be seen. 'The dramatic monologue is, in the fullest and most conscious sense, the product alienated from its producer ... The alienation of the artist from his art is seen [implicitly] ... not as a weakness of will or spirit, not as a lack of commitment or ambition; it is seen as the only way for the artist to exist and produce within the capitalist market.... [This poem] makes explicit the logic of the poet's need to bring the dramatic monologue into being' (Martin 1985: 47).

Here is food for thought. Martin brings out in an effective way the depth of the issues that reside in the poem. Art does not exist in its own private sphere, but only as a part of society, and is therefore subject to society's wider values. The poem's speaker is caught on the horns of an impossible dilemma, not created by his own spiritual inadequacy, but rather created by changes in society and in society's perceptions of what art actually is.

(iv) Rescuing Andromeda: ironic and heroic readings of 'Count Gismond'

As we saw in Part II [76–8], the story of 'Count Gismond' seems at first glance romantic and heroic. The monologue is given no specific date, but from the world it creates we can roughly imagine that we are in the France of the fifteenth or sixteenth century (perhaps exactly at the same time as 'My Last Duchess'). The speaker is a French countess, living in the south of France, in Aix en Provence, the country, we may note, of the troubadours. In conversation with her confidante Adela, she is looking back to events of roughly ten years before, when she lived somewhere further north in France. Then she was unmarried, and about to be crowned 'Queen' at a tournament, when unexpectedly she was slandered by Count Gauthier, who accused her of fornication with himself (55–60). Count Gismond (then quite unknown to her) at once stepped forward and defended her honour. He brutally defeated Count Gauthier in a duel, got him to confess his slander publicly, and then – in the confused aftermath – quietly carried her off to his home in Provence. From the security of a loving marriage, the (now) Countess Gismond looks back with hurt, wonder, and gratitude to the extraordinary day on which her married life began. This straightforward reading takes for granted that the poem exists in a world of high chivalric romance, a world urgently brought to life with properties like the tournament, ladies in flower-garlands, armour, penance-sheets, torture-engines, and falconry.

What is interesting in the critical approaches to the poem is the persistence of ironic readings, i.e. readings that seek to subvert the reading outlined above. Then, contrary to these, there are strong rebuttals of the ironic readings. And then, after ironic reading and anti-ironic reading, the poem has been left to fall into a kind of limbo. The ironic readings commenced with John Hagopian (1961), and they have continued on at least to Ryals, who declares that 'In the last analysis we cannot accept the lady's story as true' (1983: 155–9).

Ironic readers think we should be as sceptical of the Countess's words as we are of the Duke's in 'My Last Duchess'. They believe that the Countess did have a sexual relationship with Count Gauthier, and that she was happy to cover it up in a self-righteous and deceptive manner. At the tournament she pretends to be a chaste virgin, is mortified when her lover exposes her, and then is quite satisfied to see him murdered within the ludicrous honour-and-combat code of the day. She marries Count Gismond, but her eldest son with his 'clear | Great brow' (121–2) is probably Gauthier's child, and the ending of the monologue, where she lies to her husband about what she has been talking about to Adela, is an indication of her general duplicity (123–6).

Sidney Coulling sought to discredit the ironic reading in an important article in 1986, pointing out that Browning's pairing of the poem with 'My Last Duchess' created 'two sides of the Andromeda myth'. In 'My Last Duchess' a tyrannical husband, a dragon if you like, succeeds in destroying an innocent woman, whereas in 'Count Gismond' a chivalric hero definitively rescues an innocent woman. What Coulling wanted to discuss was the motivation behind the ironic reading: 'Dissatisfaction with the traditional reading of the poem seems to have derived first of all from the belief that it made "Count Gismond" too "simple" and hence inferior to the complex monologue ['My Last Duchess'] with which it was originally paired' (Coulling 1986: 77). In 1988, in the *Oxford* edition, Ian Jack is scathing about the 'influential' ironic reading, describing it as 'a view which would surely have astonished Browning' (*Oxford* iii.189).

If we choose to agree that the ironic reading is untenable, is 'Count Gismond' just a naive romantic poem? or at least not as interesting as 'My Last Duchess'? Here the perspective of Coulling and other critics is helpful.

The story is a remarkably vivid piece of story-telling in verse, but more than this, as Coulling suggests, its central concerns are in ironic dialogue with 'My Last Duchess'. When Gauthier accuses the future Countess of fornication – when, that is, she is publicly humiliated – and when Gismond then steps forward to defend her honour, what is interesting is the Countess's lack of worry or anticipation. We might expect her to think that she was far from out of the woods, that Gismond (the good knight) might not defeat Gauthier (the lying, evil knight), or, even if he did, that the result might not be conclusive: people might still think her chastity impugned. In fact, at what we might expect to be a moment of continuing suspense and worry the speaker relaxes. At the first sight of her champion 'I knew | That I was saved':

> I never met
> His face before, but, at first view,
> I felt quite sure that God had set
> Himself to Satan; who would spend
> A minute's mistrust on the end?
> (68–72)

She is completely sure, in other words, that Gismond will win and that her honour will be vindicated. Coulling observes that at this point the monologue has almost the air of a medieval morality play, with God versus Satan, truth versus falsehood, and belief versus doubt, and that there are other lines that reinforce this impression.

The Countess is a religiously-minded lady, whose very first words are a conventional but heartfelt prayer for her husband's soul (1–2), and who, contemplating the dying Gauthier and his load of sin, says piously 'Gauthier's dwelling-place | God lighten! May his soul find grace!' (119–20) – in other words, may he not go to Hell, may his soul rise up through purification in Purgatory. At the centre of the crisis, her faith is so strong that she 'enjoyed | The heart of the joy' (79–80) because of her sure knowledge of God's defeat of evil. So she was able to notice every detail of her champion's preparations for combat:

> Did I not watch him while he let
> His armourer just brace his greaves,
> Rivet his hauberk, on the fret
> The while! His foot ... my memory leaves
> No least stamp out, nor how anon
> He pulled his ringing gauntlets on.
> (85–90)

Anxiety is non-existent; time stands still. What the lady enjoys here is a long, detailed gaze at her future husband. We remember, by contrast, how the Duke in 'My Last Duchess' was maddened by the fact that the Duchess's 'looks went everywhere' (24). The Duke gazes at and tries to control his Duchess's portrait, just as he wanted to control her gaze while she was alive, whereas here the future wife looks at and enjoys, sexually, the sight of her future husband. Her gaze is free to notice and to celebrate the details of the moment.

From a small point like this, the wider dialogue between the two poems becomes more apparent. Here 'God had set | Himself to Satan' (70–1), but taking 'Count Gismond' in conjunction with 'My Last Duchess', it is obvious that – except in fairytales – good does not always and unequivocally defeat evil. When the Duke started seething, and in the end reached the pitch of controlled fury that led him to order his Duchess's murder, there was no obvious divine intervention to stop it happening. Surprisingly, however, this fact does not call into question the Countess Gismond's religious faith. In her life story, as she understands it, God's intervention is wonderfully and clearly visible: it is an instance of God's will at work in the world, and is clearly acted out by his agent, Count Gismond. Within the same overall and conventionally Christian viewpoint, 'My Last Duchess' is simply an instance where the Devil has his way.

We could compare the dialogue between the two poems to that between William Blake's states of 'Innocence' and 'Experience' in the *Songs of Innocence and Experience* (1794). The Countess Gismond may seem naive (to the 'experienced' reader) and to some extent may indeed be so, but her religious understanding of her own life story is nonetheless validated. The Duke of 'My Last Duchess', on the other hand, is a master of the world of 'experience' and is victorious in his own terms. It is hard to imagine someone more cynical and knowing, more completely sceptical of higher values or ideals. Yet, acting so ruthlessly to enforce the demands of his own ego, and with nothing else to satisfy but his own ego, he is nonetheless uneasy at some level: the sheer goodness of his Duchess resists his demand to stamp it out. Something in her generosity, warmth, and virtue cannot be completely extinguished, so that – as so many readings have suggested – she remains a profound contradiction to his whole viewpoint.

In the last moment of 'Count Gismond', Gismond returns to his wife the tercel (male hawk) he has borrowed from her – a simple instance of husband-and-wife reciprocity and exchange. The Countess says casually to her husband

> And have you brought my tercel back?
> I just was telling Adela
> How many birds it struck since May.
> (124–26)

For ironic readers like Hagopian and others, these lines are a sinister cover-up. For Coulling, however, they are a direct and loving exchange, a piece of trusting marital chit-chat. The contrast is again with 'My Last Duchess', where it is impossible to imagine the Duke ever speaking so simply and informally. His intimacy-freezing egotism would demand a stilted, controlled exchange.

(d) THE MIDDLE PERIOD WORK

Men and Women (1855) and *Dramatis Personae* (1864), the two collections that lie at the middle of Browning's career, present one major problem to criticism: their sheer variety. This issue was addressed briefly in Part II (d), but needs to be considered again.

In these volumes Browning is not just presenting a chocolate-box-like confection of different characters and historical periods, he is also exploring different styles, modes, and tones of poetry. (The variety of stanza forms is an indication of this, since stanza form is one determinant of tone and mood.) Some of his speakers are full of bumptious energy, reflected in the buoyant rhythms of their voices (Bishop Blougram for example); others are depressed, almost exhausted and overcome by ennui (Andrea del Sarto). Some speak in earnest tones (the lover of 'Love Among the Ruins'), others in tones altogether more rollicking, within a comic-grotesque mode ('Holy-Cross Day', 'The Heretic's Tragedy'). In one famous instance, 'Caliban upon Setebos', the savage Caliban, only recently having acquired language at all, speaks his own semi-animal version of English. As well as encountering this variety of tones, we are also bounced around through levels of decorum: from the dignity and *gravitas* of the death-speech of St John ('A Death in the Desert'), to the unseemly speech of a fraudster spiritualist trying to apologize for his trickery ('Mr Sludge, "The Medium"'). To read well we have all the time to shift our sensitivities, not to confuse the romantic with the grotesque, the comic with the tragic or tragicomic.

In response to this variety, criticism in the last twenty years has tended towards specialisation, so that each of the major poems has become a separate force field of particular concerns. In 'Fra Lippo Lippi', for example, that force field is Florence in the fifteenth century, and, related to this, debates in the nineteenth century about Renaissance art in the context of history and religion. For 'A Death in the Desert' the context is Browning's study of nineteenth-century Bible scholarship and Higher Criticism, writings that were beginning to historicize an understanding of the Gospels and to open out debate about who Christ really was (simply a primitive Jewish prophet or, in theological terms, both fully human and fully God?). The debate about the Higher Criticism was also, centrally of course, a debate about how we read texts, in this case the texts comprising the Bible.

The following sections will enter into detail about some of the critical debates on particular poems, but, in doing this, they try to keep in mind the larger question of a potential centre of concern. In *Men and Women* and *Dramatis Personae*, as later in *The Ring and the Book*, Browning pulls us in two directions at once. On the one hand he relativizes knowledge, throwing the reader into a confusion of experience (comprising different historical periods, different speakers, different world-views, etc.), on the other hand, he seems to be pulling all this variety back towards a centre, a centre rooted in beliefs underpinned by his liberal Protestant Christianity.

These volumes are centripetal and centrifugal, with individual poems working in the same way. A given monologue will throw us into a particular historical setting, into the mind of an individual and his or her preoccupations, into particular ways of thinking and speaking – manifestly different from our own: we visit, as it were, another consciousness historically situated. Yet we are expected to deduce from this experience something relating to Browning's own core of beliefs. This tactic variously exhilarates or annoys critics, depending on their own belief-systems.

(i) 'A Toccata of Galuppi's': deconstructive vs. historical readings

---

A brief outline of this stanzaic dramatic monologue is given in Part II **[94]**. The speaker of the monologue is a nineteenth-century scientist, or at least amateur of science, who imagines the life of Venice in the eighteenth century. He has either heard or himself played a fast piece of music, a toccata, by the Venetian composer Baldassaro Galuppi (1706–85), and it is this music that sets his mind buzzing with images of Venice.

The speaker patches together an extraordinary image of the city, comprised of properties like the Doge in the *bucentoro* (his grand golden barge) throwing a ring into the sea to 'wed' it at the special annual festival (6), the dances and masques of the Carnival season (10–12), and a pair of young lovers (13–18). The piece of music survives from this past, and can now be played a hundred years after its original composition, while 'Venice and her people' have passed away (40). The Republic of Venice lost its independence in 1797, first to the French, and then to the Austrians. The young people of the city, their lives devoted to pleasure, have also passed away, leaving 'not a rack behind'. And so the speaker meditates on death and the ruins of time, a meditation on which the poem ends.

Herbert Tucker, a critic associated with deconstruction, tends to exclude referentiality or context from his readings. (The significance of this is examined later.) Tucker reads the monologue in relation to his larger thesis, and in a highly reflexive way. Browning's main

170

problem, as Tucker sees it, was to grow beyond his major influences – Tucker, following Bloom, takes the major precursor poet to be Shelley – and so open out his own poetic space. Having begun to open out this space and begun to write, Browning had to continue to open out new space, to resist closure: he had to open out more imaginative space rather than drawing his work to a conclusion. Browning had to resist, in this view, internal conclusions or lines that would inhibit further explorations of his imaginative world.

Tucker sees 'A Toccata of Galuppi's' as a miniature enactment of this thesis, the speaker of the poem, on the one hand, seeking to impose a conclusive moral judgement on eighteenth-century Venice by interpreting Galuppi's toccata in a reductive way, and on the other hand being betrayed by his deeper imaginative responses into a prolonged reverie. If the speaker succeeded quickly with the reductive reading of the toccata's meaning that he proposes in stanza 1 the poem would simply stop. But then Tucker feels that (for the speaker, as for Browning) the 'possibility of closure' is then pushed away by the 'desire' that awakens within the speaker's poem.

Take the opening stanza:

> Oh Galuppi, Baldassaro, this is very sad to find!
> I can hardly misconceive you; it would prove me deaf and blind;
> But although I take your meaning, 't is with such a heavy mind!
> (1–3)

The speaker seems to say here that he has completely understood the music, grasped its one-and-only meaning, and that that meaning makes him 'heavy' or sad. Looking later in the poem, we can see what the one-and-only meaning is. It is basically 'Dust and ashes' (35, 43). Galuppi's music has a sad strain in it, sad sequences of harmonies (19–20) which (in the speaker's view) should have been heeded by the Venetians who first heard it. Galuppi's music contains, as it were, a warning about death (24), and so a call to seriousness, which the speaker (being a serious person) believes he immediately understands, but which he is sure that the original Venetian listeners must have ignored (28–30). The Venetians devoted their lives to sex and pleasure and could not encompass an awareness of death, and they therefore passed blithely on their way to 'dust and ashes'. In the same manner, eighteenth-century Venice itself – saturated in hedonism – headed straight on towards its political doom.

Tucker reads the speaker in ways similar to his interpretation of the Duke in 'My Last Duchess'. At first the speaker is determined to impose his reductive interpretation on Galuppi's toccata, but then, almost immediately, finds the 'erotic energies' of his own imagination generating more complicated, less reducible, images and meanings. In the opening of the monologue the speaker sets out to simply condemn the young Venetians' hedonism, but then, in the central stanzas, he finds himself almost falling in love with them.

It is worth pausing over the central stanzas because of their difficulty. The speaker has been building up for himself an image of eighteenth-century Venice, and at the heart of that image is a typical man and woman, lost (as he sees it) in the mires of sensuality and decadence. The young woman, with the 'superb' breasts (15) is partnered by the young man who sits fidgeting with his sword (17). The scene, we have to imagine, is set in about 1750, in a grand Venetian saloon. The couple are supposed to be listening to Baldassaro Galuppi playing on the clavichord (18). Instead they are engaged in a flirtatious discussion about their own love-affair, oblivious (as the speaker sees it) to the hints about death present in the music.

The speaker's comments on the death-hinting tones of the music modulate into his imaginative recreation of their sexy conversation:

> What? Those lesser thirds so plaintive, sixths diminished, sigh on sigh,
> Told them something? Those suspensions, those solutions –
> 'Must we die?'
> Those commiserating sevenths – 'Life might last! we can but try!'
>
> 'Were you happy?' – 'Yes.' – 'And are you still as happy?' –
> 'Yes. And you?'
> 'Then, more kisses !' – 'Did I stop them, when a million seemed so few?'
> Hark, the dominant's persistence till it must be answered to!
> (19–24)

The speaker only hears in Galuppi's music an obsession with closure, a sure knowledge of endings (whether of a piece of music or of life). However, it is his own erotic imaginings that create a world with seemingly no endings, where kisses go on forever, even beyond a million. But in speaking of seriousness / death, and of eroticism / beauty, the speaker is really speaking about different parts of himself, his own inner being. As Tucker says, 'Browning's complex speaker unsteadily commiserates or condemns the various intentions that make him up':

This speaker is quite capable of conducting a partial critique of his own conclusive rigidities; what enables him to do so is the irrepressible erotic susceptibility that surfaces in the central stanzas quoted above. It is only through his imagination in those stanzas that the ghosts of the Venetian lovers present themselves and make their haunting speeches; and it remains a moot point whether, even in the speaker's own mind, the mutual responsiveness of their playful questions and answers may not scold him more than the sober responsibility of his intrusive 'Hark' scolds them.

Although in the penultimate movement of the poem [stanzas 12 to 14] the speaker safely distances himself from his imagined lovers, regarding them collectively as a dying generation 'born to bloom and drop' in 'mirth and folly' (40–41), the delicate specificities of his earlier stanzas have already given such deterministic generalizations the lie. He has heard in Galuppi's music not the monotone of a single meaning, ... but the different meanings of antiphonal voices.

(Tucker 1980: 191)

In lines 35–42 the speaker imagines the music directly 'speaking' its meaning to him, though really of course these lines are just his interpretation of what the music is saying. The music seems a direct condemnation of the Venetians and a validation of his own seriousness. But then again, in the final lines (43–5), imagining the lovely blonde hair of the Venetian women ('the gold | Used to hang and brush their bosoms') the speaker again becomes (in Tucker's terms) 'unsteady', commiserating with rather than condemning them.

This summary of Tucker's reading points to one of the main characteristics of his critical approach: its concern with rhetoric and reflexivity, and its relative reluctance to refer outwards to biography, history, or politics. If we were to treat this reading in unsympathetic terms we could say that the gist of it lies in the conflict between the speaker's thoughts about death and his thoughts about sex. The speaker starts with death-filled, serious thoughts, then moves in the middle stanzas to life-filled erotic thoughts, and then, via stanzas 12 to 14, collapses back to thoughts of death and loneliness: 'I feel chilly and grown old' (45). Stripped of a sophisticated critical framework, the poem becomes a meditation on the limits of life and the sadness of death.

In the work of Tucker, John Maynard, Warwick Slinn and others, deconstruction in various forms and in various nuances has been a significant vein in Browning criticism over the last twenty years. But, as with criticism on other writers, biography, history, politics, etc. have been making a significant return. Tucker's reading leaves out of account some simple questions. What did Browning think of his speaker? What did he intend his readers to think of his speaker? What did Browning think about eighteenth-century Venice? Addressing these kinds of questions, critics opposed to deconstruction tend to take a more positive view of Browning's speaker, seeing him as a man we can at least *partly* trust.

In an after-dinner conversation in 1863, with Edward Bulwer-Lytton, Edward Ward, and Henry Adams (the American writer), Browning gave his views about the importance of seriousness and the afterlife. A version of what he said was recorded by Henry Adams, and it is a useful context for 'A Toccata of Galuppi's':

> Browning went on to get into a very unorthodox humor, and developed a theory of spiritual election that would shock the Pope, I fear. According to him, the minds or souls that really did develop themselves and educate themselves in life, could alone expect to enter a future career for which this life was a preparatory course. The rest were rejected, turned back, God knows what becomes of them; these myriads of savages and brutalized and degraded Christians. Only those that could pass the examination, were allowed to commence the new career. This is Calvin's theory, modified; and really it seems not unlikely to me.
>
> (14 May 1863) (Levenson 1982: i. 355)

For critics opposed to deconstruction, a passage like this provides a gloss on the poem. Browning is here presenting a modified version of the views of the afterlife in Plato's *Phaedo*, one of his favourite books. He is also clearly echoing one aspect of 'A Toccata of Galuppi's': the speaker's view that he, as a serious person, developing his abilities in physics, geology, and maths (37–8), may be properly educating his soul to pass upwards to higher stages after death, whereas the Venetians may simply cease to exist at death, because they have lived their lives as thoughtlessly as 'butterflies':

> 'The soul, doubtless, is immortal – where a soul can be discerned' (36),
> 'Butterflies may dread extinction, – you'll not die, it cannot be!' (39).

This is *not*, of course, to collapse the gap between Browning, the poet, and the dramatic speaker of the poem. As various critics have noted, aspects of the speaker's character make him quite dissimilar to Browning. Ian Jack describes him as a 'rather limited autodidact', who has 'never been "out of England", knows little of the layout of Venice, and is remarkably complacent' (*Oxford* v. 55). Others have noted how his speech is dominated by metaphors derived from money (35) and by a scientific emphasis on rationality (31–2), and also his slightly querulous, awkward air (Hawlin 1990b). In this, and various other ways, Browning oversees the speaker's character ironically, just as he oversees the characters of Andrea del Sarto and Fra Lippo Lippi. Despite all this, Browning's own emphasis in the passage above on the importance of developing and educating oneself in this life in preparation for the spiritual life to come does make an obvious connection with the speaker, and means that, though the speaker is clearly narrow-minded in some respects, as readers we are basically expected to be on his side. The speaker is endorsed by Browning in a similar manner to his earlier endorsement of Paracelsus. The speaker's serious quest for knowledge and understanding is valued (though with caveats) in opposition to the unexamined lives of the Venetians.

(ii) Historical readings of 'Fra Lippo Lippi'

As this discussion should make clear, one trend in Browning criticism has been to bring back 'referentiality', i.e. a sense of how poetry should be read in the context of biography, history, and politics. John Woolford and Daniel Karlin, for example, speak of how they welcome the 'rehabilitation of context as a legitimate and urgent subject' (Woolford and Karlin 1996: vii). This tendency can also be seen in treatments of 'Fra Lippo Lippi'.

In this monologue, as in so many of the monologues, Browning is using historical knowledge to recreate a particular historical moment and a particular individual within that moment. In this case, as described earlier **[84–7]**, it is a spring night in the Florence of the 1440s, and the individual is the painter-monk Fra Lippo Lippi caught at that particular point in time. In other monologues it is other people, times, and locations: in 'Epistle of Karshish' an Arab physician on a particular day in AD 66 in Palestine; in 'Holy-Cross Day' a Jewish man on a christian feast-day in Lent in 1600 in Rome; in 'A Death in the Desert' the apostle St John, in about AD 100, somewhere in a desert cave near the Greek town of Ephesus. Browning, in other words, is a historicist, concerned to situate some of his dramatic speeches in an exact context and to understand them as growing out of those contexts. He also shows, to some extent, the second reflex of historicists, a consciousness doubling back on itself 'to explore the extent to which any historical enterprise inevitably reflects the interests and bias of the period in which it was written' (Hamilton 1996: 3).

New historicism and historicism generally is one of the significant critical emphases of the last twenty years, an emphasis that has led to the relationship between literary works and their historical contexts being explored in interesting, sometimes tendentious, ways. Its biggest single effect has been to problematize how we look at the historical past and how we reconstruct it. Broadly speaking, it has made critics very aware of how they approach the past with their own preoccupations: '[New historicists] seek to minimize the distortion inherent in their perceptions and representations [of the past] by admitting that they see through preconceived notions; in other words, they learn to reveal the color of the lenses in the glasses that they wear' (Murfin 1996: 224). Within this context, critics have become more sensitive about how Browning represents history and what exactly he thinks he is achieving through this endeavour.

The best short treatment of this subject is Joseph Bristow's 'Histories and Historicism' (in Bristow 1991: 67–127). Bristow takes as his starting point the statement that 'the nineteenth century was the age of historicism' and J. Hillis Miller's influential assertion that 'the dramatic monologue is par excellence the literary genre of historicism' (Miller 1963: 108). Bristow then explores the ways in which history as a subject opened out in the nineteenth century, both in a simple sense in the study of geology, which was gradually making clearer the ancientness of the planet, and in a subtler sense in the Higher Criticism (the work of David Friedrich Strauss, Ernest Renan, Benjamin Jowett, and others) which was gradually setting the Bible texts more and more in their historical context and understanding them from within that context. Some of that historicism can now be seen to be naive, but nonetheless in its time it represented a major shift of awareness.

In 'Fra Lippo Lippi' Browning goes out of his way to recreate something of the otherness or relativity of the past, the presumptions and preoccupations of a different era, and how people might have thought in that era. Because we now tend to meet the historical monologues in well-annotated modern editions (which explain all the historical references) this aspect of them may be lost on us. But consider: Lippi's Florence is one where the Medici family wield great political influence, where the law is maintained by 'the Eight' (121), and where, when happy, one might sing a *stornello* (53–7); it is a world of Black Friars and White Friars (145), of Carmelites, Camaldolese, and Dominicans (139–40), of carnival, antiphonaries, and the importance of Latin. More importantly it is a world in which art is discussed in religious terms, where someone like the Prior (anticipating the views of the Dominican preacher Girolamo Savonarola later in the fifteenth century) can accuse Lippi of materialism and sensuality in his painting (174–98). If, however, Browning recreates the otherness of the past, relativizes it in relation to his own times, casting readers into another epoch in which they have to find their bearings, so – as surely and completely – he aims to deliver definitive judgements which he expects his readers to pick up. For a critic like Joseph Bristow this represents a not altogether satisfying paradox. Browning, in his poems about the Renaissance and about the times of Christ, is

> ... identifying forms of divine revelation – in high art as well as Christ's miracles. And in both Browning finds it extremely difficult to handle the problems of metapoetic authority invested in the claims he is making about God's evolutionary plan. This is perhaps his major epistemological problem. For he has to take up a highly authoritative position, one set over against his personae, to indicate how and why he is correct, while they, more often than not, remain in error. His generous receptivity to the findings of the historicists is counter-weighted by his overinterpretive desire to impress the idea that his historical model, which is also God's, is the right one. At times, the liberal-minded Browning can haunt his speakers' voices in tones that verge on the dogmatic. Each poem under discussion here ['Fra Lippo Lippi', 'Andrea del Sarto', 'Karshish', 'Cleon'] exposes the considerable tension that builds up between his interest in relativising human truth claims (allowing a variety of opinions; giving the individual freedom of speech; enabling irony to disrupt relations between intention and meaning) and a religious concern with encircling these ever contingent beliefs beneath an incontestable faith in divine truth (God's historical plan; the poet's privilege to reveal it; and its magnanimous capacity to absorb all objections to its unstoppable movement towards the millennium).
>
> (Bristow 1991: 72)

This is an excellent (if hostile) description of how a poem like 'Fra Lippo Lippi' works. First, there is the 'relativizing of human truth claims'. Lippi is the underdog in the poem, a square peg in a round hole. Within his particular social situation he is apparently a complete failure. As a supposedly celibate monk, he has been caught by the police near a brothel. He admits generally that, particularly in Carnival time, he finds it virtually impossible not to 'kiss the girls' (225). As a novice, he has proved useless at learning Latin, the official language of the church (108–9). He often finds the religious subjects he is obliged to paint dull and repetitive (48–9). He is not on the best of terms with his present patron, Cosimo the Elder, who has had to lock him in a room to keep him at this work (47–8). Moreover, within the poem, he has to argue his case for the innovative style of naturalism against the Prior's insistence on purism (i.e. the superiority of the styles of Giotto, Lorenzo Monaco, and Fra Angelico). The Prior, as the head of the monastery, has all ecclesiastical authority on his side; Lippi is powerless.

Pulling the other way to all this, is Browning's concern 'to encircle these ever contingent beliefs beneath an incontestable faith in divine truth' (Bristow 1991: 72). So, out of this unenviable situation, Lippi's passionate defence of naturalistic art eventually wins out, particularly in the wonderful centre of the monologue at lines 270–92, and his rumbustious, vivid character wins our sympathy, overpowering the sterilities and hypocrisies of his opponents. Outside the monologue, he is vindicated by history: his art is now (in the nineteenth century) revered (at least by some), and the underdog of the poem has his paintings in the most important art galleries of Florence. His advocacy of naturalism, which looks frail, actually (as the monologue implies) puts him on the side of progress in art, setting the ground for the achievements of the High Renaissance (Raphael, Leonardo, Michelangelo). And, of course, his defence of naturalism is partly Browning's defence of his own art, an art which only makes its way towards high ideals by letting in the complexity, resistance, ugliness and evil of real experience.

So far, so good. But what historically-based criticism has also been able to show about 'Fra Lippo Lippi' is how it is part of a complex debate within the nineteenth century about the relationship between history, art, and religion: that is to say, it is not 'innocent' historical reconstruction, but a document within a religious-aesthetic argument in its own time. David DeLaura (1980) was the first to make this fully clear, and his findings have been deployed since in most readings of the poem. This background is complicated and nuanced. The following brief account draws on DeLaura, Bristow (1991), and Bullen (1994).

To start with, we have to remember that nineteenth-century Protestants did not always take easily to religious art that was explicitly Roman Catholic in its subject-matter. England was still a strongly Protestant nation, and Italian Renaissance art, in being focused around explicitly Catholic subject-matter (the Madonna, saints, the Sacrament of Communion, etc.), was still not easily or unguardedly appreciated:

[T]he assimilation of medieval art in English taste was as much bedevilled by religious (rather than political) issues as by those aesthetic considerations which I have already discussed: pure or monkish, rising above the superstition of the age or contributing to it? Endless arguments were deployed on both sides, and it was – during the first half of the nineteenth century – certainly difficult to express very warm feelings for early Italian art without committing oneself to other allegiances as well. [i.e. without being sympathetic to or directly aligned with High Anglicanism or Roman Catholicism]

(Haskell 1976: 65)

Liberal Protestants like Browning, of course, did not find it difficult to appreciate the art of paintings whose Roman Catholic subject-matter they did not directly endorse, nonetheless this negotiation remains a significant background presence in the poem: one of Lippi's arguments, after all, is that his paintings are inspired by a love of the world's beauty, not by a particular veneration for the Virgin Mary or the saints.

What heightened this subtle tension between the Protestant viewer and Roman Catholic art was an ultra-Roman Catholic reading of the Renaissance by the art critic Alexis Rio, *De la poésie chrétienne* (1836; 'The Poetry of Christian Art', translated 1854). Rio distinguished between the earlier and later phases of fifteenth-century Italian art, and he identified what he saw as a gradual (if uneven) decline from a purist, idealised, or spiritual style of painting (Fra Angelico is its greatest exponent) to a more pagan, sensualized, materialistic, or naturalistic style of painting; even Raphael's work, for Rio, was finally ruined by this unspiritualized realism, an idolatry of the inner resources of art rather than a devotion of art to the worship of God. Lippi, perhaps because of his known profligacy and his seduction of the nun Lucrezia Buti, became the central villain in this history of decline: 'Lippi may be considered, in many respects, a *mannered* artist, and without injustice may be reproached with having sown the first seeds of decadence in the Florentine school' (Rio 1854: 91). Rio describes how this naturalism – 'a development that might almost be called fatal' – broke up the previous unity of purpose that had characterized the body of artists:

some continuing to receive their inspirations from above, while the others, who formed indeed the greater number, fell into the snare spread for them by naturalism, and no longer sought to connect their arbitrary creations with that centre of unity from

whence painting, like all the other Christian arts, had originally
proceeded.

(Rio 1854: 114)

This view was widely influential, not necessarily concentrated on
Lippi, but as a general reading of Renaissance art. The art critic Anna
Jameson (1794–1860), who was Browning's friend, repeated it in her
Memoirs of the Early Italian Painters (1845). Following Rio, she also singled
out Fra Lippo Lippi:

This libertine monk was undoubtedly a man of extraordinary
genius, but his talent was degraded by his immorality: he adopted
and carried on all the improvements of Masaccio ... but the
expression he gave to his personages, though always energetic, was
often inappropriate, and never calm or elevated: in the
representation of sacred incidents he was sometimes fantastic and
sometimes vulgar.

(Jameson 1845: 113–14)

In 'Fra Lippo Lippi' itself, the views of the Prior (175–98, 316–19)
present, in a weakened and caricatured form, a version of Rio's argument.

Browning's poem, in other words, is part of a complex nineteenth-
century debate about art and religion, a debate which addressed more
fundamental issues than the simple merits or demerits of Fra Filippo
Lippi as a painter. How, for instance, does Christian art work? Is there
such a thing as a specifically *Christian* art?

In Alexis Rio's understanding, paintings of religious subject-matter
served a *directly* spiritual function: a painting of a saint could help you
pray to that saint; a painting of the Madonna of the Seven Sorrows
could help you contemplate the Madonna's sufferings and help you
pray to her. Paintings help to insert their viewers into the life of religious
grace: they could educate viewers in the realities of Bible stories and
hence inspire the viewers' lives, they could help them towards the
contemplation of divine mysteries, and they could lead their minds
towards prayer. Paintings are spiritual pathways. Rio quotes with
approval the words of Buffalmacco: 'We painters occupy ourselves
entirely in tracing saints on the walls and on the altars, in order that
by this means men, to the great despite of the demons, may be more
drawn to virtue and piety' (Rio 1854: 69).

This view of art as a direct spiritual medium and agency is caricatured by Lippi at lines 313–35, an indication of how Browning is aware
of this view and is arguing with it. In this sense Browning's reading of

Lippi's paintings (implicit in the poem) is a profound reflex of his liberal Protestantism. His view is clearly opposed to Rio's. In Browning's view religious paintings do not help us contemplate specific religious teachings, neither do they improve our lives by helping us contemplate the exemplary lives of saints, nor are they *immediate* aids or pathways to prayer. Rather they work in more diffuse and general aesthetic terms, awaking us to the beauty of the human form and face, and awakening us to the loveliness of the physical world. They alert us to

> – The beauty and the wonder and the power,
> The shapes of things, their colours, lights and shades,
> Changes, surprises, – and God made it all!
> (283–5)

Only via this aesthetic pleasure do they lead us (implicitly, and indirectly) to a potential consideration of God. In this way, as a Protestant, Browning frees himself to read and appreciate paintings with specifically Roman Catholic subject-matter. His manoeuvre within the poem is essentially similar to that of his friend Anna Jameson who distinguished strongly between 'poetic' and 'religious' readings of Roman Catholic art:

> I hope it will be clearly understood that I have taken throughout the aesthetic and not the religious view of those productions of art which, in as far as they are informed with a true and earnest feeling, and steeped in that beauty which emanates from genius inspired by faith, may cease to be Religion, but cannot cease to be Poetry; and as poetry only I have considered them.
> (Jameson 1848: xi–xii)

This is, in effect, nineteenth-century code for 'I am not a Roman Catholic'!

This reading of 'Fra Lippo Lippi' takes us a long way. Browning, the historicist poet, has himself been historicised, and his poem set within the Catholic–Protestant art debates and tensions of his own time.

(iii) 'Childe Roland': psychoanalytic vs. historical readings

---

'Childe Roland', Browning's most enigmatic poem, takes us further into the problems of reading him. Initially we might be tempted simply to leave it alone. It is clear enough how it has its origin in the line from

Edgar's song in *King Lear* (III. 4. 182), and how it presents the voice of Childe Roland, a quester knight, relating his journey through a blighted landscape. But the usual signs and signals are missing. This is not a historicist poem in any meaningful sense: it has only a vague medieval setting and no clear date. Moreover, ambiguously, the knight Roland speaks to us about events in the past, yet he breaks off his narrative at what appears a thrilling, climactic moment. Isn't this monologue just atypical of Browning's work, only a product of some strange welling up of the unconscious? Can't we ignore it?

In Part II **[94–6]** some of the perplexities of criticism were outlined, yet at the same time it was made clear that this is one of Browning's most discussed works. Critics come back to it again and again, as somehow being central. Turning from the almost lush eroticism of 'A Toccata of Galuppi's' (see stanza 4 for example) or from the lyrical climax of 'Fra Lippo Lippi' (280–92) to the world of 'Childe Roland' is like moving from some sunny impressionist painting to the most macabre of Albert Dürer's etchings. Yet it is just this vitality of the grotesque that has so fascinated critics, its sharp visual brilliance enacted in an often rough, frictive language. The famous instance is the blind horse:

> One stiff blind horse, his every bone a-stare,
> Stood stupefied, however he came there:
> Thrust out past service from the devil's stud!
>
> Alive? he might be dead for aught I know,
> With that red gaunt and colloped neck a-strain,
> And shut eyes underneath the rusty mane;
> Seldom went such grotesqueness with such woe;
> I never saw a brute I hated so;
> He must be wicked to deserve such pain.
> (76–84)

Line 80 clinches this description, but no one is quite sure what 'colloped' means. A collop is a slice of meat, so one synonym often suggested is 'raw', yet 'colloped', subtly reacting with 'red' and 'gaunt' (words whose meaning we do know), is more forceful. It suggests, I think, that the sinews or muscles of the neck are somehow exposed, as in a stark anatomical drawing.

Two of the best recent readings of 'Childe Roland' are by Daniel Karlin and Donald Hair, and I want to compare and contrast them. Karlin's reading is primarily psychoanalytical: it concentrates on the emotions happening within the poem (and, implicitly, within the poet). It is also intertextual (it relates 'Childe Roland' to another Browning poem 'The Englishman in Italy'). Hair's reading is historically based, it refers outwards more overtly. It relates the poem to Browning's Protestant religious sensibility and to his readings in seventeenth-century Emblem books. Which reading should we prefer?

Karlin's first move on 'Childe Roland' is startling: he relates it to 'The Englishman in Italy' in *Dramatic Romances and Lyrics*, a poem originally called 'England in Italy'. 'The Englishman in Italy' looks at first like an innocent travelogue. We know that on his 1844 journey to Italy Browning stayed (probably with a peasant family) in the beautiful Sorrento peninsula south of Naples, and the poem seems to be (with only a thin dramatic gloss) his own account of the sights and sounds of the countryside in autumn. Karlin notices, however, that the poem describes a journey by mule through that countryside, up the side of Mount Calvano and on down to the sea and a view of the so-called Sirens' islands or Galli. The sinister mountains of lines 181–96 seem to anticipate the mountains of 'Childe Roland' (165 f.), but, more strikingly, on one of the islands 'the strange square black turret | With never a door' (219–20) anticipates Roland's 'round squat turret, blind as the fool's heart, | Built of brown stone' (182–3). With this intertextual link, we can see that we have two journeys towards towers, though the things seen during these two journeys appear very different: in the one case almost excessively beautiful, in the other case intensely ugly and nightmarish. But Karlin sees similarities. In both cases, there is a similar kind of energy in the descriptions, and in both cases the descriptions seem self-reflexive – they are metaphors for the inner emotions of the speaker as much as they are objective observations.

Because of this, the beautiful descriptions of 'The Englishman in Italy' sometimes come close to toppling over into the grotesque world of 'Childe Roland'. The best instance is the speaker's description of his listener's brother as he struggles to tread down the grapes in the wine vat:

> In the vat, halfway up in our house-side,
>   Like blood the juice spins,
> While your brother all bare-legged is dancing
>   Till breathless he grins
> Dead-beaten in effort on effort
>   To keep the grapes under,
> Since still when he seems all but master,
>   In pours the fresh plunder
>   (73–80)

If this passage is read innocently, it is just a description of the abundance of the grape-harvest and of a boy struggling to cope with the excess. But the image of the wine as 'blood' and of the boy as 'dead-beaten' with exhaustion, almost drowned in the flood of grapes, suggests an intensely beautiful image tipping over into something more sinister. In another passage, lines 150–61 – about the speaker's journey by mule up Mount Calvano – parts of the description again have sinister overtones. There are, for example, the 'piles of loose stones | Like the loose broken teeth | Of some monster which climbed there to die' (153–5) and 'dark rosemary ever a-dying | That, 'spite the wind's wrath, | So loves the salt rock's face to seaward' (159–61). These images, says Karlin, would require only a small shift of context to become nightmarish and Roland-like:

> In both 'Childe Roland' and 'England in Italy' ['The Englishman in Italy'] a daemonic energy informs the descriptions, though in one poem the mode is orgiastic and in the other grotesque or perverse ... Perhaps the most disturbing thing about such images is the very imaginative energy which informs them. Roland is erotically drawn to death, worships the power whose cruelty appals him, finds hatred, in the end, a more animating idea than love; but his *mode* of perception brings him closer to that of the speaker of 'England in Italy' than is comfortable for either of them.
>
> (Karlin 1993: 244–6)

Both poems, as it were, are erotically charged, one positively, the other negatively. In Roland's case there is a 'horrific displacement of the erotic across the physical features of the landscape' so that all the time the knight is encountering images of bestiality, mutilation, impurity, and disease (p. 255). That blind horse, emphasized earlier, once part of the 'Devil's stud' – i.e. *once* sexually vital and capable of siring other horses – is a case in point. The speaker hates the horse so passionately 'that his self-identification with it is almost too forcibly suggested' (p. 256). He is himself, as it were, the 'blind' knight 'Thrust out past service from the devil's stud' – in Roland's case thrust out from 'The Band' (39), the company of his fellow knights that has long since dissolved. Roland, like the horse, is exhausted, lonely, and impotent.

Karlin's comparison between 'The Englishman in Italy' and 'Childe Roland' brings out the essential loneliness of the two speakers, and the highly self-reflexive, even solipsistic mode of these poems. (The speaker of 'The Englishman in Italy' technically has a listener, the girl Fortù, but for much of the poem she is asleep and absent from the monologue's action, and in the end the speaker hardly relates to her at all.) In both poems the speakers journey on alone, defining their inner emotional worlds by means of the landscapes, showing 'an erotic preoccupation with the self, solitary and exposed' (p. 256). What Karlin is challenging here is a too simple notion of Browning as a poet of love and relationships. 'Childe Roland', like 'The Englishman in Italy', is about the lonely perceiving self, which is so starkly alert to its own inner condition – via the medium of the landscape – just partly because it is so fully on its own. To put it simply, the energies of these poems are intensely introverted, and we should keep a sense of the power of that introversion as part of their meaning.

Donald Hair's reading of 'Childe Roland' points the way to a wholly different kind of criticism. There is not space here to relate his reading in the same detail as Karlin's, but a brief outline can set the reader on the track. For Hair, Browning's Protestantism is crucial to reading the poem, as is his love of seventeenth-century Emblem books. Hair's 'Childe Roland' is not an introverted, self-preoccupied narrative of awkward sexuality, but rather a poem of religious questing, through despair, sin, and the awareness of sin, to some kind of self-knowledge and affirmation. Hair agrees with Karlin about the essentially reflexive nature of the descriptions – that is to say, 'the inner action of the poem is interpretation', the speaker's responses to the landscape are really his inner responses to his own heart and soul – but he sees a religious framework (rather than a Freudian-sexual framework) as the context in which we should read these images.

In Hair's reading the varying qualities of the speaker's acts of seeing and interpretation through the course of the poem become a mapping out of his inner spiritual journey. For example, the words that the speaker attributes to 'Nature' in stanza 11 are really about himself: 'It nothing skills: I cannot help my case' (64). These words reflect his own passivity at this stage, and they are also the deeply traditional cry of the religious soul lost in sin without a knowledge of God. Hair sees such phrases through the poem as one of the ways in which it maps out a religious journey: 'quiet as despair' (43) ... 'He must be wicked to deserve such pain' (84) ... 'The round squat turret, blind as the fool's heart' (182). At the start of the poem, the 'hoary cripple' is less an objective fact than 'a projection from within Roland', a figuration of his own crippled self-understanding. In Roland's ensuing spiritual progression, Hair's reading of the blind horse is strikingly different from Karlin's:

Roland's conversion begins with the sight of the 'stiff blind horse.'
He names the details of the animal's appearance, and then proceeds
from such images to interpretation: 'He must be wicked to deserve
such pain' (84). That interpretation leads Roland to a conviction
of sin, the first stage in conversion.

(Hair 1999: 105–6)

The reading of the tower is similarly different. What is important
to Hair is that it is a 'round squat turret': 'towers conventionally are
associated with range and comprehensiveness of sight … [whereas here
the tower] dwindled and shrunk – a parody of a watch tower … is
associated with limited perception'. Then:

The phrase 'blind as the fool's heart' is crucial. The poem itself
defines the word 'fool' in the parenthesis in stanza 25: '(so a fool
finds mirth, | Makes a thing and then mars it, till his mood |
Changes and off he goes!)' (147–9).The fool is changeable in mood,
making and lightly discarding images without grasping their
significance; the wise man (as in Carlyle) stares fixedly at the thing
until its meaning reveals itself.

(Hair 1999: 107)

The poem's ending marks a moment of self-knowledge, where
Roland finally frees himself from the dark landscape of the soul that
lies at the centre of the poem. This reading clearly responds strongly
to the shift of mood, the tone of grim triumph, in the final stanza:

There they [the spirits of my fellow knights] stood, ranged along
    the hill-sides, met
To view the last of me, a living frame
For one more picture! in a sheet of flame [the sunset]
I saw them and I knew them all. And yet
Dauntless the slug-horn to my lips I set,
And blew. '*Childe Roland to the Dark Tower came.*' (199–204)

This sketch of Hair's reading needs to be hedged with caveats. Hair
is not reducing the poem to a religious allegory (confusion, despair,
inner lack of knowledge, awakening self-consciousness, the rejection
of spiritual blindness), but he is suggesting that the poem mirrors some
of the patterns of belief that Browning drew from his Protestant
(specifically Congregational) background. Ideas of spiritual insight,
moments of self-understanding and conversion, are deeply written into

the Christian sensibility, and when Roland encounters the tower he does seem to be naming and triumphing over something within himself. The 'dark tower' is as 'blind' or unperceiving as the fool's heart, – the allusion is to Psalm 14: 'The fool hath said in his heart, There is no God' – and such an allusion, at this point, lifts up the ending and contributes to its feeling of hope.

Hair would be quite happy for us to see the poem as essentially a surreal inner phantasmagoria of intense visual power, but he would want to insist that patterns concerned with despair and the escape from despair are rooted in Browning's religious outlook. The *'came'* (204) in the last line of the poem, which repeats the title, is for him a layered word. The knight has not just 'come' in the sense of changing geographical location. Hair sees the word taking on, if only metaphorically, other definitions (which he takes from Johnson's *Dictionary*): 'to attain any condition or character', 'to change condition either for better or worse', 'to advance from one stage or condition to another' (pp. 108–9).

(iv) 'The Heretic's Tragedy' and the grotesque

I want to end this section by thinking about a relative blindspot in recent Browning criticism: an appreciation of the grotesque, and to concentrate this discussion on a particular poem exemplary of this mode. The grotesque was famously defined by John Ruskin, Browning's contemporary, in 'The Nature of Gothic' (1853), and it was well defined in the twentieth century by various critics, particularly Mikhail Bakhtin, who saw it as a mode contrary to a neoclassical aesthetic of harmony, grace, and perfection. The word is usually used of a comically exaggerated and distorted mode that lets in dark and tragic elements, or – more exactly perhaps – that mixes tragedy and comedy, grace and ugliness, the smooth and the guttural, in surreal or unstable combinations. In a more limited sense, the word has been associated with Browning from at least the time of Walter Bagehot's essay 'Wordsworth, Tennyson and Browning; or Pure, Ornate, and Grotesque Art in English Poetry' (1864). Bagehot's emphasis was mainly on questions of style and vocabulary: he characterized Wordsworth as having a 'pure' style (plain, limpid, direct), Tennyson as having an 'ornate' style (sonorous, elaborate), and Browning as 'grotesque' (i.e. often deliberately difficult, awkward, and ugly). Adam Roberts has taken up this theme in his *Browning Revisited* (1996). He quotes an earlier critic, J. Hillis Miller, who wonderfully evokes how Browning's twisted, frictive language often gives his poetry a dense physicality:

Grotesque metaphors, ugly words heavy with consonants, stuttering alliteration, strong active verbs, breathless rhythms, onomatopoeia, images of rank smells, rough textures, and of things fleshy, viscous, sticky, nubbly, slimy, shaggy, sharp, crawling, thorny, or prickly – all these work together in Browning's verse to create an effect of unparalleled thickness, harshness, and roughness.
(Miller 1963: 119-20)

Even a little experience of the poetry gives us access to this aspect of Browning's language. The cleft in the tree 'like a distorted mouth that splits its rim | Gaping at death' ('Childe Roland' 155), '*Bang-whang-whang* goes the drum' ('Up at a Villa' 63), 'freaked fawn-coloured flaky crew | Of toadstools' ('By the Fire-Side' 64), 'each softling of a wee white mouse | *Weke, weke*' ('Fra Lippo Lippi' 10), or, from the same poem, the oath 'Zooks' (3, 392). Examples are legion. This element of style is evident throughout the work, though – and this is an important point – it is variable between poems. In some poems about love, for example 'Love Among the Ruins', 'A Woman's Last Word', or 'Respectability', grotesqeries hardly appear at all. In 'Andrea del Sarto', whose smooth tones and images help create the artist's depressed emotions, again what we might call the 'Zooks' or 'Gr-r-r' or 'Ugh' element is kept well out of the way. When this particular kind of linguistic energy helps to create the image of a tree's cleft, the sound of a drum, the texture of mushrooms, we relish its vividness, but this kind of energy can also be considered in darker contexts: the satiric, tragi-comic evocation, for example, of a public burning in 'The Heretic's Tragedy'. Browning, as much as Shelley, explores different levels of decorum, so the high ideal that predominates in, say, 'By the Fire-Side' or 'A Toccata of Galuppi's', exists as far from the world of 'The Heretic's Tragedy' as Shelley's 'Ode to the West Wind' from his *Oedipus Tyrannus*.

Browning's 'The Heretic's Tragedy' pretends to be a medieval musical play or 'interlude', written originally by a Master Gysbrecht of Ypres, in Belgium, and then passed down, through various manuscripts, into its present form. We are overseeing, as it were, a piece of medieval church music on the subject of the burning of the Grand Master of the Templar Order, Jacques du Bourg-Molay, in Paris in 1314.

The poem has various musical indications: it is divided between different voices and a chorus, and has notes for accompaniment on organ, lute, and 'clavicithern'. It does not really have one speaker in the sense of other monologues, but it seems that we are to assume that Master Gysbrecht – whose description of the burning we hear – is the central consciousness of the poem. It is perhaps this mock-medieval frame that has set some readers on the wrong track. Ian Jack starts his commentary on the poem by describing it as 'one of Browning's studies in the perversions of religion' (*Oxford* v. 441), which is true, but leaves out of account other important aspects. The comment might lead the casual reader to think the poem is primarily a liberal Protestant satire on the practices of medieval Catholicism, a satire on a time and a culture that somehow thought that burning heretics was a good idea.

Certainly Browning oversees his speaker with irony. Black humour, and the grotesque style that enacts it, is one aspect of the poem. Who, we might ask, is this Master Gysbrecht, this churchman, who can so calmly write a composition about such horrible suffering? And who are the people who have thought it worthwhile to perform his interlude and to preserve its manuscript? The paraphernalia of the notes for performance bring out this aspect of the poem well: 'Preadmonisheth the Abbot Deodaet', '*Organ: plagal-cadence*', 'One Singeth' in their stateliness and deliberation contrast to macabre effect with the subject-matter they help to describe. So far, so good. But the more important point is that, within the poem, Browning also inhabits the voice of Master Gysbrecht.

One reading of the poem would be to assume the innocence of Jacques du Bourg-Molay in keeping with the general tendency of modern research. The assumption would be that he was not really corrupt (as his accusers stated) and that the whole suppression of the Templar Order, of which he was the head, was essentially a grab for money and land by Philip, King of France. In fact, Browning assumes Bourg-Molay's guilt and indicates this clearly in the poem.

The Bourg-Molay of the poem is cynical and worldly, and only begins to think about calling to Christ for help when he is completely trussed up by his executioners (37–44). Moreover, he is a ruthless crusader who has himself brutally and thoughtlessly executed 'infidels' (i.e. Arab people) throughout his military career. (We might notice here Browning's liberal Protestant reading of the crusades.) His prayer to Christ to save him from burning is self-righteous and couched in almost hectoring tones:

> Now it was, 'Saviour, bountiful lamb,
>   I have roasted thee Turks, though men roast me!
> See thy servant, the plight wherein I am!
>   Art thou a saviour? Save thou me!'
>
> (49–52)

Bourg-Molay is right to call for Christ's help at this terrible moment, but the question that is being begged is the quality of his prayer. In the next stanza what mitigates God's 'menace' or anger towards human evil is the figure of Christ, called by his name from the Bible, 'Sharon's rose' (Song of Solomon 2: 1). The point is that Bourg-Molay, 'the mocker', is calling on this gentle Christ in a thoroughly cynical and hypocritical way, and that at the moment of his death, Christ *does* come to meet him in answer to his prayer but in a most unexpected way.

Stanzas 9 and 10, therefore, have an extraordinary two-way effect, in keeping with the 'liberal' and 'dogmatic' elements in Browning described earlier by Bristow. In stanza 9, as the flames surround him and ignite his body, Bourg-Molay himself becomes a terrible 'rose' which unfolds petal by petal and anther by anther (74–5). This is, as it were, the liberal Browning's critique of medieval Catholicism. But in stanza 10, just at this heightened moment, Christ, the just and merciful Judge of all humankind, gradually appears to Bourg-Molay within the flames, first as a 'Name', then as a 'Person', then more intimately as a 'Face' (84). Bourg-Molay's voice (and person) 'died' (88) in the face of this overwhelming vision, which suddenly makes clear to him the reality of the religious truths he has treated so superficially throughout his life. This second aspect of the monologue is Browning's own assertion of his liberal Protestant Christianity.

We may well step back amazed at the two-way pull on us here. To put it simply, Browning is both outside and inside the voice of Master Gysbrecht. From the outside he conducts a liberal-Protestant satire on Catholicism. From the inside he touchingly approves Master Gysbrecht's sense that religious vision is real, and that Bourg-Molay was a man who had cynically used religion for the ends of wealth and power. In the end Browning's second voice, from inside the poem as it were, is the dominant one. The last line of the poem escapes from the comic-grotesque energy that precedes it, and makes itself into a ringing statement: 'God help all poor souls lost in the dark!' (89). Since it is Abbot Deodaet who prays this last line, we may view it partly as ironic: it is self-righteous and inappropriate to the occasion. But, in another sense, this really is Browning's own prayer, and the slowing of the ending makes this clear. It is a conventional, heartfelt prayer for all those 'lost in the dark', whether the dark of evil, or, as in the case of this monologue, the dark aggressions of false religion. It is a prayer for the heretic burners as well as for the corrupt Jacques du Bourg-Molay.

(e) *THE RING AND THE BOOK*: A NOVEL POEM

At 21,116 lines in length, almost exactly twice as long as *Paradise Lost*, *The Ring and the Book* is a massive poem, one that takes a lot of effort to come to terms with. Given its form, it is not necessary to read it all to get a sense of how it works. Even to read Books I to IV will give some appreciation of what is interesting and important.

The issue of the form has dominated the critical debate. Here, as we have seen **[100–15]**, Browning views the same murder-story through the eyes of nine major characters and some minor ones, each character giving different and conflicting accounts. These viewpoints grow out of their different personalities and moral presumptions. Each viewpoint is stained by the moral, emotional, and spiritual lenses with which the individual speaker looks at the events. Two main questions have arisen. Is the experiment in form a success? And should the poem be read in a transcendental or a non-transcendental way, i.e. should we read it religiously or sceptically?

The second question can look a surprising one given Browning's own presentation of the poem in Books I and XII. What Browning claims to be doing, through the multiple viewpoints, is showing us the difficulty of apprehending and telling the truth. The events of the murder-story come to us refracted through the consciousnesses of different personalities. Half-Rome (Book II), himself a wife-hater, feels that Guido was perfectly within his rights to murder a wife on suspicion of adultery. Other Half-Rome (Book III), a sentimental romantic, is sure that Pompilia is an innocent victim and Guido unjustified – and so on. Browning lets the truth of things become enmeshed in a carnivalesque confusion of claim and counter-claim, insight and distortion, showing how easily, in a world partially ruled by evil, truth can be subverted or destroyed.

But, contrary to this, Browning is absolutely sure that there is an objective truth out there to be perceived. The conflict of good and evil, and truth and falsehood implicit in the original events of the murder, is played out again in the way people perceive and judge the murder, but, over all things, sits God. The poet's aim, and our aim, must be to see through the smoke of lies and confusion to the truth of things, which is there to be perceived if we try hard enough. In the concluding section, Book XII, Browning (or the poet-speaker) claims for art the ability to transcend its linguistic limits and infer the elusive transcendent truth that escapes the 'mediate word', the word so often compromised by lies and distortion:

Why take the artistic way to prove so much?
Because, it is the glory and good of Art,
That Art remains the one way possible
Of speaking truth, to mouths like mine, at least....
                        Art may tell a truth
Obliquely, do the thing shall breed the thought,
Nor wrong the thought, missing the mediate word.
So may you paint your picture, twice show truth,
Beyond mere imagery on the wall, –
So, note by note, bring music from your mind,
Deeper than ever the Andante dived, –
So write a book shall mean, beyond the facts,
Suffice the eye and save the soul beside.
                                (xii. 837–63)

Given the later revision of line 861 to 'Deeper than ever e'en Beethoven dived' the very strongly felt allusion here is presumably to the slow movement of the last piano sonata (a work Browning comments on elsewhere). One critic hostile to what the poet claims to be doing, describes the method thus: 'The philosophical and aesthetic moral of the poem is: "By multiplying points of view on the same event, you may transcend point of view, and reach at last God's own infinite perspective"' (Miller 1963: 149). This, though, is overstating the case in order to debunk it. Browning is not claiming to reach an 'infinite perspective', but he is claiming to assert, that, despite humankind's moral frailty and self-deception, objective truth is something there to be fought for and achieved.

This view of the poem is one that a whole strain of post-structuralist and deconstructive criticism sets out to subvert. The critics' arguments, though often expressed in complex terms, can nonetheless be expressed simply.

Browning, say these critics, relativizes truth in the poem, and does so radically. In showing us 'the truth' made into different versions, he shows us that there is not really a fixed, absolute, or transcendent truth out there to be perceived. For these critics, truth is always 'truth' or 'truth claims' or 'contingent and provisional'. The Browning who, in Books I and XII, tells us that Pompilia is virtually a saint, and Guido virtually a devil, is really only another monologist within the poem, with strong limits on the validity of his perspective. All the emphasis in these readings in on just how elusive the 'truth' has become. So, Susan Blalock argues that the succession of monologues gradually takes us further away from a perceivable centre:

[E]ach monologue speaker seeks to canonize his or her version of the facts as truth ... In such an environment even the most stable facts become elusive and indeterminate ... The reader is forced to reformulate his judgments with every repetition and absorb an increasing amount of uncertainty instead of arriving at a firmer grasp on 'true events.'

(Blalock 1983: 44–5)

The most out-and-out of these readings is that by E. Warwick Slinn, who, exploiting one particular deconstructive vein, manages to make *The Ring and the Book* into an extreme essay in philosophical scepticism:

There is ... another structural principle in the poem which contradicts the truth claims of apparently fixed patterns: the principle of the supplement, or serial textualisation. By placing separate and distinctive monologues after one another, Browning employs a structure which produces a floating irony rather than fixity, indicating the gaps and differences between texts as well as within them. Each new text alters the context and therefore the signification of the previous text and that is a process that can be repeated indefinitely ... As each text produces a context which extends and alters the meaning and 'truth' of the previous one, the poem perfectly enacts the deconstructionist point that there is no meaning without context while at the same time that context is boundless ... Browning ... [weaves] a pattern of weavers weaving. It is not, therefore, the pattern of any exclusive or singular truth that is the point of the poem, not the establishing of any privileged viewpoint that displays a transcendent truth; but rather it is the pattern of patterning, the process of meaning in process, the form of forming formulations, that is the key to the poem's structural method. In this work, the singularity, the controlling thread, of an omniscient narrative is replaced by the variegated wefts of men and women who view the world through a fabric woven in language ... Meaning remains elusive, if by meaning we expect some singular, conclusive and verifiable abstraction.

(Slinn 1991: 138, 140)

Of course there have been common-sense objections to this position. Isn't it simply exaggerating the poem's relativism and playing down its religious faith to accord with the critic's own philosophical presuppositions? Adam Roberts, in a subsection called '*The Ring and the Book* and Modern Theory', makes this point clearly:

[A deconstructive critic] might argue that there is no recoverable objective truth at all. All ten [monologues] are equally false, or true; and that the extent to which we are able to assign qualities such as 'true' or 'false' wholly depends, is wholly relative. Yet this extreme levelling of value is not what we find in *The Ring and the Book* ... Browning may allow the relativist point that 'every man [is] a liar,' (12. 648) but he is equally adamant not just that 'God is truth' but that it is possible to approach closer to truth in an undeniable, objectively supportable manner ... The relativism of *The Ring and the Book* is maintained safely within a larger area – a ring, we might say – of absolute certainty.

(Roberts 1996: 101–2)

This argument cannot, of course, be resolved completely within Browning criticism. Ultimately, one will have to step outside the local debate, to the larger debate about the value or otherwise of deconstructive criticism and postmodern criticism generally, to read Jacques Derrida, and to read some of his opponents (Terry Eagleton (1996) for example, or better Nicholas Boyle (1998)). For E. Warwick Slinn, Browning is a thrilling poet just because he anticipates aspects of postmodern thought and sensibility. For a critic like Adam Roberts this position is insupportable just because, implicitly, it leaves out of account the liberal Protestant Christianity that clearly underpins the poem.

The danger of this debate – and Roberts, for one, is aware of it – is that it distracts attention from a more fundamental question: Is this vast experiment in form a success? Busy elucidating, expounding, quarrelling over critical practices and modes, it is easy for specialist critics to lose sight of this question, or simply not to consider it worthwhile. A few non-specialists, however, have raised this matter, and I want briefly to consider the views of one of the acutest of them.

Barbara Everett (1986) views Browning as an important and significant poet, but not, somehow, a poet in the first league. Everett sees both Browning and Tennyson as partaking of the 'philistinism' and provincialism of English Victorian culture. Browning's best work, according to Everett – and she clearly thoroughly loves this best work – 'really only comprises *Men and Women* and some outworks' (she means some of the poems in *Dramatic Lyrics, Dramatic Romances and Lyrics,* and *Dramatis Personae*), and *The Ring and the Book* is ultimately a failure. Browning's attraction to spontaneous, impromptu speech was an attempt to avoid an overly precious 'Art' or artiness, but it meant that in the end he also failed to deploy the highest rational resources of art – that he was, in some sense, 'an undisciplined poet'. So, *The Ring and the Book* shows 'spawning undisciplined scale' and 'randomness' within it. Conceding that Books VI and VII may be among the best things Browning wrote, she nonetheless goes on:

> ... the retelling of this same story, in its lineaments both bald and cruel, more than ten times over through the medium of speakers foolish and boring when not actually incapable of truth is – despite the linguistic and rhetorical brilliances and the neat angles of character that occasionally occur – largely unendurable, the kind of bright 'idea' that comes to a civilization simply out of touch with the realities of art in practice. One can almost think Guido's self-description meant to echo defeatedly the structure of the whole: 'I am one huge and sheer mistake'. James wrote the perfect review of the poem when, in *Notes on Novelists*, he circled the work with gloomy, delicate prevarication. 'We can only take it as tremendously interesting.' In its lack of correspondence with the actual, *The Ring and the Book* – for all its genuinely impressive theoretical magnificence – is reminiscent of other and baser Victorian misunderstandings about the nature of the aesthetic, from wax-flowers under glass to models of the Crystal Palace constructed out of matchsticks.
>
> (Everett 1986: 173)

This criticism is all the more devastating for being so serious. The parentheses clearly show that Everett appreciates at least some of the qualities enjoyed by the poem's admirers; however, this does not stop her from rounding her paragraph to the mordant wit of its ending. For E. Warwick Slinn, *The Ring and the Book* is simply Browning's 'masterpiece'. For an acute generalist critic like Barbara Everett, Browning shows 'something like real artistic intensity' in roughly the two decades from 1844 to 1864. Thereafter was decline, and *The Ring and the Book*, characterized in these terms, is part of it.

The three book-length studies of the poem in the last twenty years – by Buckler (1985), Brady (1988), and Rigg (1999) – though different in critical approaches, all provide ammunition against Everett's viewpoint, particularly in what they are able to show about the total imaginative texture and timbre of the work. In what follows, I am not summarizing these ranging studies in a small space, but I am drawing on some of their arguments and perceptions to suggest a different judgement.

In reading *The Ring and the Book* we have our eyes on two things at the same time: first the story of Pompilia Comparini, her marriage and murder, and second the presence of the particular monologist who is speaking to us (depending on which book of the poem we are reading). The central events of the marriage and murder run from 1693 to 1698, but we are quite often taken back to preceding events which give context to this central period. We see, for example, Guido's luckless life in Rome seeking some kind of preferment from Cardinals and nobles, Pompilia's childhood world, or the very comfortable bourgeois life of the Comparini prior to their daughter's wedding. At the same time as this, we are seeing into the inner psychological life of the particular monologist, his foibles and distortions, his moral and spiritual condition, revealed through particular ideas and perceptions, particular local preoccupations, an individual style of language and imagery. Which of these two focuses is the dominant one?

Everett takes very seriously the poem's form: she foregrounds the monologists and the fact that we are therefore seeing the 'same' story from different viewpoints. A better way of reading, perhaps, is to foreground the murder-story itself, and to see each monologue as simply providing further ramifications, an ever-widening view, an accumulation of physical detail and moral nuance. The monologues do not simply repeat each other. Different monologists know or imagine different parts of the story in varying degrees of detail. As in Browning's earlier use of the dramatic monologue, so here also, we are endlessly decoding the ironic structures of individual monologues to see through to the truth, and so we are adding to our knowledge of the story. We add all the time to our wider knowledge of the setting of the story. More and more physical and social details accrue, giving the world of late-seventeenth-century Italy a thick imaginative reality. At the same time, the cross-referencing and implicit interactions between the monologues deepen our understanding of the story's moral dimensions.

The monologists are partly like narrator figures in a novel, like Lockwood in *Wuthering Heights* or Nick Carraway in *The Great Gatsby*. Of course these narrator figures are interesting in themselves, but more importantly they are windows onto the central story. The fact that the narrators see the story in a particular way because of the bias of their character is less important than the fact that we quickly decode or see through that bias of character: because we see through the eyes of a living consciousness, this adds an element of interest, but it is still *what we see* that is most important for us. The monologists who are not direct actors in the story – the voices of public opinion (Books II, III, and IV), the lawyers (Books VIII, and IX), and the Pope (Book X) – all act to inscribe and reinscribe the story itself, tracings over tracings, but never give us simple repetition. Their characters are not so much facts or centres of interest in themselves, but rather additions to the total imaginative world in which the story takes place, another thickening of the fictional reality.

Take one vivid example, from Book IV. This is how Tertium Quid imagines the scene when Violante, the respectable middle-class housewife, visits a prostitute in a slum of Rome in order to negotiate to buy the child in her womb:

> And so, deliberately [Violante] snaps house-book clasp,
> Posts off to vespers, missal beneath arm,
> Passes the proper San Lorenzo by,
> Dives down a little lane to the left, is lost
> In a labyrinth of dwellings best unnamed,
> Selects a certain blind one, black at base,
> Blinking at top, – the sign of we know what, –
> One candle in a casement set to wink
> Streetward, do service to no shrine inside, –
> Mounts thither by the filthy flight of stairs,
> Holding the cord by the wall, to the tip-top,
> Gropes for the door i' the dark, ajar of course,
> Raps, opens, enters in: up starts a thing
> Naked as needs be – 'What, you rogue, 't is you?
> Back, – how can I have taken a farthing yet?
> Mercy on me, poor sinner that I am!
> Here's ... why, I took you for Madonna's self
> With all that sudden swirl of silk i' the place!
> What may your pleasure be, my bonny dame?'
> Your Excellency supplies aught left obscure?
>
> (iv. 146–65)

Browning, we might say, has been learning from his love of the great French novelists (his favourite was Balzac). This is our first detailed view of this incident, and it adds vividly to our understanding of the whole story. Of course, it does tell us something about Tertium Quid's character. It is perfectly in keeping with what we know about the upper-class Tertium Quid that he should be the one to give us this glimpse of Rome's underside: we can well believe that he is the kind of man who uses prostitutes, hence his vivid evocation of their world. Yet, even in this short passage, how quickly we leave the voice of Tertium Quid behind: the voice within the voice takes over, and, for her six lines (159–64) the prostitute's own voice is in the foreground.

The scene is vividly realized. The prostitute, only just having been left by her pimp, jumps up when she assumes he has returned. Next, both superstitious and guilty, she momently thinks that she is seeing a vision of the Virgin Mary who might have come to reproach or save her, because – comically – Violante is wearing such a fuss of lace and silk. Then, realizing her mistake, realizing that there is an ordinary middle-class woman in her room – an unusual happening – the prostitute asks the arch, insinuating question 'What may your pleasure be, my bonny dame?' The change of tone marks the whole change in the situation: no longer fearful, the prostitute sees Violante, in her awkward gentility, as her potential victim. Clearly Violante is up to no good, and in one way or another there may be money to be made.

Theoretically this vignette is only Tertium Quid's imagining, and it is his knowing worldly tone that makes it so vivid (the door 'ajar of course' is a particularly egregious touch). But, once we have heard this vignette, we completely believe it and add it to our total knowledge of the story. It is something added, in particular, to our knowledge of Violante and to the origins of the later tragedy. Violante, deceiving her husband into thinking that she is going to church, heads straight for the prostitute's house, going against instinct and inhibition, in order to buy a baby to pass off as her own. In this way she secures the Trust fund (or *fidei commissum*) that would otherwise pass to relations, and also lights up her husband's old age with a baby. But she also – and the passage implicitly enacts this, through its dark, Dickensian feel – sets going the workings of guilt that will later help to create the tragedy. Just because she knows that Pompilia is really a prostitute's child, so she longs to cleanse the deception. Consequently, later, she too eagerly grabs at the prospect of Pompilia's marriage to Franceschini just because it would (as it were) transform the girl, make her forever respectable as a count's wife. When, in other words, in other passages, in other monologues, we are given descriptions of Violante's role in bringing about Pompilia's marriage, this is one of the passages that comes back into our minds as a necessary background.

Similarly, we hold this passage in our minds in relation to Pompilia herself. When in her monologue, in Book VII, Pompilia thinks about her prostitute mother, it is also to this passage that we imaginatively recur. At VII. 847–73 Pompilia describes how she lost her virginity to a husband who hated her and who showed this through the nature of the sexual intercourse. Pompilia now knows what it feels like to be sold and used, and her telling language about her real mother's degradation is a reflection of her own. In the passage above, we have already seen that degradation, seen its depths and its meaning, and it adds a dimension to our empathy with Pompilia's thoughts. Ann Brady, who has been criticised as ahistorical and unnuanced for the terms of her wider feminist thesis, is nonetheless excellent concerning this kind of novelistic interlinking and interaction (see Brady 1988: 42–62).

Tertium Quid gives us this description of Rome's underside when he is standing in a fashionable saloon, surrounded by the upper-class of Roman society: beautiful women with patches, Cardinals playing cards, marquises and counts idling away an evening in gossip and intrigue. His view of the prostitute's room is comfortable and voyeuristic, the imagination of the lower-class world which he will only ever come in contact with if and when he wants to. And to say this, is again to say something about how the poem works. The passage adds detail to our knowledge of the main story, but it also adds one more piece to the patchwork of moral intuitions with which we perceive it.

The description is a piece of worldliness from one of the worldlings of the poem, an image which (in its moral value) contrasts with and helps us assess less cynical and more idealistic views. Tertium Quid, his upper-class saloon, and his view of the underside of Rome, are all parts of the world in which Guido and Pompilia have to live out the central story. When, for example, Pompilia (as a loyal daughter) describes Pietro's little pilgrimage around the cribs of the seven churches of Rome (vii. 250–67) – a tender Christmas ritual – we are aware that Pietro, the mildly virtuous, partly selfish bourgeois, does this modest act of religious devotion in exactly the same world in which Tertium Quid attends the self-conscious soirée, a world of seeing and being seen, of social advancement. The imaginative texture is being thickened all the time in the manner of the inner workings of a novel, with event talking to event, and scene talking to scene. One of the things that Browning takes from his long readings in the French novelists is a desire to create a total social world, from prostitutes to high-up Cardinals, from society ladies being instructed in cards by gallant priests, to the Pope at lonely evening prayers in his study. All the monologists, in small ways or large, are characters within this much larger ethical and imaginative panorama.

It is partly because of all this that Susan Blalock has called the poem a 'novel-in-verse' (Blalock 1988: 43), and Book I, which in parts is highly novelistic in its descriptions, is really an indication of this. The poet Gerard Manley Hopkins (1844–89) complained about one of the descriptions in Book I to his friend Canon Dixon, commenting in a letter on what he saw as its formless verve. Browning's description of the Florence street-market is, he says, 'a pointless photograph of still life, such as I remember in Balzac, minute upholstery description; only that in Balzac … all tells and is given with a reserve and simplicity of style which Browning has not got' (12 October 1881) (Abbott 1935: 74). The reader might like to try out the truth of this on the passage to which it refers, Book I, lines 38–100. Really, this great jumbled and inclusive description is a precise indication of the poem that is to follow, where the thread of the story of Pompilia's marriage and murder is to be surrounded by a whole imaginative world, made up, in part, of apparent inconsequences like the prostitute scene. This is the kind of view that tends to be taken up by those critics opposed to deconstruction. These critics want to insist that the poem is *not*, firstly, a poem about 'how we find out "truth"' or 'whether we can find out truth'. Its main interest is less exactly philosophical. So, Adam Roberts, for example:

> 'Truth' is perhaps the central issue, and since truth is something that needs to be determined, or interpreted, *The Ring and the Book* becomes in effect a gigantic hermeneutic epic, arguably the first epistemological poem. But seeing the poem in these terms, however valid such a critical perspective is (and however often critics have brought his sort of analysis to it) runs the risk of overlooking the supreme humanity of Browning's achievement. As portraits of character and as recreations of a historical period, these monologues have few equals, in the nineteenth century or elsewhere.
>
> (Roberts 1996: 99)

We might add, simply, that approached as an unusual novel-in-verse the poem will simply yield much more to the reader.

Further reading

The best study that gives an overview of Browning's changing reputation over the last century or so is O'Neill (1995). An even better way of getting a sense of the changing nature of criticism in relation to Browning would be to read the major collections of critical essays: Litzinger and Knickerbocker (1965), Bloom and Munich (1979), and Gibson (1992). John Maynard, best known for *Browning's Youth* (1978), has been one of the main scholarly reviewers over the period, and his work is collected together in *Browning Re-viewed: Review Essays, 1980–1995* (1998), which is something more than simply a collection of review articles: it gives a sense of movements and trends within the appreciation of Browning over the period, with many intelligent insights of the author's own.

From the rate at which they are referred to above, the best studies of Browning in the last twenty years should by now be apparent: they are Tucker (1980), Ryals (1983), Woolford (1988), Bristow (1991), Gibson (1992), Armstrong (1993), Karlin (1993), and Hair (1999). The best three with which to start are probably Bristow (1991), Gibson (1992), and Tucker (1980), in that order.

CHRONOLOGY

1812– Robert Browning (RB) born in Camberwell, then a village south of London, the eldest child of Robert Browning, a clerk at the Bank of England, and Sarah Anna Browning.

1814– RB's only sister, Sarianna, born.

1819–26 RB attends Peckham School as a weekly boarder, receiving a classical education from Rev. Thomas Ready.

1826– in this year or the next RB gets a present of Shelley's *Miscellaneous Poems* (1826), precipitating a deep engagement with Shelley's poetry and a Shelley-influenced period of vegetarianism, atheism, and political radicalism.

1828–29 RB attends the newly-founded London University for six months (Oct. 1828–May 1829).

1832– (Oct.) Moved by Edmund Kean's performance of Richard III at the King's Theatre, Richmond. Inspired to write *Pauline*.

1833– (Mar.) *Pauline* published anonymously.

1834– RB travels to St Petersburg. Probably begins work on *Sordello*.

1835– (Aug.) *Paracelsus* published.
(Nov.) RB introduced to the actor-manager W. C. Macready, leading to an intense effort to write plays for the contemporary theatre.

1836– (Jan.) First dramatic monologues, 'Porphyria's Lover' (then called 'Porphyria') and 'Johannes Agricola' published in the liberal-radical journal *The Monthly Repository*.

1837– (May) *Strafford*, RB's first play for the theatre, performed at Covent Garden, with Macready in the title role.

1838– (May–July) First trip to Italy: to Venice and the surrounding areas.

1840– *Sordello* published. It is poorly received and accused of being unintelligible.

1841– *Pippa Passes* published.

1842– *King Victor and King Charles*, and then *Dramatic Lyrics*, published.

1843– *The Return of the Druses*, and then *A Blot in the 'Scutcheon*, published. *A Blot in the 'Scutcheon* performed at the Drury Lane theatre. RB's relationship with Macready breaks down over disagreements in the production.

1844–   *Colombe's Birthday* published. Aug. to Nov. second trip to Italy: to Naples, the Sorrento peninsula, Rome, Pisa, Livorno, and Florence. (Aug.) Barrett's *Poems* published; RB reads them on his return from Italy.

1845–   (Jan.) RB writes for the first time to Elizabeth Barrett. A romance develops which she keeps secret from her father because of his irrational objections to marriage.

1846–   (Sept.) RB and Barrett are privately married. They then flee secretly to the continent.
          (Oct.) Set up home in Pisa.

1847–   (Apr.) Move to Florence.
          (July) Take a lease on Casa Guidi, in the south of the city. This eventually becomes their long-term home in Florence.

1848–9   Year of revolutions. Grand Duke Leopold flees Florence and is then repressively restored to power by Austrian troops in May 1849.

1849–   (Mar.) Birth of only son, Robert Wiedemann, usually called Penini or Pen.

1850–   *Christmas-Eve and Easter-Day* published.

1851–2   Long visit to Paris and London. Dec.1851 RB and Barrett in Paris at the time of Louis Napoleon's *coup d'état*.

1853–4   In Florence RB writes most of the poems comprising *Men and Women.*

1855–   *Men and Women* published, but has little success.

1856–   Barrett's novel-poem *Aurora Leigh* published, and achieves considerable success in the following years.

1859–61   RB and Barrett follow the military and political events of the struggle for the unification of Italy as a nation state (the Risorgimento), a cause they both ardently support.

1861–   Barrett dies after a short illness. RB decides to break up their home at Casa Guidi, and settle in England.

1862–   (Mar.) Takes lease on 19 Warwick Crescent, London.

1864–   (Oct.) Commences serious work on his 21,000 line epic *The Ring and the Book.*

1868–69   *The Ring and the Book* published in four vols. RB's reputation has been growing during the 1860s. Now, for the first time, he receives wide public recognition.

1871–   (Aug.) *Balaustion's Adventure*; (Dec.) *Prince Hohenstiel-Schwangau.*

1872–   *Fifine at the Fair.*

1873–   *Red Cotton Night-Cap Country.*

1875–   (April) *Aristophanes' Apology*; (Nov.) *The Inn Album.*

1876–	*Pacchiarotto and How He Worked in Distemper: With Other Poems.*
1877–	Translation of *The Agamemnon of Aeschylus.*
1878–	*La Saisiaz: The Two Poets of Croisic* (two works in one volume).
1879–	*Dramatic Idyls.*
1880–	*Dramatic Idyls, Second Series.*
1881–	The Browning Society founded in London.
1882–	DCL. from the University of Oxford.
1883–	*Jocoseria.*
1884–	LLD from University of Edinburgh. (Nov.) *Ferishtah's Fancies* published.
1887–	*Parleyings with Certain People of Importance in Their Day.*
1888–89	*The Poetical Works* (in sixteen volumes), the last full edition of his lifetime, carefully corrected by RB.
1889–	*Asolando* published 12 Dec.; RB dies at his son's Palazzo in Venice later that day.
	31 Dec. buried in Westminster Abbey, near Chaucer and Spenser.

BIBLIOGRAPHY

Abbott, C. C. (ed.) (1935) *The Correspondence of Gerard Manley Hopkins and R. W. Dixon*, London: Oxford University Press.

Abrams, M. H. (ed.) (1993) *A Glossary of Literary Terms*, 6th edn, New York: Harcourt Brace College Publishers.

Altick, R. D. and Loucks, J. F. (1968) *Browning's Roman Murder Story: A Reading of 'The Ring and the Book'*, Chicago: University of Chicago Press.

Armstrong, I. (ed.) (1969) *The Major Victorian Poets: Reconsiderations*, London: Routledge & Kegan Paul.

—— (1974) *Writers and their Background: Robert Browning*, London: Bell.

—— (1993) *Victorian Poetry: Poetry, Poetics and Politics*, London and New York: Routledge.

—— (2000) *The Radical Aesthetic*, Oxford: Blackwell Publishers.

Auerbach, N. (1984) 'Robert Browning's Last Word', *Victorian Poetry* 22, no. 2: 161–73.

Bagehot, W. (1864) 'Wordsworth, Tennyson and Browning; or pure, ornate, and grotesque in English Poetry', *The National Review* 19: 27–67. Often reprinted.

Barrett, E. B. (1844) *Poems*, 2 vols, London: Edward Moxon.

Barrett, R. A. (2000) *The Barretts of Jamaica*, Waco, Tex.: Armstrong Browning Library of Baylor University.

Barry, P. (1995) *Beginning Theory*, Manchester: Manchester University Press.

Berman, R. J. (1972) *Browning's Duke*, New York: Richards Rosen Press.

Besier, R. (1930) *The Barretts of Wimpole Street*, London: Victor Gollancz.

Bidney, M. (1984) 'The exploration of Keatsian aesthetic problems in Browning's *Madhouse Cells*', *Studies in English Literature, 1500–1900* 24: 671–81.

Blalock, S. (1983) 'Browning's *The Ring and the Book*: "A Novel Country"', *Browning Institute Studies* 11: 39–50.

Bloom, H. (1974) 'How to read a poem: Browning's Childe Roland', *Georgia Review* 28: 404–18.

—— (1971) *The Ringers in the Tower: Studies in Romantic Tradition*, Chicago and London: University of Chicago Press.

—— (1973) *The Anxiety of Influence*, Oxford and New York: Oxford University Press.

—— (1975) *A Map of Misreading*, Oxford and New York: Oxford University Press.

Bloom, H. and Munich, A. (eds) (1979) *Robert Browning: a collection of critical essays*, Englewood Cliffs, NJ; London: Prentice-Hall.

—— and Trilling, L. (eds) (1973) *Victorian Prose and Poetry*, London and New York: Oxford University Press.

Booth, W. C. (1974) *A Rhetoric of Irony*, Chicago and London: University of Chicago Press.

Bornstein, G. (ed.) (1985) *Ezra Pound Among the Poets*, Chicago and London: University of Chicago Press.

Boyle, N. (1998) *Who Are We Now? Christian Humanism and the Global Market from Hegel to Heaney*, Notre Dame, Ind.: University of Notre Dame Press.

Brady, A. P. (1988) *Pompilia: A Feminist Reading of Robert Browning's 'The Ring and the Book'*, Athens, Ohio: Ohio University Press.

Bristow, J. (1991) *Robert Browning*, Harvester New Readings series, New York, London, etc.: Harvester Wheatsheaf.

Brown, S. E. (1998) 'Browning's *Sordello* and Ezra Pound', unpublished D. Phil Thesis, University of Ulster at Coleraine.

Buchanan, R. W. (1869) '*The Ring and the Book* by Robert Browning', *The Athenaeum* 2160 (20 Mar.): 399–400.

Buckler, W. E. (1985) *Poetry and Truth in Robert Browning's The Ring and the Book*, New York and London: New York University Press.

Bullen, J. B. (1972) 'Browning's *Pictor Ignotus* and Vasari's "Life of Fra Bartolommeo di San Marco" ', *RES* 23: 313–19.

—— (1994) *The Myth of the Renaissance in Nineteenth-Century Writers*, Oxford: Clarendon Press.

Chesterton, G. K. (1903) *Robert Browning*, London: Macmillan.

Coulling, S. (1986) 'The Duchess of Ferrara and the Countess Gismond: Two Sides of the Andromeda Myth', *Studies in Browning and His Circle* 14: 66–84.

Curle, R. (ed.) (1937) *Robert Browning and Julia Wedgwood: A Broken Friendship as Revealed in Their Letters*, New York: Frederick A. Stokes Co.

Davies, N. (1996) *Europe: a History*, Oxford: Oxford University Press.

Davis, N. Z. (1983) *The Return of Martin Guerre*, Cambridge, Mass., and London: Harvard University Press.

DeLaura, D. J. (1980) 'The Context of Browning's Painter Poems: Aesthetics, Polemics, Historics', *PMLA* 95: 367–88.

DeVane, W. C. (1927) *Browning's Parleyings: The Autobiography of a Mind*, New Haven: Yale University Press.

—— (1955) *A Browning Handbook*, 2nd edn., New York: Appleton-Century-Crofts.

DeVane, W. C. and Knickerbocker, K. L. (eds) (1951) *New Letters of Robert Browning*, London: John Murray.

Drabble, M. (ed.) (2000) *The Oxford Companion to English Literature*, 6th edn, Oxford: Oxford University Press.

Drew, P. (1970) *The Poetry of Browning: A Critical Introduction*, London: Methuen.

—— (1990) *An Annotated Critical Bibliography of Robert Browning*, New York and London: Harvester Wheatsheaf.

Eagleton, T. (1996) *The Illusions of Postmodernism*, Oxford: Blackwell.

Edel, L. (1962) *The Conquest of London*, vol. ii of *The Life of Henry James*, Phil.; New York: J. B. Lippincott Co.

Eliot, T. S. (1957) *On Poetry and Poets*, London: Faber & Faber.

—— (1969) *Selected Essays*, 3rd enlarged edn, London: Faber & Faber.

Erdman, D. V. (1957) 'Browning's Industrial Nightmare', *Philological Quarterly* 36: 417–35.

Erickson, L. (1984) *Robert Browning: His Poetry and His Audiences*, Ithaca and London: Cornell University Press.

Everett, B. (1986) *Poets in Their Time*, London and Boston: Faber.

Forster, M. (1991) *Lady's Maid*, Harmondsworth: Penguin.

Friedland, L. S. (1936) 'Ferrara and *My Last Duchess*', *Studies in Philology* 33: 656–84.

Froula, C. (1985) 'Browning's *Sordello* and the Parables of Modernist Poetics', *English Literary History* 52: 965–92. Reprinted in Gibson (1992).

Garrett, M. (2000a) *A Browning Chronology: Elizabeth Barrett and Robert Browning*, Basingstoke, Hants: Macmillan Press Ltd.

—— (ed.) (2000b) *Elizabeth Barrett Browning and Robert Browning: Interviews and Recollections*, Basingstoke, Hants: Macmillan Press Ltd.

Gest, J. M. (1927) *The Old Yellow Book, Source of Browning's The Ring and the Book: A New Translation with Explanatory Notes and Critical Chapters upon the Poem and Its Source*, Philadelphia: University of Pennsylvania.

Gibson, M. E. (1987) *History and the Prism of Art: Browning's Poetic Experiments*, Columbus, Ohio: Ohio State University Press.

—— (ed.) (1992) *Critical Essays on Robert Browning*, New York: G. K. Hall & Co.

Golder, H. (1924) 'Browning's *Childe Roland*', *PMLA* 39: 963–78.

Greer, L. (1952) *Browning and America*, Chapel Hill: University of North Carolina Press.

Gridley, R. E. (1982) *The Brownings and France*, London: Athlone Press.

Griffin, W. H., completed and ed. Minchin, H. C. (1938) *The Life of Robert Browning*, 3rd edn, London: Methuen.

Grove, W. (1927) 'Browning as I Knew Him', in *The Sunday Express*, 4 Dec.

Hagopian, J. V. (1961) 'The Mask of Browning's Count Gismond', *Philological Quarterly* 40: 153–5.

Hair, D. S. (1972) *Browning's Experiments with Genre*, Edinburgh: Oliver and Boyd.

—— (1999) *Robert Browning's Language*, Toronto: University of Toronto Press.

Hamilton, P. (1996) *Historicism*, London and New York: Routledge.

Haskell, F. (1976) *Rediscoveries in Art*, London: Phaidon.

Hassett, C. W. (1982) *The Elusive Self in the Poetry of Robert Browning*, Athens, Ohio: Ohio University Press.

Hawlin, S. (1990a) 'Browning, Shelley and "On Worming Dogs" ', *Essays in Criticism* 40, no. 2: 136–55.

—— (1990b) 'Browning's "A Toccata of Galuppi's": How Venice Once Was Dear', *Review of English Studies* 41: 496–509.

Hill, G. (1991) *The Enemy's Country: Words, Contexture, and other Circumstances of Language*, Oxford: Clarendon Press.

Hochberg, S. (1991) 'Male Authority and Female Subversion in Browning's "My Last Duchess" ', *LIT: Literature Interpretation Theory* 3, no. 1: 77–84.

Hodell, C. W. (1908; 2nd edn 1916) *The Old Yellow Book, Source of Browning's The Ring and the Book, in Complete Photo-Reproduction, with Translation, Essay, and Notes*, Washington: Carnegie Institution of Washington.

—— (trans. and ed.) (1911) *The Old Yellow Book: Source of Robert Browning's The Ring and the Book*, London: J. M. Dent; New York: E. P. Dutton.

Holloway, M. M. (1963) 'A Further Reading of *Count Gismond*', *Studies in Philology* 60: 549–53.

Honan, P. (1961) *Browning's Characters: A Study in Poetic Technique*, New Haven: Yale University Press.

Hood, T. L. (ed.) (1933) *Letters of Robert Browning Collected by Thomas J. Wise*, London: John Murray.

Horne, R. H. (1844) *A New Spirit of the Age*, 2 vols, London: Smith, Elder.

Hudson, G. R. (1992) *Robert Browning's Literary Life: From First Work to Masterpiece*, Austin, Texas: Eakin Press.

Hutchinson, T. and Matthews, G. M. (eds) (1970) *Shelley: Poetical Works*, London: Oxford University Press.

Huxley, L. (ed.) (1929) *Elizabeth Barrett Browning: Letters to her Sister, 1846–1859*, London: John Murray.

Ingersoll, E. G. (1990) 'Lacan, Browning, and the Murderous Voyeur: "Porphyria's Lover" and "My Last Duchess" ', *Victorian Poetry* 28: 151–7.

Irvine, W. and Honan, P. (1975) *The Book, the Ring, and the Poet: A Biography of Robert Browning*, London: Bodley Head.

Jack, I. (ed.) (1970) *Browning: Poetical Works, 1833–1864*, London: Oxford University Press.

—— (1973) *Browning's Major Poetry*, Oxford: Clarendon Press.

James, Henry (1903) *William Wetmore Story and His Friends*, 2 vols, Boston: Houghton, Mifflin.

—— (1914) 'The Novel in "The Ring and the Book" ', in *Notes on Novelists*, London: J. M. Dent & Sons.

Jameson, Anna (1845) *Memoirs of the Early Italian Painters*, 2 vols, London: Charles Knight & Co.

—— (1848) *Sacred and Legendary Art*, 2 vols, London: Longman.

Jones, H., Sir (1891) *Browning as a Philosophical and Religious Teacher*, Glasgow: Maclehose & Sons.

Karlin, D. (1985) *The Courtship of Robert Browning and Elizabeth Barrett*, Oxford and New York: Oxford University Press.

—— (1989) 'Browning's Poetry of Intimacy', *Essays in Criticism* 39: 47–64.

—— (1993) *Browning's Hatreds*, Oxford: Clarendon Press.

Kelley, P. and Coley, B. A. (1984) *The Browning Collections: A Reconstruction With Other Memorabilia*, Waco, Texas: Armstrong Browning Library.

Kenyon, F. G. (ed.) (1897) *The Letters of Elizabeth Barrett Browning*, 2 vols, London: Smith, Elder.

—— (ed.) (1906) *Robert Browning and Alfred Domett*, London: Smith, Elder.

King, R. A, jun. (1957) *The Bow and the Lyre: The Art of Robert Browning*, Anne Arbor: University of Michigan Press.

—— (1968) *The Focusing Artifice: The Poetry of Robert Browning*, Athens, Ohio: Ohio University Press.

Kintner, E. (ed.) (1969) *The Letters of Robert Browning and Elizabeth Barrett Barrett 1845–1846*, 2 vols, Cambridge, Mass.: Harvard University Press.

Korg, J. (1983) *Browning and Italy*, Athens, Ohio, and London: Ohio University Press.

Langbaum, R. (1957) *The Poetry of Experience: The Dramatic Monologue in Modern Literary Tradition*, New York: Random House.

Latané, D. E. (1987) *Browning's* Sordello *and the Aesthetics of Difficulty*, English Literary Studies Monograph Series, no. 40, Victoria, BC: University of Victoria.

Leavis, F. R. (1932) *New Bearings in English Poetry*, London: Chatto & Windus.

Levenson, J. C., Samuels, E., *et al.* (eds) (1982–88) *The Letters of Henry Adams*, 6 vols, Cambridge, Mass., and London: Belknap Press of Harvard University Press.

Lewis, S. (1831) *Lewis's Topographical Dictionary of England*, 4 vols, London: S. Lewis & Co.

Litzinger, B. (1964) *Time's Revenges: Browning's Reputation as a Thinker, 1889–1962*, Knoxville: University of Tennessee Press.

Litzinger, B. and Knickerbocker, K. L. (1965) *The Browning Critics*, Lexington: University Press of Kentucky.

Marks, J. (1973) *The Family of the Barrett: A Colonial Romance*, Westport, Conn.: Greenwood Press. Originally pub. 1938, New York: Macmillan.

Markus, J. (ed.) (1977) *Casa Guidi windows: Elizabeth Barrett Browning*, New York: Browning Institute.

Martin, L. D. (1985) *Browning's Dramatic Monologues and the Post-Romantic Subject*, Baltimore: Johns Hopkins University Press.

Mason, M. (1974) 'Browning and the dramatic monologue', in I. Armstrong (ed.) *Writers and their Background: Robert Browning*, London: G. Bell & Sons.

Maxwell, C. (1992) 'Not the whole picture: Browning's "unconquerable shade" ', *Word & Image: A Journal of Verbal/Visual Enquiry* 8, no. 4 (Oct.–Dec.): 322–32.

—— (1993) 'Browning's Pygmalion and the Revenge of Galatea', *English Literary History* 60: 989–1013.

Maynard, J. (1977) *Browning's Youth*, Cambridge, Mass., London: Harvard University Press.

—— (1998a) 'Browning's Duds of Consciousness (or) No Gigadibs, No Bishop', in J. Woolford (ed.) *Robert Browning in Contexts*, Winfield, Kan.: Wedgestone Press.

—— (1998b) *Browning Re-viewed: Review Essays, 1980–1995*, New York: Peter Lang.

McAleer, E. C. (ed.) (1951) *Dearest Isa: Robert Browning's Letters to Isabella Blagden*, Austin, Tex.: University of Texas Press.

—— (ed.) (1966) *Learned Lady: Letters from Robert Browning to Mrs. Thomas FitzGerald 1876–1889*, Cambridge, Mass: Harvard University Press.

McCusker, J. A. (1983) 'A note on the last stanza of Soliloquy of the Spanish Cloister', *Victorian Poetry* 21: 421–4.

Meredith, M. (ed.) (1985) *More Than Friend: The Letters of Robert Browning to Katherine de Kay Bronson*, Waco, Texas: Armstrong Browning Library.

Millais, J. G. (1899) *The Life and Letters of Sir John Everett Millais*, 2 vols, London: Methuen & Co.

Miller, B. (1952) *Robert Browning: A Portrait*, London: John Murray.

Miller, J. Hillis (1963) *The Disappearance of God: Five Nineteenth-Century Writers*, Cambridge, Mass.: Harvard University Press.

—— (1985) *The Linguistic Moment: From Wordsworth to Stevens*, Princeton: Princeton University Press.

—— (1992) *Ariadne's Thread: Story Lines*, New Haven and London: Yale University Press.

Murfin, R. C. (1996) 'What is Deconstruction?', in *Joseph Conrad: Heart of Darkness*, 2nd edn, Boston and New York: Bedford Books of St Martin's Press.

O'Neill, P. (1995) *Robert Browning and Twentieth-Century Criticism*, Columbia, SC: Camden House, Inc.

Orr, Mrs Sutherland (1891; revised edn by Frederic G. Kenyon, 1908) *Life and Letters of Robert Browning*, London: Smith, Elder, & Co.

—— (1896) *A Handbook of the Works of Robert Browning*, 7th edn, London: G. Bell.

Paige, D. D. (ed.) (1971) *The Selected Letters of Ezra Pound, 1907–1941*, New York: New Directions.

Petch, S. (1989) 'Browning's Roman Lawyers', in *Browning Centenary Essays*, a special issue of *AUMLA* 71: 109–38.

Peterson, W. S. (ed.) (1979) *Browning's Trumpeter: the Correspondence of Robert Browning and Frederick J. Furnival 1872–1889*, Washington, D.C.: Decatur House Press.

Pound, Ezra (1963) *Literary Essays of Ezra Pound*, ed. with intro. by T. S. Eliot, London: Faber & Faber.

Rader, R. W. (1976) 'The Dramatic Monologue and Related Lyric Forms', *Critical Inquiry* 3: 131–51.

—— (1984) 'Notes on Some Structural Varieties and Variations in Dramatic "I" Poems and Their Theoretical Implications', *Victorian Poetry* 22: 103–20. Reprinted in Gibson (1992).

Raymond, W. O. (1965) *The Infinite Moment and Other Essays in Robert Browning*, 2nd edn, Toronto: Toronto University Press.

Reynolds, Margaret (ed.) (1996) *Aurora Leigh*, A Norton Critical Edition, New York; London: W. W. Norton.

Reynolds, Matthew (1998) 'Browning's Forms of Government', in J. Woolford (ed.) *Robert Browning in Contexts*, Winfield, Kan.: Wedgestone Press.

Ricks, C. (ed.) (1987) *The New Oxford Book of Victorian Verse*, Oxford: Oxford University Press.

Rigg, P. D. (1999) *Robert Browning's Romantic Irony in The Ring and the Book*, Madison, Teaneck: Fairleigh Dickinson University Press; London: Associated University Presses.

Rio, A. F. (1854) *The Poetry of Christian Art*, trans. by a lady [Miss Wells], London: Bosworth.

Roberts, A. (1996) *Robert Browning Revisited*, New York: Twayne Publishers; Prentice Hall International.

Ryals, Clyde de L. (1975) *Browning's Later Poetry, 1871–1889*, Ithaca: Cornell University Press.

—— (1983) *Becoming Browning: The Poems and Plays of Robert Browning, 1833–1846*, Columbus, Ohio: Ohio State University Press.

—— (1993) *The Life of Robert Browning: A Critical Biography*, Oxford, UK, and Cambridge, Mass., USA: Blackwell.

Santayana, G. (1916) *Interpretations of Poetry and Religion*, New York: Charles Scribner's Sons. 'The Poetry of Barbarism' (1900) is in this collection.

Siegchrist, M. (1981) *Rough in Brutal Print: The Legal Sources of Browning's Red Cotton Night-Cap Country*, Columbus, Ohio: Ohio State University Press.

Sinfield, A. (1977) *Dramatic Monologue*, the Critical Idiom series no. 36, London: Methuen; New York: Barnes & Noble.

Slinn, E. W. (1982) *Browning and the Fictions of Identity*, London: Macmillan.

—— (1991) *The Discourse of Self in Victorian Poetry*, Basingstoke, Hants, and London: Macmillan.

Stone, M. (1998) 'Bile and the Brownings: A New Poem by RB, EBB's "My Heart and I," and New Questions about the Brownings' Marriage', in J. Woolford (ed.) *Robert Browning in Contexts*, Winfield, Kan.: Wedgestone Press.

Sullivan, M. R. (1969) *Browning's Voices in The Ring and the Book*, Toronto: University of Toronto Press.

Tilton, J. W. and Tuttle, R. D. (1962) 'A new reading of *Count Gismond*', *Studies in Philology* 59: 83–95.

Thomas, C. F. (1991) *Art and Architecture in the Poetry of Robert Browning: An Illustrated Compendium of Sources*, New York: Whitston Publishing Co.

Thomas, D. (1983) *Robert Browning: A Life Within Life*, New York: Viking Press.

Toynbee, W. (ed.) (1912) *The Diaries of William Charles Macready, 1833–1851*, 2 vols, London: Chapman and Hall.

Tucker, H. F. (1980) *Browning's Beginnings: The Art of Disclosure*, Minn.: University of Minnesota Press.

—— (1984) 'From monomania to monologue: *St Simeon Stylites* and the rise of the Victorian dramatic monologue', *Victorian Poetry* 22: 121–37.

—— (1985) 'Dramatic Monologue and the Overhearing of Lyric', in C. Hosek and P. Parker (eds) *Lyric Poetry: Beyond the New Criticism*, Ithaca: Cornell University Press. Reprinted in Gibson (1992).

—— (1998) 'Browning as Escape Artist: Avoidance and Intimacy', in J. Woolford (ed.) *Robert Browning in Contexts*, Winfield, Kan.: Wedgestone Press.

Ward, J. (1985) 'Pound's Browning and the Issue of Historical Sense', *Browning Society Notes* 15: 10–25.

Ward, M. (1968) *Robert Browning and His World: The Private Face, 1812–1861*, London: Cassell.

—— (1969) *Robert Browning and His World: Two Robert Brownings? 1861–1889*, London: Cassell.

Wood, S. (2001) *Robert Browning: A Literary Life*, London: Palgrave.

Woolf, V. (1933) *Flush: A Biography*, London: L. & V. Woolf.

Woolford, J. (1988) *Browning the Revisionary*, Basingstoke, Hants, and London: Macmillan Press.

—— (ed.) (1998) *Robert Browning in Contexts*, Winfield, Kan.: Wedgestone Press.

Woolford, J. and Karlin, D. (1996) *Robert Browning*, Studies in Eighteenth- and Nineteenth-Century Literature, London and New York: Longman.

INDEX

215